D0713518

Lizzie Borden on Trial

LANDMARK LAW CASES *&* AMERICAN SOCIETY

Peter Charles Hoffer
N. E. H. Hull
Series Editors

RECENT TITLES IN THE SERIES

Prigg v. Pennsylvania, H. Robert Baker

The Detroit School Busing Case, Joyce A. Baugh

The Japanese American Cases, Roger Daniels

The Battle over School Prayer, Bruce J. Dierenfield

Judging the Boy Scouts of America, Richard J. Ellis

Fighting Foreclosure, John A. Fliter and Derek S. Hoff

The Passenger Cases and the Commerce Clause, Tony A. Freyer

One Man Out: Curt Flood versus Baseball, Robert M. Goldman

The Free Press Crisis of 1800, Peter Charles Hoffer

The Treason Trials of Aaron Burr, Peter Charles Hoffer

The Woman Who Dared to Vote: The Trial of Susan B. Anthony, N. E. H. Hull

Roe v. Wade: *The Abortion Rights Controversy in American History,* 2nd ed., revised and expanded, N. E. H. Hull and Peter Charles Hoffer

Plessy v. Ferguson: *Race and Inequality in Jim Crow America,* Williamjames Hull Hoffer

Gibbons v. Ogden: *John Marshall, Steamboats, and the Commerce Clause,* Herbert A. Johnson

The Tokyo Rose Case, Yasuhide Kawashima

Gitlow v. New York, Marc Lendler

Fugitive Slave on Trial: The Anthony Burns Case and Abolitionist Outrage, Earl M. Maltz

Capital Punishment on Trial, David M. Oshinsky

The Michigan Affirmative Action Cases, Barbara A. Perry

The Supreme Court and Tribal Gaming, Ralph A. Rossum

Obscenity Rules: Roth v. United States *and the Long Struggle over Sexual Expression,* Whitney Strub

Mendez v. Westminster, Philippa Strum

Race, Sex, and the Freedom to Marry, Peter Wallenstein

The Sleepy Lagoon Murder Case, Mark A. Weitz

The Miracle *Case,* Laura Wittern-Keller and Raymond J. Haberski Jr.

Bush v. Gore: *Exposing the Hidden Crisis in American Democracy,* abridged and updated, Charles L. Zelden

For a complete list of titles in the series go to www.kansaspress.ku.edu

JOSEPH A. CONFORTI

Lizzie Borden on Trial

Murder, Ethnicity, and Gender

UNIVERSITY PRESS OF KANSAS

Published by the University Press of Kansas (Lawrence, Kansas 66045), which was organized by the Kansas Board of Regents and is operated and funded by Emporia State University, Fort Hays State University, Kansas State University, Pittsburg State University, the University of Kansas, and Wichita State University

Library of Congress Cataloging-in-Publication Data

Conforti, Joseph A., author.

Lizzie Borden on trial : murder, ethnicity, and gender / Joseph A. Conforti.

pages cm. — (Landmark Law Cases and American Society)

Includes bibliographical references and index.

ISBN 978-0-7006-2071-5 (hardback)

ISBN 978-0-7006-2072-2 (ebook)

1. Borden, Lizzie, 1860–1927—Trials, litigation, etc. 2. Trials (Murder)—Massachusetts— New Bedford. 3. Murder—Massachusetts—Fall River. 4. Murder—Investigation— Massachusetts—Fall River. 5. Women—Massachusetts—Fall River—Social conditions— 19th century. I. Title.

KF223.B6C66 2015

45.744′02523—dc23

2014048865

British Library Cataloguing-in-Publication Data is available.

Printed in the United States of America

10 9 8 7 6 5 4 3 2 1

For Antonia, with love

CONTENTS

Editors' Preface *ix*

Preface *xi*

Prologue *1*

1. Setting: The Bordens of Fall River *6*

2. The Bordens of Second Street *23*

3. The Crime Heard 'round the Country and Beyond *51*

4. The Investigation *65*

5. Arrest *84*

6. "Probably Guilty" *104*

7. Lizzie's Long Wait *126*

8. Prosecuting Lizzie *140*

9. The Court's Heavy Hand *160*

10. Defending Lizzie *175*

11. Verdict *193*

Epilogue *211*

Chronology *217*

Bibliographical Essay *219*

Index *227*

The Lizzie Borden case is truly a tale of two cities. Fall River, Massachusetts, was a boomtown in the Gilded Age, its skyline filled with the smokestacks of cotton mills driven by the city's fast-flowing rivers. The cotton manufacturing plants had made a small group of close-knit families wealthy, and the Bordens were among them. The well-to-do lived on "The Hill" above the rivers and the coast, in substantial mansions. Closer to the mills below lived a teeming population of native born and foreign born who worked at the spindles and the bobbins. The laboring classes were heavily Irish, French Canadian, and Portuguese. Midway between the two communities lay the simple, almost austere, dwelling of emotionless and pinch-penny Andrew Borden, his second wife, Abby, and his two grown daughters, Emma and her younger sister, Lizzie, and the Irish maid the sisters called Maggie, although her name was Bridget Sullivan. The murders of Andrew and Abby shattered the placid surface of this upper-middle-class family life. The investigation of the murder and the trial of Lizzie Borden revealed the chasm that class and gender cut between the better sort and their lesser neighbors. If circumstantial evidence and her own inconsistent testimony seemed to point the finger at Lizzie, why did an experienced prosecutor worry that he had no case, and women's groups rally to her cause? When all was said and done, the jury deliberation and verdict were a sensation in themselves.

Some landmark cases change the law. Some severely test it. The murder trial of Lizzie Borden is a third type—a case that opens a window onto a time and place. In Fall River, the jarring elements of a substantially Irish Roman Catholic police force, a native-born Protestant judiciary, a frustrated feminist movement, and the clash of labor and capital all came together. In the maelstrom, Lizzie Borden was not a passive witness. She manipulated the media and reached out to family and class connections, spending the rents and investments that her parsimonious father had accumulated to insure that she had the very best defense team. One thinks of O. J. Simpson's trial for murdering his estranged wife and a young man who was in the wrong place at the wrong time. Was Andrew equally unlucky, coming back too early from his customary morning rounds, before the perpetrator could establish an alibi for the murder of Abby?

Professor Conforti has peered into every corner of the records of the town, the inquest, and the trial, looking for answers. He is especially well qualified as a detective in this case, for he comes from southern New England, his parents were the children of immigrants, he taught for many years at the University of Southern Maine, and he is a renowned scholar of the time and the region. The tale in his telling begins with the city and its industry, follows the Bordens into their home and traces their customary activities, painstakingly re-creates the crimes, and weighs the testimony of the principals and the neighbors. With the prosecutor and the police, Conforti tracks every clue. His account of the three legal steps—inquest, preliminary hearing, and trial—is a model of historical reporting, taking the reader with him. The crime was a media sensation, and Conforti's narrative presents the newspaper accounts as if we were there.

The Lizzie Borden murder case remains one of the most controversial in the history of American crime. There are many sensational accounts of it, but none so readable or so well balanced as this.

PREFACE

I am a native of Lizzie Borden's hometown. I was born less than twenty years after her death and raised in Fall River approximately a generation later. Lizzie remained very much alive in the city's collective memory and oral traditions. We all knew the site of the crime and details, many of which proved to be inaccurate, that made up the Borden story. As we grew older, we realized that outsiders usually knew of our city through Lizzie's notoriety or infamy. She stigmatized our world.

Thus I kept my distance from the blood-soaked crime as I became a historian of New England. It amounted to little more than a murder story, a mystery some said. During all of my years as a New England historian, I don't recall reading a single book about the crime. None of the many books about the Borden murders was a work of academic history. The last thing I expected was to author a work about Lizzie Borden, especially after recently publishing a book about growing up in our hometown. But I came to realize that what happened in the Borden house in the summer of 1892 amounted to more than a murder mystery, that events surrounding the tragedy and encompassing the trial revealed much about late Victorian life in Fall River and well beyond. What follows is an account of the Borden legal saga from arrest to acquittal. I also hope my narrative provides much more. I have tried to put behind me what I thought I knew about Lizzie growing up. As to her guilt or innocence, I have followed the evidence, as I see it.

Much of that evidence is contained in 3,000 pages of courtroom testimony covering three legal proceedings. I have quoted the transcripts as they were recorded, often with inconsistent or incorrect punctuation. Sometimes the lawyers didn't use proper English. I have spared the reader the repeated use of "*sic*" to note errors.

I want to thank Peter C. Hoffer for inviting me to write this book for the excellent, far-ranging series that he co-edits. Peter has not only offered constant encouragement and advice; he has set an outstanding example with his own prolific scholarship. I also want to thank Chuck Myers, Director of the University Press of Kansas, for his unflagging support.

Chuck enthusiastically embraced this project from the start, offered sound advice throughout, and helped me navigate the revisions that outside readers urged me to make. I want to express my appreciation to those two anonymous readers for their compelling, detailed evaluations of the manuscript. In countless ways they strengthened my effort to come to terms with Lizzie Borden and her world. It was a pleasure to work with the staff at the press: Larisa Martin, Mike Kehoe, and Rebecca Murray. Many thanks to Martha Whitt for her keen-eyed copyediting.

Len Rebello in Fall River generously responded to my numerous inquiries from his wealth of knowledge about the Borden case. Doug Norris set me to thinking by asking how well the Bordens were known in New York and beyond.

Finally, I want to thank my wife, Dorothy, for her patience as I devoted a second book in a row to a subject I never intended to tackle—my hometown. I dedicate this book to my daughter Antonia. She was neither born nor raised in Fall River. She now knows another piece of my hometown's story.

Lizzie Borden on Trial

Prologue

It originated as New England's crime of the century and burst into a seemingly senseless act that captivated the national press and broad segments of the American populace. The Lizzie Borden murder case abides as one of the most famous in American criminal history, immortalized by the children's rhyme passed down across generations.

> Lizzie Borden took an axe,
> And gave her mother forty whacks.
> When she saw what she had done,
> She gave her father forty-one.

In fact, Abby Borden was Lizzie's stepmother. A hatchet rather than an axe served as the butcher's weapon. Most importantly, less than half the blows of the rhyme actually battered the victims—nineteen rained down on Abby and ten rendered Andrew's face unrecognizable. Legends typically sprout with indifference to historical facts.

The rhyme does accurately record the sequence of the murders on the morning of August 4, 1892. They took place in Fall River, Massachusetts, an explosively developing textile mill city 50 miles south of Boston, 40 miles southwest of fabled Plymouth. The influx of Irish, French-Canadian, and Portuguese immigrants, among others, represented one aspect of Fall River's dynamic growth. As "foreigners" and their offspring swelled toward majority status, the Bordens and other descendants of Fall River's founding families experienced the first challenges to their control of the city. Not surprisingly, early suspicions of the murderer's identity focused on the immigrant community.

The crime shocked Fall River and then the nation for more than its sheer brutality. The assassin struck the victims at home, in broad daylight, on a busy street one short block east of Fall River's business district. There was no evident motive—no robbery or sexual assault, for example. Neighbors and passersby heard nothing. No one saw a suspect enter or leave the Borden property.

Moreover, Andrew Borden was no ordinary citizen. Like so many other Fall River Bordens he possessed wealth and claimed standing in the city. Indeed, businessmen throughout the Northeast knew of the Fall River Bordens. A week after the murders the most disturbing twist rocked the case. Andrew's thirty-two-year-old spinster daughter, a Sunday school teacher and young woman leader in her prominent church, was arrested for the brutal crime. Lizzie would remain jailed for ten months, from August 11 until her Superior Court trial in June 1893.

The popular rhyme, often referred to as "Forty Whacks," posits Lizzie's certain guilt, though the circumstantial evidence left the prosecution with major doubts about a conviction. In addition, the pursuit of justice was not simple for a well-placed, conspicuously religious Borden woman in the Massachusetts of the early 1890s. Lizzie's arrest provoked an outpouring of support, even indignation, from her affluent Central Congregational Church and the wider circle of wealthy native-born Protestant business and professional families who constituted Fall River's establishment. Then, too, women's groups in Fall River and beyond, especially suffragists, rallied to Lizzie's side. Major newspapers in New England and across the nation denounced the police and editorialized for Lizzie's innocence.

Assaying all this support and weighing potential pitfalls in police evidence, neither the local district attorney nor the Massachusetts attorney general relished prosecuting Lizzie. They explored ways of avoiding a trial. Then they put off for months setting a trial date after they found no exit.

The Superior Court seemingly set aside impartiality, a hallmark of justice. The court was not immune to Lizzie's influential support, to the clamoring of women's groups, or to the mountain of words in the press on her behalf. If the trial did not mark a turning point in American legal history, it encompassed a series of important relationships, controversial rulings, and other judicial actions whose cumulative effect gutted the prosecution's case and assured Lizzie's acquittal. In short, extra-legal considerations permeated Lizzie Borden's trial.

{ *Prologue* }

To be more precise, it mattered that Lizzie was not a working-class immigrant. A native-born, upper-class, socially active Protestant woman named Borden—these attributes of Lizzie's identity operated on her behalf. And Lizzie knew how to make the most of them in a public setting such as a court of law. In other words, she was skilled at cultivating the bearing and behavior of a genteel Victorian lady. Before a court of men, not just of law, Lizzie was far from a passive, helpless, physically and emotionally fragile lady, though she knew how to present herself that way.

A wide range of authors—novelists, dramatists, true crime writers, local historians, and Lizzie buffs, among others—have had at the case. Controversies still swirl around Lizzie's guilt or innocence. Many writers have sought to capitalize on enduring fascination with Lizzie and the crime by promoting new theories of the Borden murder mystery. The servant did it. Older sister Emma was the real murderer. Andrew's alleged illegitimate son committed the crime. The prosecution conspired to hide exonerating evidence. The murders were Lizzie's rage over childhood sexual abuse or the effects of menstruation on temporal lobe epilepsy. Thus most popular writers treat the Borden case as a mystery still in search of a solution.

This study does not advance a provocative new theory about the case. Rather, I have tried to view the crime as more than a murder mystery. I examine the family, the brutal murders, the circumstantial evidence against Lizzie, and the legal proceedings that led to her arrest and culminated in her acquittal. In other words, I try not to shortchange the criminal and legal dimensions of the case. But I also attempt to situate the story in a social and cultural context to broaden understanding of what happened. I start with the community setting to examine the Fall River that generated Andrew Borden's wealth and values as well as Lizzie's social aspirations and apprehension. At particular points in the Borden story I examine ethnic, gender, and class issues to help illuminate what transpired and why. In this way I combine criminal-legal history with social-cultural history.

Consider ethnicity. At the time of the murders and Lizzie's trial, immigrants and their offspring were surging toward a decided majority of Fall River's population. Consequently, the besieged Yankees, or multigenerational native born such as the Bordens, became more aware of and heavily invested in their Anglo-Protestant heritage. In short, the native born often spoke and behaved like a self-conscious ethnic group. Tension between Fall River's Yankee establishment and the city's immigrant-ethnic working-class families represented only one dimension of the social and cultural context in which Lizzie Borden's arrest and trial took place. From the "invasion" of the Borden house crime scene by Irish policemen to the persistent article of faith in some quarters that an immigrant must have been the murderer to the native born's mistrust of the Irish medical examiner to the near total Yankee composition of the jury—in these and other ways ethnic perceptions and actions informed the Borden case.

Similarly, important gender issues emerged in the Borden ordeal. In public, and in her lawyers' courtroom narrative, Lizzie embodied the pieties of virtuous Victorian womanhood: moral purity, physical "delicacy" and social dignity, even refinement. Lizzie's arrest, indictment, and trial for a savage domestic double murder threatened to subvert an ideal of Victorian womanhood that was already under challenge. I explore newspapers' representations of gender and Lizzie's cultivation and reaffirmation of Victorian ladyhood's touchstones before and during the trial, especially in a courtroom controlled by small-town, tradition-minded men.

Reporters described Lizzie not only as a virtuous lady; they also depicted her and older sister Emma as "spinsters." Yet single women in late nineteenth-century New England experienced ongoing upheaval in their lives. Lizzie and Emma Borden belonged to a large native-born class of single women in New England, and particularly Massachusetts, that consisted of far more than traditional "old maids" or individuals who allegedly had no choice but to remain unmarried. Women chose the single life for varied reasons. A portion of these single women became highly educated, entered the professions, and assumed the identity of the so-called New Woman. They radically modified or broke with the restrictive ideal of Victorian womanhood. Newspapers conflated the Borden sisters' spinsterhood. Yet for all the similarities of dependence on their father, Lizzie and Emma represented very different types of Victorian single women.

Of course ethnicity and gender intersected with class. In cities such as Fall River, middle- and upper-class native-born Protestant women

4 { *Prologue* }

claimed exclusive access to the cult of Victorian womanhood. The Bordens' Irish servant and the thousands of immigrant women and girls who labored in the city's mills dwelled far below the canons of prevailing ladylike respectability. As the pastor of Andrew Borden's First Congregational Church lamented on the pages of the religious *Andover Review*, in the mills too many daughters "lose the delicacy of their girlhood, and become bold in manners and rough in speech." In addition, Lizzie's social standing and wealth gave her a privileged position before the law compared to mill workers and house servants.

Why measure Lizzie Borden's historical pulse—again? First, academic historians have produced only a handful of essays on the case. They have ceded the Borden historical terrain to others. Furthermore, as suggested above, from the crime through the trial, important Victorian issues involving ethnicity, gender, and class punctuated the Borden saga. Also, Lizzie's arrest and trial erupted into a sensational media event that warrants examination. Newspapers and magazines both ginned up and catered to a broad American audience that became enthralled by what turned into a spectacle. Moreover, the Borden case is a story of the Gilded Age, a tale of bountiful wealth and entitlement on the local level.

CHAPTER I

Setting: The Bordens of Fall River

Lizzie Borden's legal ordeal unfolded between 1892 and 1893 at a distinctive New England industrial place and at a vexed moment in time. It is helpful, even crucial, to understand the Fall River of those years and the Borden clan's role in its creation. More than Lizzie's life and the virtuous Victorian womanhood that she publicly exemplified were at stake in the lurid crime and competing narratives of her guilt and innocence that grabbed national attention. The Borden family name was besmirched and so was Fall River's preferred image, burnished by elites, as a progressive industrial community. Immigrant labor unrest disrupted the elites' control of the city's reputation, and the Irish began to contest these Yankees' political dominance of Lizzie Borden's Fall River. With the city in flux, the Bordens and their fellow Yankees were not about to concede that one of their own, a genteel Christian woman, wielded a hatchet to commit the horrendous act of parricide.

The Family and Its River

The Bordens could not claim descent from the Mayflower, the gold standard of late nineteenth-century blue-blood genealogy. But they traced their New England ancestry back to the next best heroic era—the Puritan "Great Migration" of the 1630s. The progenitor of the clan, Richard Borden, disembarked at Boston in 1635. By 1636, he had settled at Portsmouth, in what would become part of Rhode Island. Two years later Anne Hutchinson, the Puritan firebrand banished from Massachusetts in 1637, and her like-minded supporters founded Portsmouth as their religious refuge. Richard may have been affiliated with them.

Over the generations the Bordens multiplied, spawning many

branches in Rhode Island and nearby southeastern Massachusetts. Some offshoots prospered more than others. When the Town of Fall River incorporated in 1803 half of the eighteen families were Bordens, including Lizzie's forbears. Until her father accumulated a fortune after decades of hard work, self-denial, and astute investing, however, Lizzie's lineage had been a stunted limb on the Borden family tree.

By 1892, the *Fall River Directory* listed 128 Borden heads of households. Spouses and children bolstered the Borden ranks. They also included single adult women like thirty-two-year-old Lizzie and her forty-one-year-old sister Emma. The unmarried daughters continued to live under the only patriarchy they had known since childhood.

Members of the extended Borden family had long controlled the Quequechan River, the catalyst for Fall River's industrial odyssey from mill town to industrial behemoth. The clunky, almost unpronounceable name "Quequechan" is an English version of the Pocasset Indian word for "falling river." "Fall River" is an adaptation of that translation. Quequechan actually designated a river of less than two miles that flowed from east to west toward Mount Hope Bay. Within less than half a mile, the Quequechan cascaded over eight falls that descended an impressive total of 130 feet. In the center of what became Fall River, the Quequechan's Great Falls made a dramatic 68-foot plunge toward the bay.

In the eighteenth century Bordens had harnessed the Quequechan's waterpower for sawmills and gristmills. In the early nineteenth century they came to realize that the river was a distinctive, exploitable New England industrial site. The Quequechan offered significant waterpower at a coastal location with ocean access to major textile markets in the Northeast. Geography bestowed another competitive asset on Fall River. Baled southern cotton and, after midcentury, mid-Atlantic coal for steam-powered mills could be more easily and cheaply delivered to Fall River than to major inland industrial locations. To reach Lowell, Massachusetts, on the Merrimack River, for example, ships had to sail around Cape Cod's extended arm.

Nathanial B. Borden, Holder Borden, Jefferson Borden, and especially his brother Richard Borden, a cousin of Lizzie's father, spearheaded industrialization of the Quequechan. They began as men of modest means, formed partnerships, attracted investors, and laid the foundation for the next generation's fabulous wealth. Bradford Durfee, another prolific local family name, became Richard Borden's principal partner. Durfee even married Borden's sister, a common practice between the two prominent families. Intermarriage among the emerging elites and interlocking directorates in the multiplying mill corporations created an intricate latticework of family and business affiliations.

The *New York Times* later acidly yet accurately described how these ties worked in the transition from the first to the next generation.

> Fall River has been more or less controlled by Durfees and Bordens, who appear and reappear as officers in most of the corporations. Of the Fall River Bleachery, Jefferson Borden is President, Spencer Borden is Treasurer and Jefferson Borden, Spencer Borden, Richard B. Borden, Philip D. Borden, and George B. Durfee are Directors. Of the American Print Works, Jefferson Borden is President, George B. Durfee is Clerk, Thomas J. Borden Treasurer, and Jefferson Borden, Thomas J. Borden, George B. Durfee, and W. B. Durfee are Directors. Bordens and Durfees have put their sons, brothers, uncles, sons-in-law, and cousins into office, and permitted them to do nearly as they chose. This is the way the Bordens and Durfees continually breakout, like small-pox, in all the industrial enterprises of that city.

The *Times'* commentary indicates how the Bordens and Fall River were well known in New York City—and throughout the Northeast. Such name recognition would fuel journalistic interest in the slaughter on Second Street. The morning after the murders, the *Times* headed a story on page two, summoning the family name: "Butchered in Their Home/ Mr. Borden and His Wife Killed in Broad Daylight."

———

Steam, Spindle City, and "The Hill"

With the arrival of steam power, Fall River's corporate cousins consolidated their control over mills, finance, and transportation (railroads and steamships). The second act in Fall River's industrialization encompassed the Taunton River and Mount Hope Bay, the western boundary of the town. Fall River incorporated as a city in 1854 with a population of 12,000. By then the Bordens, Durfees, and their partners had harnessed all the waterpower on the Quequechan, including the Great Falls, where, over time, the granite buildings of the Pocasset Mills sloped down to the waterfront. The advent of the steam engine in the 1850s altered the geography of industrialization in Fall River and opened its floodgates.

The new technology still required water for making steam and cooling engines. But steam substantially expanded the water sites available for industrial development. Fall River's textile corporations proved more nimble in converting to steam than their large inland competitors along the Merrimack River. For one thing, it was cheaper to deliver to Fall River the thousands of tons of coal required to operate steam-powered mills. The steam engine propelled rapid industrialization along the shore of the Taunton River and Mount Hope Bay. Indeed, the city's official seal, adopted in 1854, shows the Taunton River with smokestacks—one of Fall River's calling cards and a symbol of industrial progress—proudly, even boastfully, billowing soot over the skyline.

With the rise of steam power Fall River's old and newly formed corporations maximized the city's geographic advantages over its competitors. During the course of Lizzie Borden's life leading to her trial (1860–1893), upstart Fall River embarked on a journey that took it from modest mill town to "Spindle City," the major site in the nation for the production, as well as the bleaching and printing, of coarse gray cotton cloth. By the end of the century, more than forty inbred corporations controlled nearly 100 mills and millions of spindles—the spinning wheels that wound cotton thread onto bobbins. Fall River had exploded into one of the most heavily industrialized landscapes in New England. It was a manufacturing colossus composed of numerous small to midsized mills that had arrived in a jumble, without a communal vision or a master plan—except the drive to corner the market on the manufacture of coarse cotton cloth. In short, Lizzie Borden's Fall River departed radically from the famous world of the Boston Associates—the single well-financed corporation that established large planned industrial communities in Lowell and Lawrence, Massachusetts, and Manchester, New Hampshire.

Something else distinguished Lizzie Borden's Fall River. Most of its mills, especially those closest to her home on Second Street, were constructed of granite. From Connecticut to Maine, red brick buildings defined the face of industrial New England. Even nearby New Bedford, another major textile center and the place where Lizzie would be tried, was built of red brick. In the main Fall River's industrialists built their empire in granite because it was so readily available in the city's east end. A dense gray granite industrial landscape overspread swaths of Spindle City.

One other aspect of Fall River's emerging industrial landscape deserves comment because it shaped Lizzie's social aspiration. Within a few months of her acquittal, with her father's fortune in hand, she moved to "The Hill," Fall River's silk-stocking enclave. Spindle City came to be known as the place of "hills, mills, and dinner pails." Fall River was a city of rolling hills that undulated from the Taunton River and Mount Hope Bay. In the north end of the city the landscape reached a lofty, leafy plateau. Well-fixed Fall River families prized this location beginning in the middle of the nineteenth century for its refreshing summer breezes, broad vistas, and sparkling sunsets over the water. The Hill also offered seclusion from the clusters of mills, forests of triple-decker houses, and tribes of ethnic Catholics on the flatlands below.

Bordens, Durfees, and other leading Fall River families built Queen Anne and Colonial Revival homes and mansions on large lots along The Hill's streets. Rock Street emerged as the most coveted address of the elites. It ran through the heart of The Hill and connected to downtown. Not surprisingly, the Yankee establishment's houses of worship relocated to Rock Street. Central Congregational, Lizzie's church, was the city's most impressive Protestant edifice. The 1906 official *History of Fall River* described Central as follows: "It is of brick, with Nova Scotia freestone trimmings, and is in the Victorian Gothic style. It has a regular seating capacity of 1,200, which may be increased when necessary to 1,800." In 1875, the same year Central was dedicated, the Episcopalian Church of the Ascension moved to a new stately stone Gothic building a few blocks north of the Congregationalists on Rock Street. Not to be outshone, First Congregational—which Lizzie's father attended, albeit irregularly—later moved to Fall River's street of easy wealth and comfortable conscience.

In other words, as mills sprang up like toadstools and immigrants arrived by the boatload and the train-full, Spindle City's secular and sacred landscapes shifted in response. Wealthy Yankees sought a hilltop haven from the industrial world they had created. Lizzie's father didn't give a lick about joining them.

As she grew into young womanhood, Lizzie took heed of all the activity on The Hill. Her father remained content living on a noisy residential-commercial street, one short block from the bustle of South Main Street. A self-made, well-off Borden, Andrew had earned the respect of the "Hilltoppers." He was known as a prudent businessman with a sharp eye for calculating the value of real estate. In some quarters, he possessed a reputation for cold-heartedness. Like the corporations that used mill housing to control workers, evicting them for any job action, Borden's tenants could suddenly find themselves on the street for a missed rent payment. As an investor in mill stock and later as director of several mills and banks, Andrew knew and endorsed Fall River's hard-boiled industrial practices that yielded substantial profits, including to himself. In short, Andrew's personal business values and practices were not exceptionally cold-blooded; in the main they reflected the way corporations ran the mills and treated their overwhelmingly immigrant workers.

<hr>

The Fall River System and Matt Borden

It required much more than interlocking directorates and elite inter-marriage for Bordens, Durfees, and new families like the Braytons to ride herd on multiple corporations operating sundry mills. Yankee overlords devised what Mary Blewett in *Constant Turmoil* has called a distinctive "Fall River Industrial System." Through institutions such as the Board of Trade and the Fall River Manufacturers Association, mill owners crafted and enforced a set of flinty Yankee practices. All New England textile manufacturers benefited from a protective tariff on imports that stood at 40 percent in the 1880s. Within this protectionism, Fall River's mills specialized in the production of gray cotton cloth that needed to be bleached before it could be printed. Fall River's mills were constructed of gray granite, but Spindle City was built on gray cotton cloth.

The city's numerous mills turned out more cloth than local print works could handle. Possessing clear transportation advantages over rival cities, Fall River supplied gray cloth as well as printed goods to markets throughout the Northeast. With a vast production capacity, Spindle City's mill corporations dominated their corner of the textile market. Overproduction kept goods cheap, thereby discouraging potential competitors. The Fall River System also squeezed workers. The corporations exploited loopholes in a ten-hour workday law. They also managed to evade child labor laws, often with the complicity of desperate immigrant parents. Dickensian conditions prevailed in the mills. Thousands of children ten years of age and younger along with women—both of whom were paid less than men—labored for low wages around hazardous machinery in air filled with cotton fibers. In brief, specialized production, low prices, child labor, and slender wages underpinned the Fall River System, the lifestyle of people on The Hill, and much of Andrew Borden's wealth.

Still there was more. The mill corporations regularly relied on that hardy perennial of labor relations in Spindle City: the wage cut. When the economy slowed or profits failed to meet expectations, mills slashed wages. If a strike ensued, as it often did, the corporations always had an inventory of cotton goods to help them withstand the strife. Fall River came to be known among New England mill workers as a place of measly wages and chronic labor discord—a stark counter-image to the one cultivated by Spindle City's business community.

One headstrong Borden challenged the Fall River System, though he was unable to dethrone its kingpins—many of whom were his relatives. Matthew Chaloner Durfee Borden (1842–1912)—MCDB to the public, "Matt" to his employees—outstripped every other Borden as the most powerful and accomplished of all Fall River's industrialists. It is one of the ironies of Fall River's history that MCDB surpassed his ancestors and contemporaries as the most dynamic and distinguished Borden the city had ever seen, at the same time that Lizzie, his distant cousin, brought unwelcomed, far-flung notoriety to the family name.

MCDB was the youngest son of Richard B. Borden, the pioneering first-generation industrialist who became one of the richest men on The Hill. Matt followed the custom of his country and married a Durfee. Something of a maverick, though, he shunned The Hill. He built and ran his Fall River empire from New York City, another way the family gained prominence in Gotham.

Matt Borden acquired sole ownership of mills that his father and partners had established along the Taunton River. He demolished most of the buildings and opened up nearly twenty acres on the waterfront for industrial development. He was determined to wrest as much control of the coarse cotton cloth market as he could from the architects of the Fall River System. MCDB despised the system because local mills often drove hard bargains before they agreed to supply cloth to his American Printing Company. Such business tactics more than rankled; they inflamed the Borden competitive spirit. He resolved to create his own massive cotton mill complex on the east bank of the Taunton River, using his financial and marketing connections in New York City to advance his industrial empire.

Between 1889 and 1904, Borden constructed seven large cotton mills along the Taunton River and added buildings to his American Printing Company. By the time he was done, Matt Borden had created by far the largest cotton mill plant in Fall River, with perhaps unrivalled capacity in the country to produce, bleach, and print cotton cloth. Once all of his mills were up and running, each week the Borden complex processed 1,500 bales of cotton, produced 100,000 pieces of printed cloth, and consumed 1,600 tons of coal.

In 1895, when Lizzie was comfortably settled on The Hill finding ways to spend her father's money, Matt Borden donated $100,000 to Fall River for charitable purposes, including the construction of a boys' club and an old age home. He may have been trying to discomfort his well-heeled relatives on The Hill. One scours the Borden biographies in Fall River's official history for evidence of philanthropy or civic accomplishment. Charles F. Borden led the effort to establish a YMCA. Some Bordens held local political office or served terms in Congress. Borden mayors pushed for civic improvements such as extending gas and water lines, which benefited business as well as residential neighborhoods. Yet Borden benevolence, when it surfaced, appears to have been confined to the Central and First Congregational churches. After Andrew Borden was hacked to death, his obituary listed his business accomplishments and affiliations, but little else—certainly not civic associations or a trace of charitable contributions. MCDB's Fall River philanthropy overshadows Borden family history, like his towering 350-foot smokestack—by far the tallest of the scores of others that dominated the city's skyline.

Natives and Immigrants

The industrialization of Fall River, and of New England as a whole, proved to be a devil's bargain for Yankee mill owners and civic leaders, who were often one and the same. A steady supply of cheap immigrant labor, for example, served as the lifeblood of the Fall River System. Most textile jobs required little or no skill. Technological improvements in the late nineteenth century even made it easier to train illiterate immigrants to operate machinery. Thousands of immigrants became productive cogs in the industrial system that sustained life on The Hill. But the arrival of successive waves of immigrants altered the social and civic fabric of communities like Spindle City and provoked not only labor unrest. It stirred ethnic and racial animosities with the native born. Reverend William W. Adams, long-serving minister of the First Congregational Church and member of the local School Committee, fumed in print about what immigrants were doing to places such as his Fall River. In 1886, he published an essay in the *Andover Review* titled "The Spiritual Problem of the Manufacturing Town." The review was the publication of one of the leading Congregational seminaries in the country. It reached a national audience of influential ministers.

For Adams certain large immigrant groups constituted a plague, even though their labor surely helped pay his salary. "The parents have no education whatever," he complained; "they do not appreciate education for their children." Adams failed to acknowledge how child labor served as a means of family survival in a low-wage economy. Rather, as he saw it, parents marched their children off to the mills, which enabled the father "to live without labor," to become "a lounger at the rum-shops, or a 'political worker.'" Of course, he had the Irish in mind, who were "seldom of high grade."

Adams discerned in the growing French Canadian presence, "on average," "the lowest grade in the development of humanity." The dark-skinned Portuguese did not register on Adams's racial ranking of humanity. They had not yet flocked to Spindle City in 1886.

For Rev. Adams and the people for whom he was a spokesman, Catholic education was a travesty. In schools like St. Mary's, just up the street from the Bordens' residence in an expanding Irish neighborhood, the nuns "not infrequently" were "phenomenally incompetent." They squandered "half their time upon the church catechism and the prayer book." Indoctrination rather than education governed Catholic schools.

Adams's nativist outburst was bred from the conviction that the immigrants who descended on cities like Fall River would never be morally and intellectually fit for citizenship. Six years later, Adams would rally to Lizzie Borden's side and never doubt her innocence in public. If we assume, with fair certainty, that many in the Central Congregational Church shared brother Adams's sentiments, one wonders about Lizzie's Sunday school teaching. Her students were the children of immigrant Chinese laundrymen and women, the most alien people in the city.

Nativism like that of Adams was provoked by more than the perceived unfitness of new immigrants for informed citizenship. In the decades after the Civil War, New England Yankees represented the slowest-growing ethnic group in the entire country. Middle- and upper-class women, some influential men argued, bore much of the blame for the plight of the region's Yankee race. They practiced family limitation through contraception and abortion. They also increasingly extended their educations, with detrimental consequences for their physical health, especially their reproductive organs.

Though some highly educated women were beginning to enter professions formerly reserved for men, other respectable Victorian Yankee women no longer performed work within or outside the home. They also limited their exposure to the rigors of childbirth. One consequence, some doctors argued, was that the New Woman and well-to-do spinsters like Lizzie Borden became overly "delicate," that is, physically weaker than their Yankee ancestors—and, ironically, than the despised immigrants. The newcomers' women worked in mills and bred their young by the brood. In other words there were unresolved tensions within the Victorian elevation of female delicacy and anxieties over Yankee womanhood's physical decline.

Women advocates challenged the notion that their sisters, particularly those who pursued higher education, were contributing to Yankee "race suicide." They pointed to the high infant mortality rate among immigrants, while ignoring the living conditions that fostered this tragedy. They disputed the notion that too much education over-cultivated women. Yet the fact remained that New England Yankees were facing their demographic demise, and medical experts supported strengthening and enforcing pre–Civil War laws against abortion and contraception as one solution.

The debate over the physical delicacy of refined Yankee womanhood bears more than relevance to the nativist anxieties it excited. It is pertinent to the Lizzie Borden case. She was a highly cultivated young woman. A recurring question followed the crime: moral capacity aside, did delicate Lizzie possess the physical strength to wield a hatchet in such a vicious double-murder, delivering repeated blows with skull-cracking force?

Lizzie and her deeply rooted New England family were not immunized against the anti-immigrant and anti-Catholic prejudice that swirled around them. Dr. Michael Kelly lived next door. He had emigrated from Ireland when he was fourteen and settled in Fall River. Kelly graduated from Holy Cross College, trained as a doctor in New York City, and returned to Fall River in 1885. Five years later Irish Mayor John Coughlin appointed Kelly City Physician. The Bordens tolerated but avoided their impressive Irish immigrant neighbor and his family. If Andrew came face to face with the Kellys on Second Street, all he could summon was a clipped Yankee "How do?"

Consider what happened when Lizzie discovered her father's brutalized body. She yelled for "Maggie," the Bordens' Irish servant. Lizzie sent Maggie across the street to summon Seabury Bowen, the family doctor. He was not home. Apparently Lizzie never considered finding out if the Irish City Physician next door was at home. (He was actually out of town attending a medical meeting.) Nor did Lizzie seek the aid of J. B. Chagnon, the French-Canadian doctor who lived diagonally behind the Bordens, separated by a six-foot fence crowned with barbed wire. (He was also not at home.) Instead, Lizzie ordered Maggie down to nearby Borden Street to notify a friend, Miss Alice Russell.

Or consider Maggie. Her real name was Bridget Sullivan. Lizzie and Emma, unlike their parents, persisted in calling her Maggie, the name of their previous servant. It was almost as if to the daughters, and to many Yankees such as Rev. Adams, all Irish girls or women were "Maggies" or "Biddies" (Bridget), not individuals but members of a stereotypical group. In fact, the Irish were often referred to as "Paddy"

(Patrick) or "Micks," an undifferentiated mass with so many common names—McDonald, McCarthy, McMahon, and Mike, for instance. At Lizzie Borden's trial before the Superior Court, Bridget Sullivan was a witness for the prosecution. Lizzie's lead lawyer seized on the name "Maggie," trying to ferret out any hostility Bridget bore toward the defendant for not calling the servant by her proper name. He knew, as a former governor of Massachusetts, that the Irish resented being tagged Maggies and Micks. But Bridget refused to acknowledge any ethnic animosity, which would have undermined her credibility in court.

Q. You were called Maggie?
A. Yes, sir. . . .
Q. Not at all offensive?
A. No, sir.
Q. Did not cause any ill feeling or trouble?
A. No, sir.
Q. Did Mr. and Mrs. Borden call you by some other name?
A. Yes, sir, called me by my own right name.
Q. Did you have any trouble there in the family?
A. No, sir.

Bridget was a much more confident witness than she had been at the inquest and preliminary hearing ten months earlier.

It would be a mistake to assume that the people on The Hill and their supporters were losing their grip on Spindle City. They would continue to control mill investment, banking, and transportation—and they would not share, let alone relinquish, political control without a fight. Yet as Fall River fragmented into a patchwork of inward-looking mill villages with immigrants and their American-born children swelling toward majority status, the politically awakened Irish contested the Yankees' stranglehold on Spindle City's government.

Significantly, the Irish Catholic working-class daily, the *Fall River Globe*, was founded in 1885, the same year Spindle City elected its first Irish mayor. The *Globe* proved more combative than the older Irish Democratic newspaper, the *Fall River Herald*, founded in 1872. Dr. John Coughlin was one of the *Globe*'s directors. The newspaper helped him get reelected mayor in 1892, the second of his four consecutive terms.

He defeated The Hill's candidate, Philip H. Borden.

As well as competing for mayor, the Irish also made inroads on the Board of Aldermen. Then, too, the Irish gained a strong presence on the police force.

There was an unintended ethnic consequence to the shocking bloodshed in early August 1892. The Bordens had nothing to do with the Kellys next door, yet Lizzie and Emma were compelled repeatedly to answer questions or endure multiple searches at the hands of Irish police officers—Doherty, Mahoney, Mullaly, and Riley, among others— who overran their home.

Beyond the heavily Irish police force, other Sons of Erin intruded on the Bordens. Mayor John Coughlin took a lead in the investigation, continually returned to the scene of the crime, and met with Lizzie, Emma, and Maggie. The Bristol County Medical Examiner—Irishman Dr. William Dolan—assumed control of the mutilated corpses of Andrew and Abby. He was the first doctor to slice into the murder victims, cutting out body parts for laboratory examination. He also participated in the complete autopsy a week later at Oak Grove Cemetery, the Protestants' fashionable nineteenth-century rural burial ground. The bodies were decapitated. Skin would be removed from the heads, allowing the skull wounds to be clearly, and sensationally, presented in court. Andrew's death had precipitated the most invasive intimacy one could imagine between the Bordens and the Irish, from whom he had shrunk during his life.

An Ethnic Hierarchy

After the Borden murders, the pugnacious Irish *Fall River Globe* unrelentingly attacked Lizzie's credibility and assumed her guilt. In turn, over the ten months that stretched from accusation to acquittal, the extended Borden kinfolk, the Central and First Congregational churches, The Hill, and their house organ, the Republican *Fall River Evening News*, the oldest city newspaper, militantly championed the persecuted "girl," the virtuous "young Christian woman." Still, it would be an oversimplification to arrange the Borden case too neatly across a public divide between Catholic immigrants and the Protestant native born. For one thing, Spindle City's immigrant house of labor was ethnically and racially divided against itself.

Let us return to Maggie, or Bridget Sullivan, to begin a brief sketch of Spindle City's ethnic hierarchy in 1892. After the discovery of the crime, she apparently pointed the finger at a Portuguese from over the river because police asked about the presence of such a farm worker around the house that morning. Bridget was referring to a man who worked on one of Andrew Borden's Swansea farms, the second town westward across the Taunton River ten miles from Fall River. Lizzie quickly corrected her and pointed out that the man was actually Swedish. Nevertheless, Bridget's hasty accusation suggests where the recently immigrating Portuguese stood on the hierarchy of Spindle City's major immigrant groups—at the bottom with an undeserved reputation for violence.

Fall River's ethnic hierarchy became increasingly unyielding as the immigrant population skyrocketed in the 1890s. Between 1890 and 1893, the year Lizzie was tried, Spindle City's population grew by almost 10 percent. Over the course of the decade the population swelled from 74,918 to 104,863. According to the Federal Census of 1900, Fall River had the highest percentage of immigrants in its population of any city with more than 100,000 people.

Among Spindle City's immigrants, the English and Scottish occupied the top tier of the ethnic hierarchy, even though many were experienced, militant trade unionists coiled to contest the Fall River System. The Irish, the earliest group of Catholic arrivals who controlled the bishopric and the church, clung to the next rung. As successive waves of large Catholic immigrant groups arrived in Fall River, they threatened to undercut the wages of those who preceded them. This was especially true of French-Canadians, who abandoned infertile farms in Quebec by the tens of thousands and sought work in New England's post–Civil War burgeoning mill cities. French Canadians were first recruited as strike breakers. They were considered clannish and committed to preserving their language, the linchpin of their culture, across generations. They did rank above the mostly dark Portuguese, who emigrated primarily from the Azores and whose numbers were just beginning to grow at the time of the Borden murders.

Other immigrant groups, as well as Fall River's native born, typically considered the Portuguese as less than white or part "negro." Tensions and violence among immigrants roiled mill yards and spilled over onto streets. Headlines describing "Race Wars" screamed from the local press. "Portuguese and French Canadians Collided in French Town with Serious Results," one daily informed its readers.

For our purposes, Maggie's snap judgment about the Bordens' murderer is telling. The Portuguese came under particular suspicion during the earliest stages of the investigation. Within hours of the murder a Portuguese was arrested a few blocks from the Borden house. The *Fall River Herald* reported, "At 2:15 a sturdy Portuguese named Antonio Auriel was arrested in a saloon on Columbia Street and brought into the police station." Auriel was only released after he secured a reliable character witness. Other Portuguese were brought in for questioning on thin reeds. One raised suspicion because, a bank reported, he was withdrawing a significant amount of money. Across the Taunton River in Somerset, a Portuguese was interrogated because someone saw him with a bloody axe. Joseph Silvia established that he was not in Fall River on the day of the murders. His axe rested on a woodpile with no signs of blood.

The *Herald* described an encounter between Andrew Borden and a Portuguese farm worker on the day of the murders. This immigrant was nothing more than a figment of the fevered local imagination. The *Herald* claimed that the laborer went to Borden's house around 9 a.m. and asked for wages that were owed him. "Mr. Borden told the man he had no money with him, to call later." The implication of this unsubstantiated story was that this suspect needed to be found, arrested, and grilled. But "nobody around the house seemed to know" this man or his name.

The managers of Borden's two farms in Swansea may have hired Portuguese day laborers. It is highly unlikely that Andrew would have directly employed a despised Portuguese. After all, Andrew maintained a starchy relationship with his Irish neighbor who was a doctor.

Even after Lizzie was arrested, the slaughter on Second Street was represented as a masculine crime. Her defense hewed to this argument. In one narrative, a demented man had stolen into the house, hidden in a closet, and, almost miraculously, slipped away undetected. Though never fully articulated after the initial investigation was complete and police relied on strong circumstantial evidence to snare Lizzie, given the bloodbath on Second Street, her supporters and lawyers still conjured the murderer as a big, strong unhinged man and most likely a working-class immigrant. Instead, the authorities had arrested an upper-class Borden—a physically delicate, genteel Protestant "girl" of unblemished character and impressive engagement with institutions of moral reform. In other words, the police had locked up a paragon of virtuous Victorian ladyhood. And, then, as we shall see, only days before Lizzie's Superior Court trial, ten months after her arrest, a Portuguese immigrant did use an axe to murder the daughter of his employer on a Fall River farm. The new brutal crime sent a tremor through Fall River. Was the real assassin of the Bordens still on the loose?

Spindle City of 1892 was a vastly different and more widely known place from the Fall River of three decades earlier when Lizzie had been born. Business connections and riches had spread the Borden name well beyond Spindle City and Massachusetts. With members of the family in the forefront, the Fall River landscape had become far more heavily industrialized, gritty, and sooty. Wealth was far more highly concentrated. The Hill had evolved as a privileged precinct safely segregated from the overflowing triple-decker working-class quarters below. Immigrants poured into the city, and the Irish broke the Yankees' grip on the mayor's office and the Board of Aldermen. The entrenched Fall River System provoked strikes, which mill owners and agents accepted as a cost of doing business.

Lizzie's trial engaged issues of ethnicity, gender, and class, not to mention family name and the city's image. By 1892, her father had profited handsomely from his mill town's transformation into a cotton cloth empire. He was not nearly as wealthy as the richest Bordens on The Hill, shielded from immigrants and labor unrest behind granite walls and wrought-iron fences. Andrew rubbed shoulders with Hilltoppers as a director of mills and officer of banks. At the same time, Lizzie was emerging as one of the young leaders of the Central Congregational Church, located on the right side of town. At home things followed a different trajectory. It would be too much to say that family relations were as toxic as the overworked Quequechan River. Yet as they matured Lizzie and her sister, Emma, had grown distant from their stepmother. And for five years preceding the murders, family relations in the Borden household had turned permanently frosty.

CHAPTER 2

The Bordens of Second Street

The ghastly horror that transpired at 92 Second Street on the muggy morning of August 4, 1892, blew open the Borden family's triple-locked front door. The crime offered the public uninvited entrée into the domestic life of a prominent, wealthy Yankee family. Relatives, friends, neighbors, business associates, ministers, and investigators volunteered comments that were carried by the three local dailies. These newspapers published special editions as they tried to out-scoop one another, increase their readership, and satisfy the public's craving for details about the crime, the family, and the investigation. Boston, Providence, and New York papers, among others, joined the journalistic fray. Initial legal proceedings as well as Lizzie's Superior Court trial swelled the tidal wave of printed words devoted to the crime.

These and other sources enable us to document the poisonous atmosphere that pervaded the Borden household. Whether it proved lethal, as the police and prosecution argued, became a more difficult legal proposition to establish, especially in a court controlled by judges who were sympathetic to the defendant. Women numerically dominated the Borden home. No one, however, seriously challenged Andrew's prerogative to preside over the family. Lizzie did make a run at it. A hard-shelled self-made man, Andrew lived beneath his means and kept his business affairs to himself, most importantly, the future disposition of his estate. He tightly controlled the family purse strings, doled out the same weekly allowances to his wife and adult daughters, and paid his servant half as much. Yet despite his legendary penny-pinching, Andrew from time to time bestowed gifts and stock on his daughters and conveyed to them one controversial piece of property. In the last case, and probably on other occasions when he relaxed his miserliness, Andrew sought to ease mistrust between the daughters and their stepmother, restoring some emotional equilibrium to domestic life. A man of few words, Andrew also deployed money and gifts as his way of expressing love for Lizzie and her older sister, Emma.

Andrew's second wife, Abby, was the most lamentable member of the family. In particular, her efforts to win the love and respect of her stepdaughters ultimately came to naught. At forty-one, Emma was deep into the habits of spinsterhood and financial dependence on her father. Lizzie, nine years younger than her sister, was the second most forceful personality in the Borden family next to her father. She shared some of Andrew's makeup—at least behind the closed doors and shuttered windows of the Borden residence, an undistinguished structure even for Second Street. Bridget Sullivan, the twenty-six-year-old well-versed Irish maid, rounded out the household.

Andrew

Andrew perished just short of his seventieth birthday. He was a respected if unvarnished member of the Fall River business community who boasted that he had never borrowed a cent. Through austerity, industry, and the avoidance of debt he had cobbled together a fortune consisting of diverse investments. Andrew owned stock in mills and banks, rental property on and near the South Main Street business district, and two farms in Swansea. One farm served as a country retreat. To the west and east of Fall River, well-to-do families sought rural havens from Spindle City's industrial grime and unwashed immigrants. In fact, at the time of the Borden murders, Lizzie had planned to join friends in several days at Dr. Benjamin Handy's summer place in Marion, on Buzzard's Bay at the head of Cape Cod.

Andrew always sought a return on real estate investment. His main Swansea farm most likely turned a profit and provided the family with a weekend and vacation refuge from Spindle City. Andrew had a can of fresh milk from Swansea deposited on his side doorstep each day at approximately 5 a.m. His farmhands must have delivered milk, and probably eggs, to other Fall River households as well. They also harvested hay for sale.

Andrew's most important and highly valued piece of real estate was a three-story red brick building, trimmed in cast iron and located in the heart of South Main Street, which was constructed a few years before his murder. The top two floors held offices and businesses occupied the street-level space. Andrew inscribed his name on the building. Other well-to-do Fall Riverites emblazoned mills with family names. In a sense, Andrew outdid them. The A. J. Borden Building stood in the busiest part of town for all shoppers to see.

At the time of his demise, Andrew was president of the Union Savings Bank, a director of the B. M. C. Durfee Safe Deposit and Trust Company, and a director of the First National Bank. He also served as director of the Globe, Merchants, and Troy mills. Andrew's estate was worth well over $300,000, the equivalent of $8 to $10 million dollars today. From nothing he had accumulated an impressive sum; yet it didn't approach the wealth of the richest families on The Hill or that of Matt Borden in New York City.

Unlike Matt Borden, Andrew was not handed a head start in life. Born in 1822, Andrew was the son of Abraham Borden and a cousin of Richard B. Borden, Matt's fabulously wealthy father. Abraham numbered among the less successful Bordens. He is variously listed as a "gardener," a "laborer," and finally a "fishmonger," his more enduring occupation. Andrew's father did manage to acquire a modest house. It stood in a working-class neighborhood below the crest of a hill that descended to the waterfront. The Borden homestead was near the center of the city and only several blocks from where Andrew's life would come to a brutal end. He lived at home until he was thirty-one, even after he married and his daughter Emma was born. Andrew squirreled away his money and then invested it shrewdly when opportunities arose in his booming textile town.

The ambitious businessman spurned alcohol. Tobacco was another matter. At the time of his death, Andrew's pocket contained a "partly used package of fine cut chewing tobacco," one of his few daily indulgences.

Contrary to his father, Andrew showed some of the Borden drive. He trained as a cabinetmaker and found ready work in construction. Then with a partner, he opened a furniture store in 1845 on a corner of South

Main Street in the center of Fall River. The business quickly prospered, and before the age of thirty he had begun investing profits in real estate—both his own money and the partnership's. He became adept at buying and selling property. Later in life, clients called on his skill as an astute appraiser of real estate.

The furniture company branched out to the funeral business. As undertakers Borden and his partner supplied the bereaved with custom-made and stock caskets. They also rented furniture, such as chairs, for wakes. The undertaking business evolved into one of the most successful in the city. It was clear that with the furniture-funeral business the partners had combined enterprises with healthy profit margins and a steady stream of people in need.

Instead of consuming profits, Andrew continued to put his money to work, investing in mills, banks, property, and a streetcar line. In 1878, at the age of fifty-six, he sold his share of the furniture-undertaker partnership and retired to manage his investments. Still, Andrew retained a demeanor befitting an undertaker and shaped by a constellation of personal traits that seem to have been natural to him. Dressed in a black three-piece suit, even during Fall River's humid summers, Andrew was a long-faced, tight-lipped man. Standing six feet tall with little excess flesh on his erect figure, he strode down Main Street with a sense of determination in his gait and gaze. At the time of his death Borden sported a white beard that stretched from sideburn to sideburn across his chin almost in the shape of a crescent moon. His upper and lower lips and his cheeks were neatly shaved.

Andrew has been repeatedly described as an old-fashioned "Puritan" or of "Puritanical" character. Such descriptions do something of a disservice to New England's religious founders. Andrew had joined the Central Congregational Church in 1850, just as his furniture business prospered. But evidence indicates that he privileged worldly profit over religious return. Andrew was a full-blooded secular mutation of the historic Puritan—a nineteenth-century crotchety Yankee, without dry wit or any of the humor often imputed to the regional character in popular mid-century Yankee stage performances.

A story that emerged after Lizzie's arrest suggests how Andrew's devotion to the market prevailed over his bond with his religious brethren. Reverend William W. Jubb, the pastor of Central Congregational, explained in the *Fall River Herald* how Andrew became disaffected from the church. Charles Holmes, a banker, and his wife were members of Central and friends of Lizzie. Charles served as the leading deacon of the congregation. He approached Lizzie's father about a piece of property that Andrew owned and that the church corporation wanted to buy. Andrew's selling price was apparently unreasonable. He probably recognized that the well-off church had the resources to satisfy in full what he demanded. "Mr. Holmes voted against paying the price as he thought it was too high," Jubb reported, "and as a result Mr. Borden never attended the church afterward." In an act of spite, Andrew bought a pew in the First Congregational Church.

Andrew's brother-in-law, Hiram Harrington, related another story of money-grubbing, this time in the family. One has to approach Harrington's words cautiously. There were hard feelings between the Bordens of Second Street and Harrington of Fourth Street. He was married to Borden's sister, Lurana, Andrew's only sibling who survived childhood. He was not welcomed in Andrew's home. For one thing, Harrington was a blacksmith. He lacked Andrew's ambition, remaining content as a member of the working class. Hiram did nothing to enhance the Borden family's standing. Lurana remained modestly above the social level of her fishmonger father. Harrington, Lizzie later told police, was the only person she knew who bore ill will toward her father.

Despite this bad blood Hiram had a window on the Bordens of Second Street through his wife. He also had direct knowledge of how Andrew could be tightfisted even with his own sister. Harrington's characterization of Andrew is consistent with the Central Congregational Church squabble. To a *Fall River Herald* reporter he depicted Borden as "an exceedingly hard man concerning money matters, determined and stubborn." Once he made a decision "nothing could change him." Harrington went on to recount a story of petty greed or peeve. "When his father died some years ago he offered my wife the old homestead on Ferry Street for a certain sum of money. My wife preferred to take the money, and after the agreements were all signed . . . he wanted my wife to pay an additional $3.00 for a water tax upon the homestead."

Andrew reluctantly retained ownership of the homestead and rented it. But he was not finished with the property and related family problems. The homestead would be at the center of a tempest that ruptured relations between his daughters and their stepmother.

While Andrew's business career prospered, tragedy beset his personal life. In 1845, at the age of twenty-three, Andrew married Sarah Morse in Central Congregational Church. Twenty-one-year-old Sarah was a seamstress and the daughter of a cabinetmaker. An early photograph reveals a fair-skinned, plain-looking young woman with dark hair. Sarah does not bear much resemblance to Lizzie except for her light skin and full cheeks.

Emma was born in 1851. Soon the family moved out of the joint arrangement with Andrew's father but remained on Ferry Street. Then the first of two heartaches struck.

The Bordens' second daughter, Alice Esther, born in 1856, died less than two months before her second birthday. Approximately a year later, Sarah was pregnant again. The Bordens' third daughter was born in 1860. She was named Lizzie Andrew. Some have speculated about the name, which the daughter came to despise. Lizzie later changed her name to Lizbeth Andrews. Did Andrew bestow his name on his daughter because he expected and wanted a son? Given this yearning, did Andrew develop a special relationship with his younger daughter rather than with the older Emma? What kind of relationship might that have been? Lizzie gave her father an inexpensive gold ring, which he wore like a wedding band and carried to his grave. It would play a sentimental role in Lizzie's trial.

Less than three years after Lizzie was born, a greater and more disruptive tragedy than Alice Esther's death wracked Andrew's family. Sarah died at the age of thirty-nine in 1863 of what was diagnosed as uterine and spine disease. Andrew was forty years old and immersed in his business affairs. Now he was the sole parent for his two daughters, aged twelve and two. Sister Lurana helped with their care, but Andrew needed a wife.

Abby

Andrew's second wife is the most poignant character in the Borden family tragedy. He rescued her from almost certain lifelong impoverished spinsterhood. Andrew's new marriage may have been a loveless arrangement, a kind of "business" decision; he needed someone to care for his daughters. Andrew did not even wear a wedding band. Yet later he easily and permanently slipped on his finger Lizzie's gift of an inexpensive ring that she had worn. It was the only jewelry he displayed prominently, other than a silver watch and chain.

Andrew's second wife came from a working-class family. Abby Durfee Gray's father was a tinsmith. When she was thirty-two and still living at home, her mother died. Her father soon remarried, choosing a woman who was approximately a year older than Abby. Her stepmother gave birth to a daughter, Sarah, in 1864. Abby and her half-sister were thirty-six years apart in age! This generational difference underpinned a subsequent mother-daughter relationship. In fact, Sarah became her much older sister's closest friend and confidante. (She even named her daughter for Abby.) Their relationship would provide solace to Abby when Borden domestic affairs turned permanently icy. Her adult stepdaughters' resentment and mistrust eroded whatever lukewarm affection may have once abided in the household.

Andrew Borden and Abby Gray met at the Central Congregational Church. They married in 1865. If there were strong practical reasons for Andrew to take a new bride, the same was true for Abby. At thirty-seven, it may have been the last chance for her to escape from unending spinsterhood. Then, too, she lived awkwardly in a household in which her stepmother was approximately her age and her stepsister was three and a half decades younger.

Did Abby and Andrew enter into a marriage of mutual convenience? Some students of the Borden case have speculated on the murder victims' relationship. Andrew wanted a son. He was a vigorous forty-two, and Abby was five years younger. Yet she never became pregnant. Maybe he feared that Abby would die in childbirth. Perhaps it was a loveless marriage. At the inquest into the murders the district attorney, Hosea M. Knowlton, probed Emma about whether her parents were "happily united." She answered ambiguously: "Why I don't know but that they were. I think so."

Abby grew portly over the course of her marriage. She was not heavy when she wed, but she scaled at least two hundred pounds twenty-seven years later when she was murdered. Abby was often described as short because of her weight, but she stood five feet three or four, Lizzie's height. Abby, like her husband, had a set of false upper teeth. Her murderer dislodged her teeth as well as a switch of hair that probably covered a thinning spot.

Abby had become something of a recluse. She spent most of her time at home. Dusting the parlor and sitting room and caring for her bedroom and the guestroom were her primary domestic responsibilities. She left home to do grocery or household shopping. Sometimes she wore an ordinary morning dress, to the embarrassment of her stepdaughters. Like Andrew, she attended church irregularly. During the summer, the family spent weekends in Swansea; the daughters stopped visiting the farm with their parents five years before the murders.

Abby did not have close friends. When she went out on a social call, it was usually to visit her half sister. Sarah married George Whitehead, a teamster and then a produce salesman. Abby unburdened herself to Sarah as she strove and typically failed to cultivate enduring affection with her stepdaughters.

Abby led an obscure life. She remained behind the curtain in death. She merited only perfunctory mention in Andrew's obituary. Lizzie was initially indicted for her father's murder. Abby was not added until the grand jury voted, four months after the murders. At Lizzie's trial, her defense team established Andrew's murder as the axis of their case. After all he was the one with blood ties to the accused.

After the homicides, the principal of Lizzie's neighborhood Morgan Street School, Horace Benson, was interviewed by the *Woonsocket Call*, his hometown newspaper in Rhode Island. He had boarded next door to the Bordens for several years and came to know the family well. He described Abby as a "kindly hearted, lovable woman, who tried, but ineffectually, to win the love of the stepdaughters." Everyone who knew Abby, including Bridget Sullivan, agreed that she was a warm, gentle woman.

———

Andrew rationed weekly allowances the way he carefully doled out his affections. Abby received $4 per week, the same allowance as his daughters. To put this money in context, in Fall River's mills a skilled female spinner typically earned less than $5.50 for a sixty-hour workweek. There was one difference between the allowances of Abby and her stepdaughters. From her money Abby had to pay for household incidentals such as towels and curtains. Andrew stinted Abby, and she complained to half sister Sarah. Emma and Lizzie spent their allowances, and their time, as they pleased.

From his vantage point as the husband of Andrew's only surviving sister, Hiram Harrington claimed to the *Fall River Herald*, "For nearly ten years there have been constant disputes between the daughters and their father and stepmother." Circumstantial evidence indicated that five years before the murders Borden domestic affairs reached an acrimonious point of no return. Abby was at the center of this escalation of hostility, through no fault of her own. She persuaded Andrew to consummate one of the most generous acts of his life in 1887.

After Abby's father died, her stepmother wanted to sell the Fourth Street house. She co-owned the property with Abby's half-sister. Sarah did not have the money to buy out her mother's share. Sarah faced the prospect of losing her home. Somehow Abby convinced Andrew to buy the stepmother's share for $1,500. He gave the deed to Abby.

Andrew did not tell Emma and Lizzie. They found out from a friend. The daughters then confronted their father, with Lizzie as the advance party. As she testified during the inquest into the murders, "We thought what he did for her people, he ought to do for his own."

Andrew tried to placate his daughters. He conveyed to them the deed for the old Borden homestead, a rental property that was worth $3,000, the equivalent of Abby's stepsister's house. This gift would be the first of several he presented to his daughters in the years leading up to the murders. Less than three weeks before the grisly crime, in another act of generosity, or desperation, he repurchased the homestead from his daughters for $5,000!

Such generosity was so out of character that it suggests how Andrew sought to put a price on family peace, just as he did on everything else. There was little return on these investments, however. The daughters' distrust of Abby deepened. Lizzie stopped calling her "Mother" and referred to Abby as "Mrs. Borden." Lizzie and Emma snubbed Abby's half-sister whenever they encountered Sarah in public. As often as possible the daughters boycotted meals with their parents. Lizzie and Emma were genteel upper-class Victorian women. They knew proper behavior, how to control their feelings and talk through their teeth before guests and even maids. But sometimes Lizzie could not contain herself. The March before the murders, she had a cloak made by a Mrs. Hannah Gifford, who testified at her trial. Gifford had referred to Lizzie's "Mother" at the cloak-making session, and the daughter erupted. "'Don't say that to me, for she is a mean, good-for-nothing thing.' I said: 'Oh Lizzie, you don't mean that?' And she said: 'Yes, I don't have much to do with her; I stay in my room most of the time.' And I said: 'You do come down to your meals, don't you?' And she said: 'Yes, but we don't eat with them if we can help it.'"

Lizzie had grown up dependent on her sister. She had confided in Emma, not Abby. Yet over time, the sisterly relationship made a reversal. Lizzie came to dominate Emma, who possessed a more retiring temperament.

Emma

Unlike Lizzie, Emma had enduring, sentimental memories of her mother. Late in life she revealed in a rare interview to a *Boston Post* reporter what happened as her mother lay drawing her last breaths: "When my darling mother was on her deathbed she summoned me, and exacted a promise that I would always watch over 'baby' Lizzie." Lizzie acknowledged in court that she "always went to [her] sister, because she was older and had the care of [her] after mother died." Emma never doubted Lizzie's innocence, even a decade after the trial when the sisters separated for good and never spoke to one another again. Emma would protect "baby" at the trial. She shaved the truth; indeed, sometimes she took a carving knife to what other highly credible witnesses testified. For example, she would claim that she, not Lizzie, seized the initiative to challenge her father about his generosity to Abby and her half-sister.

Emma was less outgoing than Lizzie and with fewer friends. But she achieved more than Lizzie in school. She enrolled at Wheaton Female

Seminary, located between Providence and Boston, in 1867 at the age of sixteen. Modeled after Mount Holyoke Seminary, Wheaton was a Congregational institution that combined academics with religious instruction. Its biblical motto was: "Who drinks will thirst for more." Like Mount Holyoke, Wheaton produced graduates who often went into teaching or missionary work. Its alumnae also made good wives for Congregational ministers. By 1867 some graduates had begun to move into the professions.

Andrew paid for Emma's seminary education, though he did not attend church consistently and his fortune was still in the making. Perhaps he saw Emma's education as an investment that would enable her to support herself or, more likely, marry the right man. Whatever his intention, Emma remained only fifteen months or four semesters at Wheaton.

She returned home and never left. Emma was petite and not unattractive, well dressed and polite. But she doesn't seem to have entertained any serious suitors. When she turned twenty-one in 1872, Andrew left his familiar working-class neighborhood and purchased what became the infamous house at 92 Second Street. It was a better place to entertain young men, though not those from The Hill. Perhaps gruff Andrew scared off appropriate suitors. More likely Emma felt the obligation to continue "mothering" Lizzie at least into the latter's early adulthood. By then Emma was well beyond the typical age of marriage.

The years flew by and Emma found herself in early and then mid-spinsterhood. What she did with her time remains a mystery. Care for her bedroom was her principal household responsibility. She didn't travel. In Lizzie she had a domestic companion and confidante. And with $200 a year in spending money, the sisters had enough to live adequately as long as their father paid the bills at home.

Broadening the context beyond family circumstances helps us understand the Borden sisters' single lives. The familiar image of the unfortunate spinster, or so-called old maid, who remained single and lonely out of necessity, not choice, doesn't accurately encompass the female world in which Emma and Lizzie grew to adulthood. Single women in New England increased each decade over the first half of the nineteenth century, and beyond. The demographic disruption of the Civil War can't account for the fact that by the 1870s, 22.6 percent of native-born women in Massachusetts were single compared to the national average of 10.9 percent. Of course, not all of these women would remain unmarried. But the Borden sisters did belong to a multitude of Massachusetts single women.

As a group these women composed varied profiles. Their size and diversity meant that society more readily accepted and respected types of single women. Many of them elected to remain unmarried for personal reasons. For some the vaunted ideal of virtuous Victorian married womanhood appeared too demanding and confining. Others found the choice of a husband problematic. Massachusetts mill girl, teacher, and author Lucy Larcom explained why she elected the single life. Her biographer quotes Larcom's words: "marrying and giving in marriage" required women to be "sure *the* one *is* the one and no other." Larcom preferred her "life of 'single blessedness.'"

Some single women valued autonomy, the opportunity for intellectual growth, and self-fulfillment. This feminist quest typically characterized women who sought education at first-rate colleges and universities. Especially in the 1880s and 1890s, new college and university opportunities emerged for women. In particular the prominent colleges that would come to be called the "Seven Sisters" (four of which were in Massachusetts) attracted ambitious young women. Universities also began to admit women. College and university graduates flocked into the professions in growing cities. Some women continued their educations and returned to their alma maters to teach. Many educated, self-supporting, and solidly middle-class New Women remained single for life.

Still other models and motivations for elective singlehood developed during the Borden sisters' early life. Emma remained single largely because her mission in life seemed to be Lizzie herself. Emma did make a choice. Yet, in many respects, she acquired the profile of the traditional old maid. Lizzie, however, pursued a rather different single life from her sister.

———

Lizzie

Lizzie was no more than 5 feet 4 inches tall. She possessed a sturdy 130-pound frame. Her figure was appropriately feminine for the era when it was corseted by tight-fitting Victorian outfits that constrained respectable women's movements.

Horace Benson, Lizzie's former Morgan Street School principal, who believed she was incapable of committing the double murders, described her in the classroom to the *Woonsocket Call:* "As a pupil she was an average scholar, neither being exceptionally smart nor noticeably dull," he reported. "She was subject to varying moods, and was never fond of her stepmother." Others concurred with Benson's assessment of Lizzie's moodiness. Her uncle John Morse, the older brother of Lizzie's deceased mother, happened to be visiting the Bordens at the time of the murders. He gave an interview to the *New York Herald* in which he described his niece as a "peculiar girl often given to fits of sullenness." Hiram Harrington, her uncle by marriage, was more blunt, even intemperate. "Lizzie is of a repellant disposition, and after an unsuccessful passage with her father would become sulky and refuse to speak to him for days at a time."

Lizzie attended Fall River High School, completing only two years. She left during the next school year. Thus she never graduated. Even though he had supported Emma at Wheaton, Andrew apparently did not insist that Lizzie finish high school. Or, perhaps he did, and his strong-willed daughter refused. While she dressed well and became socially adept, Lizzie possessed weaker formal education than most ladies from The Hill. In a word, she was less eligible to men of her class. Lizzie lived at home with care of her bedroom her chief responsibility. She socialized with friends and during the summer spent time in Swansea where she loved to fish. Yet her adult life before she became a "joiner" belongs to those everyday activities in the private world of a privileged single woman that typically elude recorded history. Neither Lizzie nor her sister kept a diary.

Lizzie didn't fully awaken to Christ until she was twenty-seven years old, that is, after she had passed the typical age of marriage and joined the ranks of those single women who were perceived as spinsters. Then she embraced religion with the enthusiasm of a convert. To be sure, she had attended Central Congregational before then, but she was only confirmed as a member of the church in 1887, five years before the murders. At the time of the crime she had already compiled an impressive record of woman's activism in the congregation.

Lizzie served as Secretary and Treasurer of Christian Endeavor. Congregationalists formed the society in the 1880s to encourage religion among young people of their churches and to support Sunday schools. Lizzie grew close to the Reverend Edwin A. Buck, Central Congregational Church's City Missionary, who informed the *Fall River Herald* after the preliminary hearing that he had been "this girl's spiritual counselor for 20 years . . . She is as innocent as the day she was born."

Lizzie also joined the Fruit and Flower Mission, a coalition of women from leading Fall River churches. The members visited sick people, especially the indigent, in the hospital or in their homes. They brought gifts for children and adults. The Mission women performed other good deeds such as organizing Thanksgiving and Christmas dinners for poor children. Much of this activity was admirable. Nevertheless, it offered meager relief to the poor, and the upper-class women never questioned poverty's root causes, the components of the Fall River System.

Lizzie made other commitments during her outburst of civic and religious engagement. She joined the Women's Board of the Fall River Hospital. Perhaps most significantly, Lizzie became a member of the Young Women's Christian Temperance Union, a wing of the WCTU. Founded in 1874 the WCTU believed that alcohol lay at the root of many of the country's social ills, particularly domestic problems. The WCTU viewed the United States' growing immigrant population, particularly the Irish and Germans, as aggravating the country's disruptive abuse of alcohol.

The WCTU elected Frances Willard its second president in 1879. She would serve for nearly two decades. A college graduate who had successfully pursued a career in higher education, Willard had broken off her marriage engagement and claimed that she never regretted her decision. She remained single for the rest of her life. Willard added women's suffrage to the WCTU's reform agenda, making the organization more feminist and radical. Local unions possessed considerable autonomy, however, and there is no record of Lizzie's advocacy of suffrage.

For all the ways that Frances Willard embodied the figure of the New Woman, she also came from an evangelical Christian background. She believed in the spiritual and moral superiority of women. During her first presidential address in 1880, Willard referred to her single members as "our Protestant nuns," who were "once called spinsters." These Protestant nuns and married women were to work together in the WCTU; its ranks numbered approximately 160,000 in 1892.

Willard's Protestant nuns were, like Lizzie, single, churchgoing, and socially engaged. What the WCTU and her other reform activities suggest is that especially after the age of twenty-seven Lizzie flirted with an ideal of Victorian single life that resembles what women's historian Carroll Smith-Rosenberg has described as "proto-feminist": "More pious and domestic than men, the efficient housekeepers of the nation, True Women . . . could not confine their efforts to their homes and families. They must extend their 'home rule' to encompass the world—wherever children and other women needed ministrations. With these words they had justified . . . the 'Do Everything' policy of Frances Willard and the WCTU." We don't have to transform Lizzie into a suffragist or actual proto-feminist to appreciate how the WCTU's mission clarifies the way she tried to make sense of her life after she awakened to religion. Lizzie's socially engaged Christian life validated her claim on unmarried but still highly virtuous Victorian ladyhood. Yet in many respects, such a public persona stood at odds with her life at home. The five-year period—1887–1892—that marked Lizzie's flurry of activism also recorded family rancor over the purchase of Abby's sister's house and the ongoing deterioration of Borden domestic relations.

Through her religious and social commitments, Lizzie advanced her standing on The Hill and beyond. She fashioned a public profile that befit her gender and class while she built a reservoir of goodwill. The ministers of Central and First Congregational churches and their members, as well as the WCTU, would form a phalanx of supporters and even a pressure group on her behalf.

A core group of Lizzie's friends was vacationing at Marion, Massachusetts, at the time of the crime, which scuttled her plans to join them the following week. It is instructive to compare Lizzie to these eleven companions. They ranged in age from twenty-three to thirty-seven, with most in their late twenties and thirties. Only one was married. Six were teachers in Fall River's public primary schools. A seventh served as a principal and another was a former teacher. In their form of the single life such teachers sacrificed procreation to nurture other peoples' children, thereby extending "home rule" beyond their families. They also affirmed their virtuous Victorian womanhood. Unmarried teachers have been called "moral mothers." In any event, having completed only two years of high school, Lizzie fell well below the educational level of her closest peers and her sister. She had no interest in the poorly paid job of a moral mother.

In another way, however, she and nearly all of her Marion friends shared an identical profile. Nine of the eleven belonged to the Central Congregational Church and were active in its women's reform and relief societies. They, like Lizzie, assumed the public shape of the Protestant nun.

It is important to keep in mind that the less-educated Lizzie was no dowdy spinster church lady. Her worldliness extended beyond social climbing. She had a taste for fashion, which became more pronounced after she inherited her father's wealth. Two days after the murders, when the police searched the large closet at the top of the front stairs that Lizzie shared with Emma, they found upwards of eighteen dresses. Many—perhaps most—belonged to Lizzie. Eight of the ten blue dresses were hers. (She wore blue on the morning of the murders.) Lizzie also owned an expensive sealskin cape, another peace offering from her father. She possessed more fur garments, as testimony at the inquest revealed. She described "seal skin sacks" that were "hanging in a large white bag in the attic, each one separate."

Lizzie enjoyed travel, and perhaps the most expensive gift Andrew gave her was a Grand Tour of Europe for her thirtieth birthday. In the summer of 1890, Lizzie and several of her friends toured Europe: England, Scotland, France, Switzerland, Germany, and Italy. As they approached Fall River in November, Lizzie divulged her unhappiness to her cabin mate, Anna Borden, who testified at the trial. Anna related how Lizzie said that she "regretted the necessity of returning after she had such a happy summer, because the home that she was about to return to was such an unhappy home."

Lizzie liked stylish clothes more than jewelry, though she later acquired three diamond rings and other gems. In this respect, there was a suggestive burglary at 92 Second Street the summer before the murders involving money and Abby's jewelry. It has a striking parallel to the later crime. Andrew and Abby were at their country retreat in Swansea. Lizzie, Emma, and Maggie were home. A thief managed to open the locked door to the parents' bedroom and Abby's adjacent dressing room. Andrew's desk in the dressing room was broken open. Among the things stolen, according to the police report, which is published in a collection of the district attorney's papers: "$80.00 in money and 25 to 30 dollars in gold ... [Abby's] gold watch & chain, ladies [sic] chain with slide & tassel attached, [and] some other trinkets of jewelry." The investigating officer did get a "6 or 8 penny nail" from Lizzie, who said "she found [it] in the Key hole of [the] door."

Lizzie, Emma, and Maggie heard no intruder. The police combed the neighborhood, but nobody saw anyone entering or leaving the Borden property. The investigating officer reported that over the next two weeks Andrew said three times, "I am afraid the police will not be able to find the real thief." Undoubtedly, he suspected, or knew down to the core of his being, that Lizzie was the culprit in another expression of jealousy toward Abby and resistance to his patriarchal control of family affairs.

The robbery on Second Street raises the question of whether Lizzie was a kleptomaniac because of an incident that occurred four years after her acquittal. Lizzie owned two porcelain paintings from Tilden-Thurber, a fine jeweler in Providence. A friend admired the plaques and Lizzie gave her one. Later the porcelain was damaged and the friend visited Tilden-Thurber to see if it could be repaired. The store had no record of its purchase and a warrant was issued for Lizzie Borden's arrest. She apparently made restitution and the matter was settled.

Some popular writers on the Borden case argue, or simply assert, that Lizzie was a serial shoplifter. Oral tradition from a few families on The Hill who knew Lizzie passed the claim down to their children. These informants were alive as late as the early 1990s. In interviews with investigators interested in Lizzie, they transmitted what they were told about her alleged shoplifting.

Lizzie does fit the profile of the typical late nineteenth-century shoplifter. "Kleptomania" was a coinage of that century. It refers to the compulsion to steal while having no material need and with no relationship to value of the object. At the time of the robbery at Second Street, Lizzie had her regular allowance, mill and bank stock, and rental income, however small, from the Borden homestead. A year later, when the murders were committed, she had over $2,800.00 in the bank. As women historians in particular have shown, kleptomania coincided with the nineteenth-century emergence of the department store and its cornucopia of material goods, grouped by commodity and attractively displayed. The department store was a temple of consumption. Well-off women constituted its principal worshippers.

Why did comfortable Victorian women steal? Here the robbery on Second Street is intriguing. On one level, kleptomania was an "act of defiance," a form of rebellion against the way husbands and fathers controlled women's lives. The department store offered escape from women's tightly bound world. Kleptomania added excitement, as well as resistance against patriarchy, to women's shopping excursions.

On another level, however, kleptomania reinforced important Victorian gender convictions. As the label suggests, kleptomania came to be seen as a periodic semi-medical condition rather than a crime. Victorian medical authorities associated it with menstruation. Defined as a crime, kleptomania would have subverted accepted notions of true Victorian womanhood—its morally pure essence. Instead of criminals, kleptomaniacs were represented as respectable women periodically "unstable" and incapable of controlling their impulses in an emporium stocked with aisles of seductive items. Typically, husbands and fathers made restitution for pilfered goods—another display of patriarchy.

If the Borden house robbery had some of the defiant trademarks of kleptomania, does that mean Lizzie was afflicted with this "semi-medical condition"? Perhaps she did shoplift in the department stores blocks from her house and in the midst of Andrew's commercial empire—a bold act of defiance. Perhaps Andrew attempted to preempt Lizzie's shoplifting with his ongoing gifts, which, of course, would have had precisely the opposite effect. He gave Lizzie and Emma bank and mill stock, some of which they sold even though the price plummeted. Andrew's gift giving was another act of control and possibly a miscalculation that bolstering Lizzie's bank account would forestall kleptomania.

The issue never arose at the inquest, preliminary hearing, or Superior Court trial. But, then, why would it? Kleptomania was not a crime but an episodic emotional "disorder" that Victorian doctors and others reconciled with notions of true womanhood. Lizzie did possess the family background of the typical kleptomaniac. The house robbery and the Providence incident offer evidence that she was a fitful shoplifter if not a full-fledged kleptomaniac.

Even as Andrew and Abby lay dead, the murderer delivered repeated blows to their skulls. The brutality even shocked some observers of the scene who had witnessed the carnage of the Civil War. The murders manifested rage, which has led a few commentators who believe in Lizzie's guilt to suggest that incest, not greed, provoked the crime.

In many respects, the Borden family displayed the classic preconditions for incest. Andrew was a domineering father. Abby was a powerless stepmother. Andrew had a special relationship with Lizzie. He had ready access to his daughters' rooms. Privacy was at a premium, until all the inhabitants began locking, even barricading, their rooms. For fifteen months, Emma was away at Wheaton, and Andrew was alone with Lizzie.

All of this boils down to conjecture, intriguing in light of the horrific nature of the crime. In the most perceptive analysis among the mere handful of scholarly essays and chapters on the Borden murders, feminist historian Cara Robertson proposes that a nonsexual incestuous family "dynamic" among the Bordens could still have generated the murderous rage. "Like cases of incest," Robinson argues, "relations in the Borden family are marked by contradictions of protection and abuse as well as accord and submission."

Andrew rewarded and deprived his daughters. He reaffirmed his authority by bestowing and withholding gifts. This family drama unfolded as Abby was mostly a spectator. Lizzie had a special bond with her father, most visibly represented by the ring he wore. The preceding spring when the house was to be painted, Andrew told Lizzie, not Abby or Emma, to choose the color. In her own conflicted way, Lizzie loved Andrew. Yet she was completely dependent on him and deeply, and wrongly, suspicious that her passive stepmother secretly influenced Andrew on money matters. This distrust escalated when he purchased the home of Abby's half-sister.

Bridget "Maggie" Sullivan

Bridget Sullivan emigrated from Ireland at the age of twenty in 1886. She worked as a maid in Newport, then moved to Pennsylvania to live with relatives, and came to Fall River in 1888. She was hired by the Bordens in 1889 and at the time of the murders had been employed by the family for nearly three years.

Bridget was sturdily built and plain looking. Her duties included cooking, washing, ironing, and sweeping. She slept in the attic and was paid $2.50 per week. She worked six days a week. The Bordens relieved her of labor on Sunday. Increasing wealth in Fall River created a demand for experienced servants such as Bridget that outstripped the supply. Turnover was common, as Irish "girls" sought better-paying positions. The departure of a good servant threw households like the Bordens' into turmoil.

Though Bridget stated in court that she liked working for the Bordens, she told Officer Patrick Doherty a different story when he accompanied her to the police station during the inquest. Tension permeated the Borden household and she threatened to leave on more than one occasion. "But Mrs. Borden was a lovely woman, and I remained there because she wanted me to." The fifty cents in Bridget's weekly salary may have been a raise pinched from Abby's allowance. Bridget was called "the girl" when the Bordens referred to her among other people. They followed custom; maids were the "Bordens' girl" or "Dr. Handy's girl" or "Reverend Adams's girl."

Bridget left the Borden family for good two days after the murders. She testified at all four of Lizzie's legal proceedings, gaining her voice and confidence over time. At first she feared that Lizzie's lawyers would implicate her in the crime. After all, she was a lowly Irish immigrant, an unladylike "girl." Ethnicity, class, and gender were arrayed against her. Sympathetic Irish police and other investigators quickly and soundly eliminated her as a suspect. Even Lizzie stood up for her innocence.

After Lizzie was charged, however, the president of the Board of Aldermen, John Beattie, seemed to question why the police had not arrested Bridget. The *Fall River Globe* quoted Beattie on the contrast between Lizzie and her hired help: "We hate to believe, we find it hard to think, that a girl brought up as well and with the intellectual associations she has had would commit such a crime as this. I have always wondered why the servant girl was not arrested." The Irish community was thrown into an uproar, and Beattie denied that he had made such a statement.

Still, at the preliminary hearing, Lizzie's lawyer summoned the image of Bridget, the unpolished commoner, in a provocative way. In his closing argument, Andrew J. Jennings insisted that he was not accusing Bridget of the crime. In fact, Jennings claimed, he believed she was innocent. Then he asked: "In the natural course of things who would be the party to be suspected? Whose clothing would be examined, and who would have to account for every movement of her time? Would it be the stranger, or would it be the one bound to the murdered man by ties of love?" No wonder Bridget feared being drawn into the eye of the storm.

John V. Morse

Morse had the misfortune of visiting the Bordens the day before their murders, staying in the guestroom where Abby was killed the next morning and returning to the house shortly after the bodies were discovered. That night he showed his steeliness. He slept in the bed inches from where Abby's murderer had spilled her blood and brains hours earlier. He remained at the house during the investigation and was considered a suspect. However, Morse established that he was far from Second Street at the time of the murders.

Morse was the brother of Lizzie's mother Sarah and had lived in the West for nearly four decades, mostly in Hastings, Iowa. He owned farmland, raised cattle and horses. Morse acquired some wealth and returned to Massachusetts three years before the murders. He boarded in South Dartmouth, approximately 15 miles east of Fall River and kept a hand in horse trading. Perhaps this occupation formed the basis for his continuing relationship with Andrew. Horse trading required skill in estimating value. Indeed, the Yankee horse trader was a common figure in nineteenth-century popular culture. Noted for his shrewdness, the Yankee horse trader was often represented as a "sharpy," someone who easily slipped into duping people. Andrew must have admired Morse's business skills, which in many ways mirrored his own. After the crime, a

Boston Post reporter interviewed Morse's former neighbors in Iowa. They described him as "frugal" and "self-denying." He was "hard-fisted in his business dealings, almost avaricious but scrupulously honest." Not surprisingly, Andrew liked and sought the counsel of the fifty-nine-year-old Morse. They were both cut from the same bolt of Fall River cloth.

One would think that Lizzie developed a relationship with the brother of her idealized dead mother. Instead she deliberately ignored him. She seemed to resent that her father discussed his business affairs with Uncle John but not with anyone else in the family. Morse's inopportune visit did nothing to temporarily tamp down family tensions. His presence had the opposite effect. Lizzie came home on the night before the murders and went straight to her room without bothering to greet Uncle John. Nearly twenty-four hours after he first arrived, Morse finally spoke to Lizzie. Andrew and Abby had already perished.

House and Street

The Bordens moved to 92 Second Street in 1872 when Emma was twenty-one and Lizzie was twelve. The house was a step up from their dwelling on working-class Ferry Street. Still, Andrew could have easily afforded a more substantial home at a more fashionable address.

The two-family house had been built in 1845 for an overseer of a carding room in a mill, someone with a respectable position but well beneath Andrew's socio-economic standing. Andrew converted it to a single-family home. He remodeled the second-floor kitchen into his bedroom. The house had unusual features. It had been two "railroad flats," narrow, long apartments resembling a passenger car. The house was barely 20 feet wide. There were no halls on the floors. As a result, the Bordens had to pass through one bedroom to reach the next. They devised a layout to ensure some privacy and in the process they re-created elements of a two-family house. The back stairs were reserved for access to Andrew's and Abby's bedroom. One reached Emma's and Lizzie's rooms as well as the guestroom via the front stairs. At least two years before the murders, the family locked their bedrooms at night. Then Andrew and Abby secured their room even when they came downstairs for meals. Lizzie's bedroom adjoined that of her parents. They bolted it on their side and pushed a bureau against the door, which was hooked on Lizzie's side. She moved a desk that was five feet high against the door to the guestroom. Andrew kept a club under his bed. The Bordens guarded their rooms against each other like they often padlocked their emotions.

Some of their bureau drawers were under lock and key. The front door had key and spring locks and a deadbolt. The north-facing side door, the servant's entrance, was also equipped with three locks, including a bolt. The Bordens opened the door in the summer. Then they fastened the entrance's screen door with a hook. From bedrooms to house doors to bureau drawers, the Bordens remained in lock-down, even during the day. In this narrow house seething with mistrust, they sought security against the outside world and separation from each other.

When the Bordens moved to Second Street, Lizzie, as the youngest, was given the smallest bedroom, less than two-thirds the size of the others. A major change occurred in 1890. Lizzie took over her sister's room and Emma moved into the smallest bedroom. Emma later claimed that this was her own decision. She offered her room as a present to Lizzie for her thirtieth birthday. But given Lizzie's emergent personality and how she had outgrown Emma's "mothering," the exchange of rooms must have been more complicated. Perhaps Lizzie pressured her sister to switch rooms. For one thing she had mementos from her Grand Tour to display. Then, too, the Bordens had become accustomed to using domestic space to manage family relations.

The house did not have up-to-date plumbing, at least by the standard of Andrew's wealth. There was no running water on the second floor. A small sink room near the back door had running water, as did the barn, where a horse had been stabled until Andrew stopped driving his carriage approximately a year before the murders. There was a sink in the basement and a water closet with a stack of old newspapers for ready use. The bare dirt cellar floor was only covered near the sink, where there were a few boards to stand on. Without a second-floor bathroom, the family resorted to slop pails at night. They drew water in the sink room and carried it in a basin to bathe in their rooms. The dirty water went into the slop pail.

The pail had other uses. Lizzie was at the end of menstruation at the time of the murders. The slop pail was one way to carry menstruation cloths to the cellar for washing. When Inspector William Medley and Officer Michael Mullaly searched the cellar, they came across a pail with bloody cloths soaking in water. The prosecution was impeded from using such evidence, though instead of menstruation cloths they might have been small towels used to clean up after the murders. At the preliminary hearing, Officer Mullaly described seeing the pail. Lizzie's lawyer immediately jumped to his feet and reminded the district attorney: "You disclaim any connection of that matter with this case, I thought?" In turn, Lizzie's lawyers, and the defendant herself, were able to deploy her "monthly illness" a few times to frustrate the prosecution.

The house did possess some contemporary features and comforts. The windows were equipped with attractive interior white shutters that opened and closed separately on the top and bottom. There was a coal furnace in the basement that provided central heat. Andrew purchased a piano that Lizzie once played. Descriptions of the interior of the house after the murders varied. The prosecution hired a Charles A. Bryant, a mason and building contractor, to conduct a thorough search of the house before Lizzie was arrested. Bryant gave his impressions to the *Fall River Herald*. "I would say that the house was furnished very plainly—notably so," he reported. "The ordinary mechanic with an ordinary salary has his house furnished as well. There was nothing in the house to indicate the wealth of the people who lived there." Of the horsehair sofa on which Andrew was bludgeoned, the Borden family doctor, Seabury Bowen, told a reporter for the *Fall River Globe* it was the kind "commonly manufactured for high class parlors forty years ago." The piece probably had been acquired at a discount when Andrew still owned his furniture store.

Three weeks after the murders a Mrs. Percy, a reporter for the *New York Herald*, which was sympathetic to Lizzie's plight, presented a very different view of the house's interior. She most likely was invited by Emma and her lawyers to dispel rumors that the family lived amid downscale furnishings, a frustrating deprivation resulting from Andrew's miserliness. Mrs. Percy arrived with low expectations. "I was surprised to find the house extremely pretty and refined in its appointments," she reported. "Easy chairs, shaded lamps, books, well-chosen bits of bric-a-brac, cushions and draperies, an open piano, a hundred comforts and pleasing trifles tastefully disposed bespoke pleasantly the character of the inhabitants."

Did she notice the absence of electricity, the lack of a telephone for a businessman, the inconvenience of no running water on the second floor, or the privation of no bathroom on either floor? The reality of the Bordens' material world probably falls closer to mason Bryant's and the doctor's observations than reporter Percy's. Still, Andrew the penurious patriarch did not furnish his home quite as plainly as he dressed.

Mrs. Percy penned a helpful, though wrought-up, description of Lizzie's room. It was "as dainty and charming as any girl need ask for. The tiny bed had a pale blue embroidered counterpane," supposedly Lizzie's handiwork. The wall had a recess with Lizzie's washstand. Curtains afforded privacy; this was probably where she kept her slop pail. "Many books and pictures were in the room, some of them evidently gathered in that foreign [Grand Tour] journey." Mrs. Percy "read" the room as evidence of Lizzie's innocence. "How could Lizzie Borden have come in the dainty place and removed the traces of such fearful work without marring all the delicate purity of everything with which she had contact." Though we are afforded a rare glimpse of Lizzie's inner sanctum, where she spent most of her time when at home, Percy's piece ladled out too much sentiment. The *Fall River Herald* republished the dispatch of her visit to the crime scene, giving it wide local circulation.

Lizzie chose a "drab" shade of brown when the house was painted in May. At Lizzie's trial the painter described the house as "kind of dark drab." The shutters and trim were painted an even darker color. Lizzie loved blue, as witnessed by her dresses. Yet she chose a dreary color for a house from which she longed to escape.

The Borden house had no front yard. The dwelling hugged the sidewalk, separated by an attractive picket fence. Second Street paralleled nearby South Main Street. It ran north to south, climbing one of Fall River's profusion of hills along the way. The Bordens lived on the lower end, a block and a half from Pleasant Street, 900 feet from City Hall, and 1,300 feet from the police station. Andrew valued Second Street's proximity to his commercial empire on South Main Street, especially after age forced him to give up his rig.

From Main Street commercial activity spilled over to or was spawned on Second Street. The Bordens lived in a residential-business neighborhood, unlike The Hill. There were more distinguished homes on Second Street than the Bordens'. Next door, for example, Mrs. Adelaide Churchill, whose father had been mayor, occupied a large, Federal-style house. Dr. Bowen lived in a similar house across the street. Dr. Kelly's house was a Cape Cod dwelling with an addition on the back. The visual effect of these surrounding dwellings served to accentuate how narrow, clear-cut, and plain the Bordens' house appeared. It was almost as if the house made an architectural statement of Andrew's temperament and reputation.

He was by far the wealthiest man on Second Street. Professionals and shopkeepers occupied homes and businesses along the blocks. In the thick of the Bordens' neighborhood, one found in addition to two doctors, a liquor store, a grocer, a livery stable, a news store, a restaurant, a plumbing company, a paint shop, a photography studio, two Chinese laundries, and the rectory of the two Irish priests who served St. Mary's Church. The mix of businesses and residences and Second Street's location alongside Spindle City's business district generated traffic and noise. Second Street was paved in front of the Borden house. Thus, wagons rattled up and down the hill as horses pounded the pavement. Carriages conveyed people to and from South Main Street and points beyond. Everyday, all day, foot traffic passed the Borden house in both directions. Conversations in English and sometimes in French or Portuguese filled the air.

Some of the city's oldest mills were almost within hailing distance of 92 Second Street. The spindles of the Troy Mill hummed three blocks away at a falls of the Quequechan River between Third and Fourth Streets. The Union and Wamsutta mills were a stroll from the Borden house down Second Street and east on Pleasant. And six short blocks away from the Bordens, across from the Durfee Mills complex, one of Fall River's brothels did a thriving business.

Then, too, Irish and French-Canadian Catholics were altering the character of the Bordens' neighborhood. Absorbed in his business affairs on South Main Street, Andrew displayed no inclination to flee the neighborhood. Lizzie aspired to live on The Hill. She assumed, correctly as it turned out, that Andrew could well afford to live among Fall River's nabobs. Some Bordens on The Hill were even less wealthy than he.

After Lizzie's arrest, with festering domestic bitterness and greed alleged as the motive for the murders, friends mounted a public relations counter-narrative. One close friend explained why the family remained tethered to Second Street with the acceptance of Lizzie and Emma. Mrs. George Brigham spoke to the *Fall River Herald* from The Hill: "Both girls would have much preferred to live in this part of town to where they did, and often expressed the wish of course, but they said it was better for their father . . . to live where they did, as it was near his business interests and so they did not urge it." But Andrew was not unsympathetic to his daughters' yearning. "[He] told them a short time ago," Brigham claimed, "to look for a house in this neighborhood."

Andrew was a creature of habit. He no longer used his horse carriage. The Hill was considerably further away from South Main Street than was Second Street. It is highly unlikely that he had given Lizzie and Emma the signal that he was ready to move on the eve of the murders, when he was about to turn seventy. Then, again, he had done all he could, within the self-imposed limits of his character, to heal the breach in his family. Perhaps he fathomed that moving to The Hill represented a last chance to change the chemistry in his family and bring domestic peace to his final years. Before her trial, Lizzie's attorney located an insurance and real estate agent who claimed that Andrew had asked him twice about buying a new home. The witness was not called to testify.

On the other hand, a few months before the murders, Andrew told an associate: "Second Street will eventually become an overflow business highway, but it won't be in my time. I don't like to move off the street in my lifetime." In all likelihood Lizzie knew she was confined to Second Street for the foreseeable future.

Far from being an exemplary well-to-do Yankee family, the Bordens were coming apart at the seams in August 1892. According to notes recorded by Lizzie's lawyer, shortly before the murders Andrew told one business associate about disrupted plans for the summer. He and Abby would be deprived of escaping from Fall River to their Swansea farm because "his family affairs were such this summer that he would not be able to go."

Though a respected businessman, Andrew was also a legendary figure to whom some people imputed shady dealings. Lizzie admitted that her father's coarse ways of treating people embarrassed her. Her stepmother lacked refinement, too. Lizzie's avid pursuit of women's activities within and outside of Central Congregational Church fulfilled expectations for a single woman of her class. It bolstered her social and moral standing. Her outpouring of reform work imparted a kind of moral shine to a family not known for its religiosity or its polish. On August 4, 1892, strong circumstantial evidence convinced police that her energy veered in another direction.

CHAPTER 3

The Crime Heard 'round the Country
and Beyond

The inquest, preliminary hearing, and Superior Court trial generated over 3,000 pages of testimony on the Borden murders. In addition, the police recorded investigative interviews that began within approximately twenty minutes of the reported crime. Autopsies provide other important information. Newspapers have to be used cautiously because of early confusion over the crime and the keen rivalry among the press to publish the latest "revelations." The documentary record allows one to reconstruct the morning of the murders as well as the crime itself, though students of the case have not always drawn on all of the key sources. Typically, interpretations vary on the time that Lizzie would have had to commit her father's murder and dispose of incriminating evidence. In this second stage of the crime, the actual patricide, belief in Lizzie's guilt or innocence often hangs by a thread of several minutes.

The preceding day's events serve as a prelude to what unfolded on August 4. The Bordens had arrived at the threshold of a crisis. Police suspected that the footprints of Lizzie's premeditation tracked back nearly two weeks, when she had visited New Bedford and may have tried to purchase poison. But Wednesday, August 3, is a fruitful starting point to the famous crime story.

Loomings

Andrew and Abby awoke sick on Wednesday morning. Lizzie heard them retching into their slop pails sometime before midnight. Lizzie later testified that she asked Andrew and Abby through the door between the bedrooms if they needed help. Both said they would be all right. The source of their distress was not the often-mentioned spoiled mutton. Rather, it was fried swordfish that had been left out during a heat wave and warmed over from the midday meal for Tuesday evening's supper.

Abby thought they had been poisoned. Why did such fear take hold of her? Was it because of Andrew's hardboiled business dealings? Could the evildoer be closer at hand? Did Abby's alarm reflect the level of mistrust that had come to prevail in the family? Andrew dismissed Abby's fright.

Nevertheless, in an act of spunkiness or sheer panic, Abby headed across Second Street to see Dr. Seabury Bowen. In good Yankee diction Andrew declared, "Well, my money shan't pay for it." Dr. Bowen assured Abby that she had not been poisoned. It is doubtful, however, that he allayed her apprehension. Emma was 15 miles away, vacationing with friends in Fairhaven, across the Acushnet River from New Bedford. Abby may have intuited that something was afoot with Lizzie. If so, witnesses subsequently gave weight to her unease. A few hours after Abby visited Dr. Bowen, according to three witnesses, Lizzie tried to buy deadly prussic acid from a drugstore on a corner of South Main Street blocks from her house.

John V. Morse arrived unannounced around 1:30 p.m. He called on the Bordens periodically, often only weeks apart. Later that afternoon, Morse visited one of the Borden farms, returning after supper to talk with Andrew and Abby in the sitting room. Lizzie may have suspected that Andrew was considering some business transaction involving the farm, especially after Abby went to bed and left the men in the dark discussing business well into the evening. After Andrew gave up driving his horse carriage, he and Abby spent less time in Swansea—and so did Lizzie and Emma. Then, too, one or both of the farms may have become less profitable. Andrew had asked Morse for help finding a good man to run one of the farms.

That evening Lizzie left the house at six p.m. to visit Miss Alice Russell, who worked as a bookkeeper for a clothing store on South Main Street. She was a tall, dignified, forty-year-old member of Central Congregational Church. Russell had lived next door to the Bordens in Dr. Kelly's house for more than a decade. Then she moved to nearby Borden Street and remained a friend of Lizzie's and Emma's. Miss Russell became a witness for the prosecution and related in detail what happened Wednesday night.

Lizzie was on edge, revved up like a textile mill steam engine. She labored with near hysteria to stitch a few facts and more omens into a narrative of well-founded dread and despair. An agitated Lizzie feared they were all being poisoned. She thought a villain tampered with their milk. "Father has got an enemy," Russell recounted Lizzie's words in court. A man came to see Andrew and he said, "I don't care to let my property for such a business." The man left in a huff. "Father was mad and ordered him out of the house. . . . I am afraid sometimes that somebody will do something to him; he is so discourteous to people."

Lizzie went on to relate how the Bordens' barn had been broken into twice. Russell tried to reassure her that those episodes must have been boys trying to steal pigeons. The Bordens raised pigeons—until Andrew wrung their necks and decapitated most of them for good measure, in an outburst of spite against the robbers.

Russell's words failed to comfort Lizzie. She continued to pour out her forebodings. Lizzie said that she saw "a man run around the house one night when she came home." Then she described the house robbery a year earlier. "Well, they have broken into the house in broad daylight, with Emma, and Maggie and me there." Russell expressed surprise. "Father forbade our telling it," Lizzie explained. She continued her dire tale, finishing with a flourish. "I feel as if I wanted to sleep with my eyes half open—with one eye open half the time—for fear they will burn the house down over us." Thus, on the eve of the crime, Lizzie sketched out what sounded like a murder plot. She tried to follow its portentous arc with the police the next day and beyond. But something else happened after the murders. Lizzie's unruffled demeanor and inability to summon a single tear failed to mesh with her high-strung recital to her friend the night before.

Alice Russell became a credible police and then prosecution witness. She displayed her friendship by staying in the house for four nights after the murders, sleeping in Andrew and Abby's room as well as in Emma's. Lizzie's lead lawyers would invoke her monthly female "illness" to explain what happened when Lizzie visited Russell on the evening before the murders. As one lawyer put it: "We know from sad experience that many a woman at such a time as that is all unbalanced, her disposition disturbed, her mind unsettled for the time being and everything is out of sorts and out of joint and she really is disabled for a period of time."

But the police situated Lizzie's nearly three-hour visit to her friend in another context: her failed attempt to buy poison earlier in the day. It was the preferred way Victorian women committed domestic murder. In this respect, it is helpful to recall what happened in Somerville, a factory town near Boston, almost exactly six years before the start of Lizzie's preliminary hearing.

Sarah Tennant, a Protestant Irish immigrant and an impoverished orphan, arrived in America at the age of fourteen with her nine-year-old sister, Annie. Sarah married one Moses Robinson and bore him eight children, including a daughter named Lizzie. Around 1881 Sarah began a poisoning spree with arsenic the means of death. It seems to have started with her landlord and then concentrated on her family. Her husband and three of her children, Lizzie among them, perished. She eluded authorities for five years until a brazen series of poisonings in 1886. Sarah was tried for six murders, though the actual number may have reached eleven. She was convicted and sentenced to hang. Under pressure from women's groups, the governor commuted her sentence to life in prison. The press described Sarah Robinson as America's worst "poison fiend."

Beyond suggesting the ubiquity of poison in cases of Victorian-era women charged with murder, the Sarah Robinson episode is relevant to the Borden murders in at least two other ways. First, Lizzie undoubtedly knew about Robinson from the widespread press coverage. She was of the poor working class and police caught Robinson only because she killed too often and in too short a time. Second, the fear, stoked by some of her supporters and always implicit in her trial, that Lizzie would hang if convicted, was a fiction. If Robinson's sentence could be commuted, Lizzie, with far more local and national support from women's groups, would have spent the rest of her life in jail, rather than be condemned to the gallows like Salem's "witches." In any case, strong circumstantial evidence convinced police that Lizzie, stymied from acquiring poison, turned to a more ruthless, bloody means of murder.

Nineteen Whacks

Houseguest John Morse awakened first on the fateful morning. He came down the front stairs and entered the sitting room at 6 a.m., awaiting Andrew and Abby and then breakfast. The air was already warm and muggy. (The day was not as sultry as many writers have claimed. The high temperature reached about 80 degrees.) Within fifteen minutes, Bridget left her small third-floor room, which was always the hottest. She went "down cellar," as New Englanders referred to it, to retrieve kindling and coal for the cast-iron cooking range. Then she opened the locks on the side door, unhooked the screen door, took in the milk on the step and refastened the screen door. Because the milk arrived from the Swansea farm around 5 a.m., Lizzie had suggested to Alice Russell that someone could easily poison it. Maybe that had been her plan if she had been able to acquire the prussic acid she sought the morning before.

Abby appeared downstairs around 6:30 a.m., followed by Andrew a few minutes later. He was carrying his slop pail and went into the back-yard to dispose of its contents. He flung the pail's waste in the grass, not the kind of behavior one found among residents of The Hill. Andrew unlocked the barn door, where there was running water that he probably used to clean his pail. He then filled a basket with pears that had fallen from the backyard tree to the ground. He returned to the house, latched the screen door, and washed in the sink between the kitchen and the back door. The iceman delivered a 25-pound block at 6:45 a.m. Once again, adhering to household habit, Bridget unhooked and refastened the screen door.

Breakfast was served at 7 a.m., and the notorious mutton enters the story. The breakfast consisted of coffee, johnnycakes, cookies, bananas, mutton, and mutton broth. Much has been made of the Bordens' frequent consumption of mutton between Saturday and Thursday, supposedly from a single leg of meat. It would have been difficult to keep such mutton from spoiling during a heat wave. We know from court testimony that mutton was served for dinner on Wednesday. Andrew seems to have had a fondness for inexpensive mutton served Yankee style. Like the famous children's rhyme, the legend of the mutton as the cause of food poisoning and as a token of Andrew's oppressive skimping would seep into popular culture as an explanation of what pushed Lizzie over the edge. Andrew surely could have afforded more expensive cuts of meat. Still, circumstantial evidence suggested to police that if Lizzie was the lone murderess, her lethal actions did not spring from sudden impulse or the Borden family's diet.

The morning's routine continued, altered only slightly by the presence of a guest. At 7:30 a.m. Abby rang the bell signaling Bridget that breakfast was finished. The servant now ate her breakfast in the dining room and then cleared the table. Bridget began washing dishes at 8 a.m. Abby was tidying up her room and attending to morning bathing. Morse left by 8:45 a.m. with plans to return midday for dinner. He would initially come under suspicion and he was even chased by a segment of the mob that stood vigil on Second Street after the murders. Morse had a strong alibi. He walked more than a mile east on Pleasant Street to visit relatives. Once Morse left, Andrew cleaned his teeth in the downstairs sink and drew water in a basin to complete his morning bathing in his bedroom. He left the house, unseen by Bridget or Lizzie, around 9:05 a.m. He headed "down-street," as Fall Riverites put it, to Spindle City's business and civic center.

Lizzie came down from her room at 9 a.m. She always slept late, according to testimony. Bridget heard her talking with Abby, who was dusting in the dining room. The stepmother's murder was only minutes away. Lizzie entered the kitchen but had little appetite. She drank coffee, nibbled on a cookie or two, and ate half a pear. Meanwhile, Bridget returned from the backyard. She had been overcome with a headache and upset stomach. She raced out to the backyard, stayed "ten or fifteen minutes," and vomited. When she returned to the house, she finished washing dishes, cleaned the stove, and straightened out the dining room.

John Morse testified that Abby told Bridget at breakfast that she wanted the windows washed. Bridget claimed that Mrs. Borden asked her after 9 a.m., "if she had anything to do this morning?" She answered, "No, not particular." Abby told her that she "wanted the windows washed . . . inside and out, both, they are awful dirty." The exchange has Abby's ring. She was not an imperious mistress. It marked the last time Bridget saw Abby alive. After their brief conversation, Abby mounted the front stairs to change pillowcases and straighten out the guestroom.

Bridget then closed the windows to prepare for washing them from the outside first. She retrieved a pail from the cellar, filled it with water, and went to the barn to get a long handle and brush. Lizzie appeared at the screen door and the following conversation took place, according to Bridget. "'Maggie, are you going to wash windows?' I says, yes. I says, You needn't lock the door. I will be round here; but you can lock it if you want. I can get the water in the barn." It went unchallenged at the trial that Lizzie left the door unhooked.

Bridget started on the south-facing windows, which were near Dr. Kelly's house. She chatted over the fence with Dr. Kelly's Irish servant. While she was on the Kellys' side, Bridget could not see the screen door. But she testified that as she looked at and through the windows she saw no one downstairs, including Lizzie. Nor did Bridget see anyone around the Borden property while she washed the front and north side windows, the latter immediately adjacent to the screen door. Bridget passed that door five or six times to get water from the barn.

Bridget found the screen door unhooked when she entered the kitchen for a "dipper" to splash water on the soapy windows. She did not see Lizzie downstairs. Neither was Lizzie in sight when Bridget came in the back door to wash the windows from the inside.

Lizzie and Abby were alone in the house for at least an hour while Bridget worked outside. The only alternative account proved brittle at many points: the screen door was open and out of Bridget's vision when she was on the Kellys' side; someone managed to enter the house undetected; he eluded Lizzie and killed a more than 200-pound woman who fell with a thump; this phantom probably hid in the house, undiscovered for an hour. He then butchered Andrew and departed unseen by neighbors and wayfarers on Second Street.

Lizzie claimed that she remained downstairs while Bridget was outside. She probably made at least one visit to the cellar washroom and water closet. Lizzie could not credibly say she was upstairs at the time of Abby's demise. Lizzie's room was diagonally connected to the guestroom. She would have overheard the brutal murder if she had been upstairs. Yet that is exactly where she was at approximately 10:30 a.m. when Bridget reentered the house to finish her work.

Initial medical observations and subsequent autopsies agreed that Abby was murdered a minimum of one and a maximum of two hours before Andrew, that is, between 9 and 10 a.m. Since Abby went upstairs before 9:30, the next half hour was the most likely time of the murder. Abby was standing between the guestroom bed and the bureau. In a flash, she came face-to-face with her assailant. Stunned by the first blow, the stout Abby crashed to the floor. The murderer stood over her, chopping at the back of her skull as if one was splitting wood. Seventeen blows reduced the back of her head to pulp. One scalped the side of her skull leaving a flap. Still another missed its mark and cut into Abby's upper back. Blood splattered the wall and spilled onto the carpet.

Ten Whacks

Andrew was still not feeling well from Tuesday night's food poisoning and disrupted sleep when he headed down street shortly after 9 a.m. Age had slowed him more than a step, but on this day, under August humidity, the ailing Andrew ambled along, something less than the commanding figure he usually cut in Spindle City's business district. He walked one block down Second Street to Borden, then turned left for another short block and headed right, down South Main Street. Almost immediately he came face-to-face with the A. J. Borden Building, the monument to his success. Borden then stopped at the Union Savings Bank, where he served as president. The day before he had been unable to attend the board of directors quarterly meeting because he was ill. According to the *Fall River Herald* Andrew dropped into a barbershop at the head of North Main Street for his daily shave. The barber boasted a shaving mug with Andrew's name on it. Curiously, the barber was not called to testify like all the other Fall Riverites who encountered Borden that morning. Andrew made his routine visit to the post office. He was next observed in front of National Union Bank, probably around 9:45 a.m. He then shuffled over to the First National Bank, where he was a director. He stayed for ten minutes, deposited a check from the Troy Mills, and spoke briefly to a bank official. "While he was here," the banker testified, "I noticed that he looked tired and sick, . . . real sick."

From banks Borden moved on to Main Street rental property, perhaps the major investment that underwrote his wealth. He visited a store that he rented to a man who sold men's hats and clothing. The haberdasher had recently rented another store on South Main Street in the

A. J. Borden Building. That is where Andrew was seen next. He inspected repairs that two carpenters were making to the store. On the floor lay an old, broken lock. Borden picked up the lock, inspected it, put the useless object in his pocket, and turned his face up South Main Street for the last time. Banks, rental property, and a lock—Borden's last minutes were consumed with things that encapsulated so much of his life.

It was now around 10:35 a.m. Borden turned left on Spring Street and a short block delivered him to Second Street, only feet from his house. On this, his last morning, it had taken him less than an hour and a half to complete the circumscribed forenoon circuit of his daily life. Borden arrived home at approximately 10:45 a.m. His predictable morning rounds had been cut short. His life would soon be curtailed.

He went to the side door, but it was locked, which probably both frustrated and pleased him. Borden turned to the triple-locked front door. Bridget heard someone trying to enter, went to the door, and fumbled with the locks. She testified that she said, "Oh pshaw." It may have been something stronger than that because it elicited a laugh from Lizzie, who was standing on the landing at the top of the stairs only feet from Abby's body.

Bridget let Andrew in and returned to her work. Lizzie came downstairs and asked her father if there was any mail. Bridget heard Lizzie tell him "Mrs. Borden had a note and had gone out." Andrew took his room key off the mantelpiece, where he kept it, and went up the back stairs. According to Bridget, after Andrew came back downstairs Lizzie put an ironing board on the dining room table. She then began ironing eight to ten handkerchiefs. Andrew was in the sitting room, across from her, reading the *Providence Journal.*

Bridget carried her stepladder, basin, and washrag into the dining room to clean its windows. "Lizzie asked, 'Maggie, are you going out this afternoon?' I said, 'I don't know; I might and I might not; I don't feel very well.' She says, 'If you go out be sure and lock the door for Mrs. Borden has gone out on a sick call, and I might go out too.' Says I, 'Miss Lizzie, who is sick?' 'I don't know; she had a note this morning; it must be in town.'" Of course, while she was outside, Bridget saw neither the person who allegedly delivered a note nor Mrs. Borden leave the house. In addition, Abby failed to tell Bridget where she was going, which was not her habit. She often visited her half sister Sarah Whitehead. But Abby knew that Sarah would either be on a steamboat plying the waters of Mount Hope and Narragansett bays or already at Rocky Point Amusement Park on Warwick Neck, Rhode Island, miles from Fall River. In an embarrassing irony of local history, the Fall River police held their annual picnic on the day the most brutal and infamous crime in their city's history took place. Newspapers claimed that half to more than three-quarters of the department frolicked by the seashore while the Bordens were slaughtered. Still, there were enough police on duty that day to investigate and record what happened and to begin chasing down leads and questioning "suspicious" men on the street.

Finished with her washing, Bridget retreated to the kitchen to rinse her cloths and hang them behind the stove to dry. Lizzie left her ironing and came into the kitchen. She told Bridget there was a sale of "dress goods" at a downtown store either "this afternoon" or "today." Bridget could not remember precisely. "I am going to have one," Bridget replied. Feeling ill and tired, Bridget climbed the rear stairs to rest in her room. Right after the murders, she reported to police that she lay down at 10:55 a.m. At the trial she said it was "three or four minutes" before the hour. Soon after Bridget went to her room, she heard the City Hall bell signal that it was 11:00.

By then, the uncharacteristically exhausted Andrew was stretched out in the sitting room. Lizzie had helped him rest his lanky frame on the small horsehair sofa with his legs draped over the side and his feet on the floor. She claimed he removed his shoes, but autopsy photographs show otherwise. Resting on a cushion, his head was turned to the right. His assailant stood behind him and struck ten times. One blow landed from his nostril to his chin. Another crushed his eye bone. One of Andrew's eyes was sliced in half. Another strike left a hole in his skull. Several blows crushed the brain; one severed Andrew's carotid artery. Then the morning's spasms of violence ended abruptly. Blood speckled the wallpaper behind the sofa and dripped onto the cushion. Dr. Bowen would later that day describe Andrew's face as "hardly to be recognized." He told the *Fall River Globe*: "Physician that I am, and accustomed to all kinds of horrible sights, it sickened me to look upon the dead man's face."

At approximately 11:10 a.m., Lizzie yelled, "Maggie, come down! . . . Come down quick; father's dead; somebody came in and killed him." Lizzie sent Bridget across the street to get Dr. Bowen. He was not home.

When Bridget returned she asked, "Miss Lizzie, where were you? Didn't I leave the screen door locked?" Lizzie replied, according to Bridget's testimony, "I was out in the back yard and heard a groan, and came in and the screen door was wide open."

Lizzie then told Bridget to go to Alice Russell's house at the corner of Borden and Second Streets. "I can't be alone in the house," she said. Yet that was where she stood again while Bridget went to fetch Miss Russell. In the meantime, as next-door neighbor Adelaide Churchill returned from grocery shopping, she saw Bridget scurrying back and forth. Mrs. Churchill carried her purchases into her house and then observed Lizzie standing inside the screen door, apparently unconcerned that a crazed murderer might still be lurking behind her. Churchill threw open a window and asked what was the matter? As she testified, Lizzie replied, "Oh, Mrs. Churchill, do come over. Someone has killed father."

The neighbor immediately went to the house. "Where were you when it happened?" she asked. "'I went to the barn to get a piece of iron.' 'Where is your mother?' 'I don't know; she had got a note to go see someone who is sick, but I don't know that she is killed, too, for I thought I heard her come in.'" To the police, the improbability of Lizzie's claim seemed staggering. How, for instance, would Lizzie have heard Abby come in while she was in the barn or backyard, the first two of the multiple versions of her whereabouts and her actions while her father's murderer butchered him?

Apparently desperate for a doctor, Lizzie sent Churchill out to find one, but not the Irish city physician next door or the French-Canadian doctor behind the Bordens. She remained in the house alone for a third time. When the neighbor returned, Dr. Bowen and Bridget were already there. The servant knew the most likely place where one might find Abby—with her half sister. She told Lizzie: "If I knew where Mrs. Whitehead was I would go and . . . tell her [Abby] that Mr. Borden was very sick." Lizzie repeated what she had said to Mrs. Churchill. "Maggie, I am almost positive I heard her coming in. Won't you go upstairs to see?" Bridget refused to do it alone. Churchill offered to accompany her. They climbed the stairs and as they reached eye level with the floor, both women saw Abby's body under the bed in the guestroom. They would not be the only ones who observed the victim without entering the room. Recall that Lizzie was upstairs when Andrew arrived home.

Her eyes were apparently riveted elsewhere, affording nary a glance into the guestroom while mounting and descending the stairs.

By now Alice Russell had shown up. She was surprised that Lizzie did not appear to need much comforting. "I never saw her in tears that morning," she later testified. Lizzie's defenders would read such behavior as the "calm and dignified" bearing of a true lady, of a Protestant nun. Lizzie said something revealing to Russell in the hive of horror, confusion, and sorrow that engulfed the Borden house. "When it is necessary, I should like to have Undertaker Winwood [sic]." Families on The Hill preferred James Winward to lay their deceased to rest.

Dr. Bowen and then Bristol County Medical Examiner William Dolan, who arrived by 11:45 a.m., both made quick observations about the sequence of the murders. Andrew's warm body still oozed blood. Abby was cold to the touch; her blood had coagulated and turned dark. Abby died first. Once suspicion focused on Lizzie, authorities realized the implications of Abby's prior death. If the sequence of murders had been reversed, in the time between the deaths Abby would have inherited at least her widow's third of Andrew's estate, and maybe more depending on provisions in a will (which no family member knew did not exist). After her murder, Abby's family would have claimed her share of his fortune. With Andrew killed after Abby, his entire estate would pass to Lizzie and Emma.

The Brutality

If the murders were premeditated, was the gruesome violence as well? Did Lizzie try to preempt suspicion that she was the culprit? Was the brutality calculated to underscore that the crimes were a man's work— that such a delicate, refined Christian lady as Lizzie from a respectable Borden family could never engage in acts that represented "a wreck of human morals," as one of her lawyers would later put it? Two days after the murders, the *New York Herald* framed the seeming contradiction of the case rather differently. Given her breeding and her gender, if Lizzie had somehow turned homicidal she would have killed the "victims genteelly, instead of . . . [like] Jack the Ripper." The magnitude of the brutality visited on Abby, rather than premeditated, strikes one as an eruption of repressed rage. Andrew's slaughter seems of a different order—half the blows of Abby and executed out of necessity, the district attorney came to believe. Perhaps Lizzie intended to establish an alibi by leaving the house and Andrew returned unexpectedly. Maybe Lizzie was sure that, given the mistrust and hostility in the family, he would realize on the spot that she had murdered Abby. Andrew had to be sacrificed. This shocking act of patricide only added to the disbelief that a Christian Borden lady was capable of such a grotesquerie.

Andrew's death represents the real enigma within the "mystery" of the Borden murders. If Lizzie committed the murders, she had a maximum of fifteen minutes to dispatch her father. Some who argue for her innocence say that she had far less time, perhaps only eight minutes. Twelve to thirteen minutes is more likely. In that interval, she had to dexterously slay her father and avoid being splattered with blood; clean and hide the hatchet; perhaps visit the barn; and wipe off any blood on her. Why did she call Maggie so quickly when she could have devoted another five or ten minutes to mopping up the consequences of the brutish assault?

This key perplexity of the Borden case challenged the government's prosecutors. It has also invited conjecture from the wide range of detective authors and others who have delved into the murders. Lizzie could not have committed the crime. She had an accomplice. She may have donned two dresses, which expedited cleanup. Lizzie likely wore an apron, which was easier to hide than a dress. Perhaps she killed her victims in the nude, paradoxically an act of immodesty highly problematic for an apparent embodiment of the Protestant nun such as Lizzie. Maybe she was able to shield her body behind the dining room door while she hacked at Andrew. Or, more plausibly, Lizzie might have put on Andrew's long Prince Albert suit coat, which he took off before he lay down on the sofa. Furthermore, if she put the coat on backwards, it would have covered most of her body. Oddly, the coat was found folded so that it fit under the cushion on which Andrew's head rested.

Lizzie had time to clean up after Abby's murder. Perhaps she did not need to wash off much blood after killing Andrew, especially if she shielded her body in one way or another. Moreover, the blood that flowed and splattered from the smites on Abby's and Andrew's skulls did not match the brutality of the crimes. Four days after the murders, the

Fall River Herald described Medical Examiner William Dolan's puzzled reaction to the crime scenes. "Dr. Dolan says that the more he reflects on the small quantity of blood that was spilled, the more at a loss he is to account for it," the newspaper reported. "To him it seems utterly inexplicable. Ordinarily, no matter how sharp the weapon used, the rooms would have been stained crimson had such a tragedy taken place in them." The *Herald* did not use quotation marks, but it was clear that the reporter was repeating Dolan's exact words. He found "nothing to raise the suspicion that the murderer had cleaned anything, except the dripping axe." These comments from an Irish medical examiner were not well received on The Hill. Blood testimony would occupy an important place at the trial. But the experts had ultimately to acknowledge that they could not say with absolute certainty whether the murderer had been covered with the victims' blood.

The police swarmed over 92 Second Street within less than a half hour of the discovery of the bodies. They didn't suspect Lizzie at first, and that was surely what she anticipated. By the end of the first day, however, the police recorded how Lizzie's bearing and willingness to talk seemed to betray her guilt.

CHAPTER 4

The Investigation

Once suspicion gravitated toward Lizzie, newspapers near and far questioned, even assailed, the competency of the Fall River police. The crusading *Fall River Globe*, with strong ties to the force's Irish contingent, represented the principal exception. That ethnic presence among the ranks helped make the police fair game for some critics. The blistering verbal assault on the police reached a crescendo after Lizzie's arrest and continued until the end of her trial.

The Fall River police blundered. For starters, they failed to rope off the crime scene. In the hours after the murders, too many people walked through the front door. Some tracked blood from the guestroom. Others wandered around the backyard and entered the barn. The police mishandled potential evidence, which would saddle the prosecution at trial.

Despite their bungling, the Fall River police undertook an extensive investigation that persisted following Lizzie's arrest a week after the crimes. They chased down rumors and broadened their search for the killer beyond immigrants, and also beyond Fall River. The police traveled to Tiverton, Portsmouth, Bristol, and Pawtucket in Rhode Island. They interviewed witnesses or "suspicious" individuals in Boston, New Bedford, Westport, Somerset, and Swansea in Massachusetts. They even sent an officer to Albany, New York, to interview a former bookkeeper for Andrew Borden's furniture-funeral business who had been implicated in embezzlement from the company. Yet within less than ten hours the police began to consider the unthinkable. Could the murderer be in their midst? Lizzie's account of her whereabouts and actions during the slaughter seemed to lack a narrative spine.

The Police Respond

When Lizzie sent Adelaide Churchill to locate a Yankee doctor, she hurried down Second Street to Hall's Livery Stables at the corner of Borden Street. John Cunningham, the Second Street news dealer, heard about the crime, went to a nearby paint shop, and called the police at 11:15 a.m. He also notified the *Globe* and the *Evening News*. City Marshall Rufus Hilliard (the "police chief") dispatched Officer George Allen to investigate "a row up on Second Street." After a few minutes of "walking and running," Allen arrived on the scene, the first officer to view Andrew's body. He was horrified and raced back to the station to inform the City Marshal. Before he left, he checked the front door and determined that it was locked. Allen met a sign painter and Second Street resident, Charles Sawyer, and put him on guard at the side door, where he remained all day.

Allen's horrifying encounter with Andrew's battered face presaged the jolt his fellow police received when they confronted the atrocity of an old man and old woman hacked to death in broad daylight. The deaths leap from the pages of police crime reports for the week during which Lizzie was charged. The vast majority of crimes consisted of drunkenness and disorderly conduct. Assault and battery was the most serious offense. With one exception the perpetrators of criminal conduct were all members of the working class. Not surprisingly, then, immigrants comprised two-thirds of those arrested. They were mostly Irish and English-born workers; some of the latter actually claimed Irish ancestry. Even a few of the American-born offenders had Irish last names. Men made up two-thirds of those arrested.

Given the Yankee Bordens' prominence and the viciousness of the murders, the police confronted an unprecedented crime. Stunned like Officer Allen with the seemingly senseless, barbaric slaughter, the police stumbled after they descended on the house. But once the initial shock ebbed, the police embarked on an earnest, if flawed, investigation. State Police detective George Seaver assisted the local officers. By Saturday an unsavory private detective from Providence, Edwin H. McHenry, joined the investigation. Later he would instigate what turned out to be a major embarrassment for the Fall River police.

The marshal sent the shaken Officer Allen back to Second Street with patrolman Michael Mullaly. By the time they returned at 11:37 a.m., a reporter from the *Globe* and Special Officer Patrick Doherty were already there. By noon, at least a baker's dozen of the official and the curious moved about the house and property: several policemen, Drs. Dolan and Bowen, Bridget, Miss Russell, one or two reporters, John Morse, who had returned half an hour earlier from his morning visit, and Rev. Edwin Buck, City Missionary of the Central Congregational Church. The front door was unlocked, and in the aftermath of the crime relatives, friends, neighbors, and reporters gained entrance to the house.

The police quickly determined that nothing in the house had been stolen or disturbed. Andrew's pockets had not even been picked. He still possessed his silver watch and the cheap gold ring on his pinky finger. As they arrived the police conducted searches of the house, from attic to cellar, making sure that the homicidal madman was not still hidden on the property. They also searched for a murder weapon.

The police fanned out to the yards on Third Street, behind the Bordens, looking for evidence and witnesses. They came up empty-handed. They scoured Second Street but found few credible witnesses. Only one serious witness emerged early in the investigation. Dr. Benjamin Handy, who knew Lizzie and her family, rode by the Borden house a few minutes after 10:30 a.m. and described a strange, pale man acting oddly on the sidewalk. Around 12:30 p.m. Assistant Marshal John Fleet, who was in charge of the investigation, ordered police to "cover several roads leading out of town."

From police reports recorded during that tumultuous day and the trial transcript, we can reconstruct the sequence and contents of Lizzie's police interviews. To her credit, she deflected suspicion away from Bridget and John Morse. On the other hand, what option did she have? Both possessed alibis and lacked motives. Lizzie spoke to the Fall River police with the confidence bred of her class, ladyhood, and family name. Soon her words proved less than artful. Shortly after police began arriving, Lizzie went upstairs with Alice Russell and retrieved a cheap pink "wrapper" from Emma's room. It was considered a "morning dress." What Lizzie had been wearing when the murders were committed emerged as sharply contested evidence at her trial. The dress in question was not handed over until Saturday.

Patrick Doherty was apparently the first one to interview Lizzie. The thirty-two-year-old Irish special officer (a captain by the time of the trial) had a brief conversation with her around 11:30 a.m., before Dr. Bowen recommended that she rest in her bedroom. Lizzie said she was in the barn at the time of her father's murder. Doherty's brief note simply quotes her as saying that she did not "hear any noise whatever." Yet he testified that she said, "I heard a peculiar noise . . . I think it was something like scraping." (She had told Bridget the sound was a "groan.") The conflict between Doherty's notes and his testimony never came out at the trial. Perhaps in the tumult of that gore-filled day Doherty failed to record all of what Lizzie said. "Was there a Portuguese working for your father over the river?" Doherty asked. He also wanted to know if a farm worker had been around the house during the morning. Lizzie answered no to both questions. That concluded Doherty's recorded interview.

Minutes later, Doherty accompanied Officer Mullaly to Lizzie's bedroom. This was a startlingly new experience for Lizzie—to have policemen in her bedroom, and Irishmen to compound the irritation and indignity. Lizzie's bedroom was her sanctuary. Surely Dr. Bowen was the only male outside her family who had visited the room. Even Rev. Buck would never spend time alone with a young woman parishioner in her bedroom. Perhaps the policemen felt ill at ease. Mullaly did the talking after Doherty left. The interview, once again, was brief. Most importantly, he asked Lizzie if there were hatchets or axes in the house. She said there were and that Bridget would take him to the cellar. Lizzie was soon rid of Mullaly. Bridget went with him to the cellar. She pulled out a hatchet from a wooden box. Something resembling hair clung to its blade and handle. The hatchet had spots that looked like blood. Mullaly also found a second hatchet. In another part of the cellar there were two axes. One had what looked like blood stains. Mullaly spread the four potential weapons on the cellar ground for Assistant Marshal Fleet to examine.

William Medley appears to have been the next policeman to knock on Lizzie's bedroom door. Dr. Bowen, Rev. Buck, and Alice Russell were present consoling her. Perhaps that is why the lowly patrolman, who would be promoted to inspector by the time of the trial, talked only briefly with Lizzie. He asked her where she was at the time of her father's murder. She replied, "up stairs in the barn." Medley had seen a pail of water in the basement with what looked like "small towels [;] they were covered with blood." He had the temerity to ask her about them. Lizzie informed him that she had told the doctor and he said that it was all right. She claimed the pail had been there "for three or four days." Bridget contradicted her, Medley reported, for "she had not noticed the pail until that day." Nevertheless, Dr. Bowen said that the bloody towels had been "explained to him."

Interestingly, when Patrick Doherty inadvertently referred to the towels during the trial, District Attorney Knowlton told him, "Pass from those." The police strongly suspected that the towels had been used in Lizzie's clean up. But Knowlton understandably did not want to go on a fool's errand. The defense would simply counter with Lizzie's "fleas," Victorians' preferred euphemism for menstruation. Her lawyers would win the argument over blood evidence and garner sympathy for their "persecuted" client in the process.

Medley claimed he went directly to the barn after interviewing Lizzie. He climbed the stairs and came eye level with the floor. It was covered mostly with undisturbed hay dust. Medley pressed his hand on the floor and it left an imprint. Both in his notes recorded on August 4 and in his trial testimony, Medley described how he walked on the floor "but found no footprints, except what I made myself."

Assistant Marshal Fleet appeared at 92 Second Street between 11:45 a.m. and noon. Soon after, he went to Lizzie's bedroom for the first of two interviews with her that day. Miss Russell and Rev. Buck remained with her. Lizzie lay on a lounge. Fleet asked her a series of questions about the events leading to the discovery of her father's body. Most dubious to Fleet, she told him that she had "remained up in the barn about half an hour" during the time when Andrew was murdered.

Fleet then asked if she knew anyone who might have killed her father and mother. "She is not my mother, sir," Lizzie replied snappishly; "my mother died when I was a child." Throughout the day police were struck by Lizzie's seeming inability to grieve. No one described her as distraught. Her demeanor did not change from August 4 through her arrest and appearance in court. The *Fall River Herald* attributed it to a "Wonderful Fortitude," a kind of Yankee "steeliness" that befit the daughter of Andrew Borden. "Certainly in Lizzie Borden some of the weaknesses of her sex are conspicuously absent." Intended as an explication and defense of Lizzie's deportment and womanhood, the newspaper's comments could also be interpreted to suggest that she lacked exonerating "female" qualities. Once the case exploded, Lizzie displayed dignified strength of character and occasionally expected womanly sentiment. On the day of the butchery, however, her almost haughty inability to summon tears struck Fleet and his subordinates very differently from the newspaper's reading of her makeup.

Alice Russell prodded Lizzie to tell the assistant marshal what she had related the night before. Lizzie described Andrew's heated conversation with the man who came to the house two weeks earlier seeking unsuccessfully to rent a store from her father. Now she braided a new incident into her account. "A man came at nine o'clock [this morning;] I think he wanted to hire a store, talked English. I did not see him, heard father shut the door, and think the man went away." The implication, of course, was that the disgruntled visitor from two weeks earlier had returned. Andrew had rebuffed him again, possibly with deadly results. To police, Lizzie's story sounded like an improvised, loose-jointed narrative.

Assistant Marshal Fleet was not done questioning Lizzie that day. He would return in nearly two hours, or about 1:45 p.m. He went downstairs and took control of the investigation, sending his officers out into the neighborhood and monitoring the search of the house, barn, and yard.

Before Fleet interviewed Lizzie again, Patrolman (later Captain) Philip Harrington had a spirited exchange with her. He arrived between 12:20 p.m. and 12:25 p.m. He viewed the bodies. As he was leaving Abby's body in the guestroom, Harrington saw a door ajar. Through the opening he spied Lizzie and the steadfast Alice Russell. He boldly, perhaps rudely, shoved the door open completely. Lizzie's patience with the police was already frayed. Harrington's "invasion" of the bedroom must have outraged her. Lizzie reined in her sense of violation, however, and stayed self-composed. The patrolman recorded in detail what happened and then testified to much of it in court.

It is worth quoting Harrington's contrasting descriptions of the two women from his notes at the time. "Lizzie stood by the foot of the bed, and talked in the most calm and collected manner; her whole bearing was most remarkable under the circumstances. There was not the least indication of agitation, no." Russell appeared a wreck: "Very pale, and much agitated, which she showed by short [,] sharp breathing, and wringing her hands."

In response to Harrington's questioning, Lizzie added yet another twist to the shifting plot of the man who sought to rent a store from Andrew. She now claimed the mysterious figure first came to Second Street three weeks before the murder and returned a week later. With the call that morning, which she had described to Fleet, this stubborn character had now visited 92 Second Street three times, but Lizzie never saw him. In other words, under an unexpected barrage of police questions within an hour or so of the reported crime, Lizzie chose not to cast suspicion on people whose identities were known, such as house inhabitants Bridget and John Morse. Rather, she lengthened the shadow of an aggressive man who refused to take no for an answer.

Lizzie revised her story in another way. She told Harrington, "I went out in the barn. I remained there twenty minutes." She had pared ten minutes off what she had told Fleet less than a half hour before. The front of the barn, where Lizzie was supposedly in the loft, stood only 15 feet from the side door. Harrington persisted. While in the barn Lizzie said she neither saw nor heard anything. "Not even the opening and closing of the screen door?" the patrolman grilled her. "Why not? You were but a short distance away, and you would have heard the noise if any was made?"

Harrington suggested that, given the horror of the crime, Lizzie might be "in a better mental condition" tomorrow to recall something or to offer a clearer "statement of the facts." Lizzie shook her head in "Stiff courtesy. 'No, I can tell you all I know today just as well as at any other time,'" she replied. Harrington recorded in his notes what he said to Fleet after the interview: "I don't like that girl." He might have added that the feeling was certainly mutual.

The assistant marshal interrogated Lizzie again, which ended recorded questioning for the day. Fleet came with two officers primarily to search Lizzie's room, but he did interview her again. Alice Russell was still there. Dr. Bowen testified that he administered a sedative, bromo-caffeine, to Lizzie sometime between 1 p.m. and 2 p.m. Yet she proved testy in response to one of Fleet's questions. "You said this morning that you was up in the barn for half an hour. Do you say that now?" "I don't say half an hour, I say twenty minutes to half an hour." "Well," Fleet countered, "we will call it twenty minutes." Lizzie was having none of it—that is, affirmation of her conflicting times. "I say from twenty minutes to an half hour, sir."

Fleet then left Lizzie, came downstairs and went into the cellar. He examined the axes and hatchets that Mullaly had laid out for him. Fleet made another discovery, as he testified at the trial: "I found in a box in the middle of the cellar . . . on a shelf or a jog in the chimney—an old-fashioned chimney—the head of a hatchet. It had a fresh break on the handle, up near the head's eye. The rest of the handle was missing." The hatchet head and the piece of the handle were not covered with dust like the two other hatchets. The broken one looked as if the head had been washed and rubbed in white ashes. A pile of coal ash stood nearby. Fleet studied the hatchet. He had four potential weapons on the floor near him, two with apparently telltale evidence. His mind was filled with a welter of other details and questions already generated by his officers. In this fog of a shocking double murder investigation that was barely a few hours old, he placed the broken hatchet back in the box, which he returned to the "jog" in the chimney. Fleet mishandled potential, what turned out to be crucial, evidence: the hatchet that the prosecution and the police ultimately came to believe split open the Bordens' skulls. Fleet's hesitation as he inspected the broken hatchet was fraught with consequences that he could not have anticipated in the muddle of midday on August 4.

Before he turned the bodies over to the undertaker at approximately 3:30 p.m., Medical Examiner Dolan prepared four jars for Dr. Edward S. Wood, a physician and professor of chemistry at Harvard Medical School. Two contained the stomachs of Andrew and Abby. The others held samples of milk delivered on both Wednesday and Thursday.

Emma arrived by train from Fairhaven late in the afternoon. Dr. Bowen had telegraphed her at Lizzie's request. Emma had only been told that Andrew was sick. The crowd across from the house was the first indication that something more serious had happened. No one recorded how she responded to the gruesome scene. Undoubtedly, she put her faith in Lizzie's version of the day's events, though the wrinkles in her story had not been ironed out like the handkerchiefs she was tending to when her father dozed off.

———

Night fell and the mob outside stayed late, trading rumors and speculation. The *Fall River Herald* reported the next day: "From the moment the story of the crime was first told to long after midnight Second Street was crowded with curious people anxious to hear some particulars that had not been told before." Assistant Marshal Fleet stationed police officers around the house to secure the crime scene.

Officer Joseph Hyde was assigned the rear of the house and the pitch-black backyard. Early in the night, he observed suspicious movement in the cellar, which he described in his notes and reiterated at Lizzie's trial. Between 8:30 p.m. and 9 p.m., Lizzie and Alice Russell, who was carrying a lamp, entered the cellar. Russell stood back as Lizzie "went over to the sink and emptied something that sounded to me like water," Hyde noted. Then the two women went upstairs.

Fifteen minutes later Lizzie came back to the cellar alone holding the lamp. "She set the lamp on the table," Hyde wrote, "and went over toward the sink and stooped; but I could not see what she did there." This solo trip took nerve, unless Lizzie had no reason to feel on edge. The bludgeoned bodies lay in the dining room on autopsy boards, so she passed through the sitting room. Her lamp shed light on the blood-stained wall and sofa. It cast spooky shadows around the cellar, revealing the victims' bloody clothes rolled up near the sink.

Suspicion Grows

By Thursday night, as leads and "suspicious" characters failed to produce credible evidence, the police found a major witness with an apparently damning story. Since there was a possibility that the murderer had first tried to poison the Bordens, the police canvassed drugstores in the city and also in New Bedford. Several blocks from the Borden house, on the corner of South Main and Columbia streets, a clerk at D. R. Smith's Drug Store related to police an incident that occurred late on the morning of August 3. A well-dressed woman called at the store and asked clerk Eli Bence for ten cents' worth of deadly prussic acid. A small amount of this poison could kill a person quickly, without the painful, prolonged agony of Sarah Robinson's victims. The woman told Bence that she needed the prussic acid to kill moths that were eating a "seal skin cape."

Bence informed her that prussic acid was only sold with a doctor's prescription. "She then said," he testified at the inquest and preliminary hearing, that "she had bought this several times." Bence told her that prussic acid "is a very dangerous thing to handle." She left the pharmacy irked.

Bence was sure he could identify the woman if he saw her and heard her voice. He said he knew her as "Miss Borden" but did not realize she was Andrew's daughter, until one of the two witnesses to the drugstore exchange told him. Officers could not drag Lizzie to the police station and put her in a lineup, so they took Bence to Second Street, sometime after eight p.m. on the night of August 4. The police entered the side door, went into the kitchen, and left Bence at the threshold near the sink. After Bence saw Lizzie and heard her speak, he made a positive identification.

It is perhaps fitting that Officer Philip Harrington, along with Patrick Doherty, located Bence on Thursday night. That afternoon Harrington had concluded his notes of Lizzie's interview with a distressing reflection. Lizzie's demeanor "gave birth to a thought that was most revolting. I thought, at least, she knew more than she wished to tell."

The police probably wanted to keep Bence's interview secret. Either from its own sleuthing or more likely from ties to Irish officers, the *Fall River Globe* scooped its two local competitors on Friday morning with the headline: "What Did Lizzie Want of Poison?" Reporters telegraphed this sensational development in the case to newspapers in Boston and New York. The *Boston Globe*, for instance, headlined the new evidence on Friday:

DISCOVERY!
A Woman Inquired for Poison
Said That Clerk
Identified Her.

Lizzie denied that she attempted to purchase prussic acid. Moreover, she claimed she did not even know where Smith's Drug Store was located!

The police had evidence of another failed attempt to purchase arsenic and prussic acid on the Monday before the murders. The customer fit Lizzie's description. The French-owned drug store was on Pleasant

Street. Given the prejudice against the French, perhaps the owner and clerk preferred not to become entangled in a case that had begun to divide public opinion. Or possibly authorities felt that the clerk from Martel's Drug Store would be less credible because of his ethnicity.

Police reports do not disclose any interviews in the Borden house on Friday. Officers did ransack the barn, including a search of its privy vault, and carefully inspected the backyard. Marshal Hilliard called upon his entire police force to pursue aggressively rumors and potential leads. He stationed men on streets across the city in an attempt to reassure an inflamed population. People strolled up and down Second Street, gawking at the Borden house. An ever-vigilant crowd grew from hundreds during the day to 1,000 at night, according to the *Herald*, and congregated on the sidewalk, spilling into the street.

The throng displayed a bit of a lynch-mob mentality on Friday night. They targeted John Morse. To many he remained a suspicious character, perhaps complicit in the crime. He slipped out of the Borden house to go to the post office. The crowd recognized Morse and gave chase. He had to be rescued by the police and escorted back to the house.

On Friday night the Republican *Evening News* carried the following notice. The *Herald* published it the next morning:

$5,000 REWARD

The above reward will be paid to anyone who
may secure the arrest and conviction of the
person or persons who occasioned the death of
Andrew J. Borden and his wife.
Emma J. [*sic*] Borden
Lizzie A. Borden

To the daughters, Abby was simply the "wife," not a person with a name. A New York weekly later offered a $500 payment to anyone who produced the note that Abby was supposed to have received. *Once a Week* put up the reward "Strictly in the interest of Justice and in defense of American womanhood." Neither lucrative reward, in a city of paltry wages, yielded anything but a flood of rumors.

The funeral took place on Saturday morning, after a short service at home, where surprisingly, the caskets were open in the parlor. Undertaker Winward could not hide all the wounds, especially Andrew's. When Lizzie saw his body in the casket, she kissed what remained of his lips—an uncharacteristic, and ghastly, display of sentiment.

Andrew's business associates composed the bulk of the approximately seventy-five mourners who crowded into the house. They dwarfed Abby's bereaved. During the twenty-five-minute service of prayer and bible reading, the deceased were not eulogized. Coaches lined Second Street, ready to take the family and their funeral guests to the Yankee Protestant Oak Grove Cemetery, a mile and a half across The Hill. (Fall River's Irish and French had their own separate cemeteries.) Two to three thousand people, eager for a peek at Lizzie, created a crush of spectators. Twenty policemen were assigned to crowd control.

There were conflicting accounts of Lizzie's demeanor. The *Fall River Herald* reported, "she walked with a firm and steady step to her seat in the carriage" on the arm of undertaker Winward. The *New York Times* claimed that "her nerves were completely unstrung, as was shown by the trembling of her body and the manner in which she bore down on her supporter." If true, Lizzie's bearing was strikingly atypical. Neither before nor in the days immediately after the funeral did she tremble before the police or the public. After the bromo-caffeine, Dr. Bowen had prescribed a double dose of morphine at bedtime for Lizzie's nerves. But even before then anguish seemed to have spared her.

Hundreds of curious people, along with reporters, had already staked out Oak Grove when the funeral procession arrived. After a short service by the gravesite, during which mourners remained in their coaches, the caskets were taken to a receiving vault. The attorney general had ordered that they remain there until doctors undertook a complete autopsy. It did not occur until August 11, a week after the murders. Andrew's and Abby's heads would not be buried until after the trial. Lizzie and Emma would only learn in court that their father and stepmother had been disemboweled and decapitated.

On Saturday morning, the *Fall River Herald* published an interview with Lizzie's uncle Hiram Harrington. He claimed he had a long talk with Lizzie on Friday night and that he "questioned her very carefully" about what happened during the time her father was killed. Lizzie said she "went directly to the barn to obtain some lead" and cut it "into sizable sinkers." She intended to go to Marion, where her friends were vacationing, and use the sinkers on her fishing line. From seeking lead to fix a screen Lizzie had shifted the purpose of her errand to the barn. She sought cheap fishing sinkers; yet with her lines and hooks in Swansea, she intended to buy new, more expensive equipment for her Marion vacation.

The police launched a new search of 92 Second Street while the funeral was under way. It intensified in the afternoon and included the house, barn, and yard. Dr. Dolan accompanied Marshal Hilliard, Assistant Marshal Fleet, State Police Detective Seaver, and Acting Captain Dennis Desmond, Jr. They pried into every corner of the Borden property. For more than three hours in the afternoon, they opened drawers and trunks, turned over mattresses, and rifled through closets. With strong circumstantial evidence in hand implicating Lizzie, including the attempted purchase of poison, the police sought corroborating hard evidence, especially a bloody garment or a hidden weapon. "We examined everything," Dr. Dolan told a reporter, "down to the slightest bump in the wallpaper." They rummaged through the barn once again and carefully raked over the yard.

Lizzie and her lawyer, Andrew J. Jennings, observed the tenacious efforts of the police. As she had during more than one search, Lizzie asked the officers if she might be of any help. In the end, she must have read the bafflement on the faces of the police and Dr. Dolan.

For all the thoroughness of Saturday's search, the police made mistakes, as the trial testimony revealed. Neighbor Mrs. Churchill, among others, told police that Lizzie had been wearing a light blue cotton dress with a dark blue figure on it before she changed into the pink wrapper. The dress had been stained in the spring when the house was painted dark brown. Perhaps the spots resembled the color of dried blood. Seaver and Fleet pored over the dresses in the large closet at the top of the front stairs. At the trial Seaver described what happened.

Captain Fleet was there with me, and I commenced on the hooks and took each dress, with the exception of two or three in the corner, and passed them to Capt. Fleet, he being near the window, and he examined them himself, he more thoroughly than myself, and I took each garment and then hung it back, . . . all with the exception of two or three which were heavy or silk dresses in the corner.

Those garments could have hidden the one they sought. In any case, the Saturday search frustrated police. They would make one more futile attempt to find hard evidence of the crime.

They did not come away from Saturday's search completely empty-handed. They took possession of the four potential weapons still lying on the cellar floor. Dr. Dolan would hand over to Dr. Wood two axes and one hatchet—all with possible evidence on them. Marshal Hilliard asked Jennings for the dress Lizzie wore on the day of the murders. "He went away and came back with a dress which I took away with me," the Marshal testified. It would become sharply contested evidence at Lizzie's trial.

At Saturday's search of the house, a new shadowy figure appeared: O. M. Hanscom, of the Pinkerton Detective Agency's Boston office. Lizzie and Emma hired him on the recommendation of their lawyer. Hanscom remained visible for the next few days. Then he receded from view. It is not even clear how long he worked on the case. Pinkerton authorities withdrew him from the investigation.

———

The Marshal, the Mayor, and the Minister

By Saturday, Marshal Hilliard wanted to arrest Lizzie and consult with District Attorney Hosea Knowlton, who lived in nearby New Bedford. He was unavailable. Knowlton and his family were enjoying an August weekend at their summer home in Marion, where Lizzie's friends no longer waited for her to join them. On Saturday afternoon Hilliard met with Mayor John Coughlin and Medical Examiner Dolan. An inquest offered a seemingly deliberate way to proceed. Lizzie would be under oath and perhaps she could clarify her conflicting statements to police.

At the meeting the mayor and the marshal agreed to visit 92 Second Street that evening. The mayor was entrusted to speak so that what they had to say would not have the appearance of a house arrest. A crowd milled around the sidewalk directly in front of the house and blocked Second Street. The mayor and the marshal had to summon police to clear their path.

The visitors sat down with Lizzie, Emma, and John Morse. "I have a request to make of the family," the mayor recalled at the trial, "and that is that you stay in the house." The police would protect them from the restless crowd only feet away. A provoked Lizzie responded, "Why, is there anybody in this house suspected?" The mayor tried to shift the discussion to Morse's experience with a mob the night before. "I want to know the truth," she pressed him twice. Now the mayor-physician botched the visit, handing her defense and the Superior Court a pretext to help undermine the legal case against Lizzie. "Well, Miss Borden," the mayor acknowledged, "I regret to answer yes, you are suspected." "I am ready to go now," Lizzie replied according to the mayor. Then sheepish Emma spoke up. "Well, we have tried to keep it from her as long as we could."

The mayor's words would acquire a certain legal elasticity in court. They could be taken as evidence that Lizzie was already under house arrest. The unfortunate exchange established arguable grounds for the exclusion of her damning inquest testimony, the only time Lizzie was deposed under oath in court. If she was already effectively under house arrest on Saturday night, the argument went, she should have been informed of her right against self-incrimination. The prosecution would mount a vigorous case, showing how logic and precedent contradicted this argument.

On Sunday morning, while police hovered outside the house, Lizzie burned clothing in the kitchen stove. The police had no knowledge of this incident during their investigation. Nevertheless, it fills out the chronology of events following the murders and the mayor's confirmation that Lizzie was a prime suspect. Alice Russell would not tell the district attorney of this incident until the grand jury stage, when the case against Lizzie was apparently on the verge of dissolution. Later, at the Superior Court trial, she recounted in detail what happened on Sunday morning when only she, Lizzie, and Emma were present.

Miss Russell went upstairs after breakfast and then came down. "I went into the kitchen. . . . Miss Lizzie was at the stove and she had a skirt in her hand, and her sister turned and said, 'What are you going to do?' and Lizzie said, 'I am going to burn this old thing up; it is covered with paint.'" Miss Russell left the room and then returned. "Miss Lizzie stood up towards the cupboard door; the cupboard door was open, and she appeared to be either ripping something down or tearing part of the garment. . . . I said to her, 'I wouldn't let anybody see me do that, Lizzie.'"

Russell was asked if she saw the waist of the garment. "I didn't know that it was the waist, but I saw a portion of this dress up on the cupboard shelf."

While Lizzie was tearing the garment and feeding it into the stove, Russell left the room. The next morning Pinkerton Detective Hanscom asked her "if all the dresses were there that were there the day of the tragedy?" She said, "Yes." Russell also had a conversation with Lizzie while Emma was present, informing them that she had told a "falsehood." "I said to them—I said, 'the worst thing you could have done was to burn that dress. I have been asked about your dresses.' Lizzie said, 'Oh, what made you let me do it? Why didn't you tell me?'"

On the Sunday before the inquest, while Lizzie burned her clothes, Rev. William W. Jubb fired up the worshippers of the Central Congregational Church. Both inside and outside of court Rev. Jubb and especially City Missionary Buck outdid themselves as Lizzie's pastoral counselors. "Save us from blasting a life, innocent and blameless," Jubb thundered, "and keep us from taking the sweetness from a future by our ill-advised words, and let us be charitable as we remember the poor grief-stricken family and minister unto them."

Jubb harbored no doubt that a man, and probably a crazed one, cut down the Bordens. "One to commit such a murder must have been without heart, without soul, a fiend incarnate, the very vilest of degraded humanity, or he must have been a maniac." Jubb magnified Lizzie's fear of her house falling victim to an arsonist. "Why a man who could conceive and execute such a murder as that would not hesitate to burn the city."

Jubb concluded with advice to his worshippers who inhabited a city thick like the soot-filled sky with rumors and accusations. "Let us curb our tongues and preserve a blameless life from undeserved suspicions." He prayed for the "poor stricken girls" and hoped they would be "comforted" and "realize how fully God is their refuge." Jubb's sermon represented a summons to The Hill to rally behind one of their own in the face of groundless rumors and incriminations.

The day after Jubb's impassioned sermon, the Fall River police conducted their final search of the Borden house. This time they brought mason Charles H. Bryant with them. When central heat had been installed in houses like the Bordens, Franklin stoves were removed from fireplaces, which were often bricked over. Bryant's job was to check the fireplaces, unused flues, and masonry throughout the house to see if he could find any hiding places. Once again the police were stymied. Bryant found nothing suspicious. The police did confiscate the handleless hatchet.

On that Monday before the start of the inquest, Officer William Medley interviewed one of Lizzie's good friends who was willing to talk. The young women at Marion refused to answer Medley's questions. In fact, one, Lizzie Johnson, spurned Medley's efforts "to make known to me the contents of the letter she received from Lizzie Borden on the day of the murder," he recorded. This letter allegedly contained something that Johnson feared could be misconstrued in light of the murders. The *Fall River Herald* later reported that the women at Marion had told Lizzie how the axe for chopping wood was a "dull affair." She supposedly responded that she would chop wood because she had a "very sharp hatchet." Perhaps more important than whether Lizzie actually penned those words is the fact that her friends, with the exception of Alice Russell and Mrs. Cyrus Tripp, stonewalled the police. Medley interviewed Tripp three days before she was called to testify at the inquest.

Tripp had known Lizzie since grade school. They remained friends and continued to trade visits after the former Augusta Poole married and moved to Westport, a farming town that bordered Fall River on the east. Indeed, Lizzie visited Augusta nine days before the murders while returning from New Bedford. Tripp was surprisingly forthcoming with Medley. She told him that Lizzie believed her stepmother was "deceitful." Lizzie was convinced that Abby had "influence with my father," despite her denials. Andrew's secret purchase of the stepsister's house remained a domestic grievance. "She said, 'I do not know that my sister and I would get anything in the event of my father's death,'" Mrs. Tripp related. "The conversation took place at different times during former visits; nothing being said during her visit July 26th."

As a close friend of Lizzie's, Tripp volunteered the most credible account the police recorded of years-long smoldering animosity and mistrust among the Bordens. In effect, she conveyed to Medley a finely tailored explanation of a potential murder motive. Unfortunately, almost overnight Tripp's memory turned cloudy. At the inquest, Attorney General Knowlton labored futilely to get her to confirm what she had told Medley only seventy-two hours earlier.

Two legal actions added to the rush of Monday's activity on the case.

Long-serving District Court Justice Josiah C. Blaisdell called for an inquest to begin the next day. Then the marshal, convinced of Lizzie's guilt and anxious to take her into custody, had the clerk of the Second District Court issue an arrest warrant. In his mind, the question was not if but when Lizzie would be arrested. He would simply pull the paperwork from his pocket. Ultimately, Hilliard's hasty decision would buttress the defense argument that Lizzie was effectively under arrest before the inquest. Thus, she should have been read her rights. When the district attorney finally arrived in Fall River for the inquest on Tuesday morning, he was unaware that the marshal held a warm arrest warrant in his vest pocket that he was eager to serve.

At the opening of the inquest, less than five full days into the investigation, the police were caught in the crosscurrents of a savage crime that had taken place in a divided and rapidly growing and changing mill city. With the Irish Catholic *Globe* hectoring authorities for Lizzie's arrest, its working-class readers feared that a guilty Borden might escape justice, that the power and influence of the Bordens, The Hill, and the Republican *Evening News* were too much for the police to overcome. A widely circulated rumor claimed that the Bordens conspired to spend millions if necessary to assure that Lizzie would never be convicted. Once the inquest began, the *Herald* claimed that "members of the other Borden families . . . have prepared themselves for united action in whatever direction may seem necessary."

An unidentified Borden disputed the *Herald*'s story. "No true Borden," he insisted, "has ever placed a stumbling block in the way of the law." He went on to assure the *Herald*'s readers that "no member of my family will in any way hamper the police in their investigation. The statement that fifteen million of Borden money will be used in balking the authorities is untrue and ill-advised."

No such Borden denial was going to dissolve the distrust between those on and below The Hill. Persistent labor strife, nativist bigotry like that expressed by Rev. Adams in his *Andover Review* essay, glaring inequality—all this and more created rich loam for mutual mistrust between Yankees and immigrants to thrive. The Lizzie Borden case deepened these tensions.

The Hill had already lost confidence in the police department for its aggressiveness and seeming rush to judgment against a "tenderly bred young lady," as the *New York Telegram* put it. The police force's shifting composition further unsettled The Hill. The rank and file had begun to reflect the changing face of the city and the resulting jostle for political power. The Irish mayor and the predominantly Yankee Board of Aldermen tussled over appointments to the police department. For their part, the police were relieved to entrust the controversial case to Judge Blaisdell and District Attorney Knowlton. Both professed their reluctance to pass judgment on Lizzie. Later Knowlton even tried to extricate himself from a prosecution that divided the public and announced open season on him and the judge. The inquest and preliminary hearing incited local and national newspapers to pour scorn on the legal proceedings and the men who led them. Women's groups also enlisted in the campaign of vilification against Lizzie's perceived persecutors.

CHAPTER 5

Arrest

Over approximately four months, Lizzie endured three legal proceedings: an inquest, a preliminary hearing, and a grand jury investigation. Each of them possessed its own purpose, rhythm, and length. And during each of these legal opening acts the case against Lizzie could have been derailed. The curtain would have fallen before the main event—Lizzie's Superior Court trial for double murder.

District Attorney Hosea M. Knowlton and Judge Josiah C. Blaisdell knew the perils of a seeming rush to judgment given the crime and especially the identity of the suspect—not only a Borden but also one who was a prominent religious woman, perhaps Fall River's most prominent Protestant nun. More than the police, Knowlton had to thread his way between Lizzie's partisans and her adversaries. Given the extraordinary nature of the crime, an inquest would slow down the police impetus to arrest Lizzie. After all, Professor Wood of Harvard had not yet completed his tests of the victims' stomachs or of the axes and the first hatchet forwarded to him.

The inquest lasted for three days. Lizzie took the stand on each day and testified for hours. Even more than the heap of inconsistencies that the police compiled on the day of the murders, Lizzie's inquest testimony led her into a briar patch of seeming self-incrimination. As a result, the circumstantial evidence generated by the inquest gave momentum to the next two legal phases of the case.

The inquest also produced something else. It instigated withering criticism of the police, the district attorney, and the judge in local, regional, and national newspapers. In addition, the inquest mobilized Lizzie's supporters and rallied women's groups near and far to her side.

The Inquest

Judge Blaisdell, the head of the district court, was seventy-two years old and experienced in politics and the courtroom. He had followed the old-fashioned route into the legal profession of many money-less, modestly educated young men: he studied in the office of a local lawyer. He went on to serve as a state senator and representative in addition to his election as a Fall River Mayor for two years. He had been a district court judge since 1874.

A generation separated Judge Blaisdell from District Attorney Knowlton. He was forty-five years old in 1892. He had graduated from Tufts University, studied in the office of a New Bedford lawyer, and attended Harvard Law School. Knowlton also served in the state legislature as a senator and representative. He had been district attorney for more than a decade by 1892. Knowlton and Blaisdell, in other words, were seasoned hands when it came to politics and criminal prosecutions, including inquests.

The inquest was a judicial proceeding that had evolved from a coroner's inquest. Thus a judge rather than a medical examiner presided over an inquiry into the cause and time of a "mysterious" death. Moreover, if testimony permitted, the judge could determine the probable guilt of one or more individuals. At the time, all Massachusetts inquests were held in private, though judges were not strictly bound to do so. Lizzie's attorney, Andrew J. Jennings, asked to represent her at the inquest because Mayor Coughlin had identified her as a suspect. The district attorney and the judge refused. Defense attorneys didn't customarily participate in inquests. As a suspect, Lizzie certainly knew that she could refuse to testify at the proceeding. She consulted with Jennings before and between her appearances on the witness stand. In light of the suspicions swirling around her, she and Jennings knew that her refusal to testify would only substantiate the conviction of the police and a major portion of the public that she was the demonic murderess.

The inquest was held at the small district court above the police station. Besides Judge Blaisdell and District Attorney Knowlton, the principal observers were Marshal Hilliard, State Police Detective Seaver, Medical Examiner Dolan, and Mayor Coughlin. (Attorney General

Albert E. Pillsbury also made a brief appearance.) The assembled constituted a formidable array of male authority, confronting a privileged lady who led a largely unaccountable life. Now Lizzie was obligated to explain everything she said and did on the most important day of her life and to reveal intimate details of Borden family affairs. At the inquest witnesses testified alone, that is, not in the presence of other witnesses.

The proceeding did not begin without some controversy involving class and ethnicity. The police used a hack, a hired coach with drawn curtains to block the gaze of curious bystanders, to transport Lizzie from Second Street to the police station and then back. From her cousin's house in Fall River's south end, Bridget was seen walking to the police station with Officer Doherty. Both the *Fall River Globe* and the *Herald* commented on the class-inflected perceptions that this seemingly disparate treatment provoked. The *Herald* reported, "People wondered why the girl was not entitled to the same consideration that was shown Miss Borden, who was as carefully guarded from the eyes of the curious as a closed carriage could do it." Bridget explained that she had been offered a carriage, but preferred to walk. Still, the perception suggested how authorities needed to negotiate issues of class and ethnicity as well as gender throughout the Lizzie Borden case. As the inquest began the *Herald* claimed that "a remark is going the rounds that if the parties at present were poor people they would have been locked up long before now."

Bridget's extensive inquest testimony has been lost. Most students of the Borden case focus on Lizzie's widely reprinted inquest testimony with its tangled skein of responses. They then skip the rest of the inquest, rush through or set aside the preliminary hearing (once not available) for the cover story: the nearly two-week drama of Lizzie's Superior Court trial. But witnesses at the inquest and then at the preliminary hearing were important for what they divulged and what they resisted disclosing. The proceedings enabled the prosecution to weed out some weak witnesses.

Sarah Whitehead proved to be among the weakest. Abby's half sister observed, "I always thought they [Lizzie and Emma] felt above me." She offered little else about the Bordens. Knowlton asked her if Abby "seem[ed] on good terms with her daughters?" She responded that Abby

"said little about them; she was a woman that kept everything to herself."
Yet Sarah had told Officers Harrington and Doherty a different story,
including that "Lizzie did not like Mrs. Borden." Knowlton ended the
brief testimony from Sarah with a crucial question that clearly suggested she was not telling all she knew. "Was there some little friction
about property that you know about?" "Not that I know of." Sarah professed to be totally unaware of how the daughters became permanently
disaffected from Abby when Andrew purchased the half sister's home.
In fact, she had told the police that the bitterness in the family had
erupted five years earlier.

Sarah had good reason for such tight-lipped testimony. When Abby
died her property passed to Andrew. After he was murdered Emma and
Lizzie inherited Andrew's estate, including Abby's deed to her half sister's house. Thus Sarah was at the sisters' mercy, fearful of antagonizing
them. They held the deed to her home. Lizzie and Emma did eventually transfer all of Abby's property to her survivors, including the deed.
Sarah had no way of knowing this at the time of the inquest, however.
She did not testify again.

Augusta Tripp successfully parried Knowlton's questions that were
based on the interview she gave Officer Medley on the preceding Monday. She admitted that she and Lizzie exchanged visits. This included
Lizzie's weeklong stay at Westport during the previous year. Tripp had
also "called" on Lizzie at home "this year." Knowlton asked what she had
heard Lizzie say about Mrs. Borden.

A. Well, I don't know . . . for I have seen them so little. . . .
Q. I want to know what they did tell you, that is all.
A. It would be rather hard for me to remember what they did tell me.
Q. . . . Do you remember what you told the officer about it, Mr. Med-
    ley, did you have a talk with him?
A. Yes, Sir, I have had a talk with him.
Q. Do you remember what you told him?
A. I don't remember that he asked me such a question as that, I an-
    swered his questions.

Tripp went on to deny or not recall what she had told Medley about
Lizzie's wariness of Abby and fear of being disinherited. The most

Knowlton could wrest from Tripp was that Lizzie believed her step-mother had influence with her father and that the sisters "did not enter into conversations [with Abby], with each other, perhaps." Knowlton was unable to make any headway with a witness who had been so prom-ising with Officer Medley. Tripp returned to Westport's green pastures and cornfields, not to be called again. She had joined the friends who closed ranks behind Lizzie.

John Morse was more forthright in his answers to Knowlton's ques-tions. A hint of suspicion still clung to him, but he had nothing to hide. His testimony revealed his knowledge of Andrew's business affairs. He had boarded with the Bordens for a year, 1875, when he returned to Fall River temporarily from his long sojourn in the West. Andrew once had a will, Morse said. Both Emma and Lizzie testified to their knowledge of the will at the inquest. Neither had been aware that Andrew "destroyed it 15 years ago," according to Morse.

Morse said that he visited Andrew on August 3 to discuss his Swansea farms. Andrew had asked Morse if he knew someone who could "take charge of his farm." Surprisingly, Andrew talked about making "some gifts for charitable purposes." What he had in mind was giving a farm to the Old Ladies Home, "if they would take it."

Morse's testimony requires some sorting out, clarification that did not occur in court. Apparently, Andrew was referring to both of his farms, neither of which turned a sufficient profit. The new manager would take over the farm where Andrew and Abby sought relaxation and escape from Spindle City. Ostensibly, the other farm was so unprof-itable that Andrew weighed transferring it to the Old Ladies' Home. From Morse's testimony, it is difficult to determine how serious Andrew was about such an uncharacteristic act of charity. In any event, death left him bereft of any philanthropic record.

Morse claimed to have a warm relationship with Emma. She had been old enough to know him before he resettled in Iowa. They corresponded regularly. He saw her when he visited Second Street, "sometimes once a week, every three weeks, sometimes once every three months." He sel-dom saw Lizzie. Morse could not recall the last time she joined him and her parents at a meal. Then, catching himself because he believed in Lizzie's innocence, Morse claimed that they had eaten together "several times" over the previous six months. Lizzie didn't cultivate a relationship with her uncle. Unlike her, he was privileged to know something of Andrew's business affairs.

Lizzie Testifies

Lizzie testified for an hour and a half on Tuesday, for half a day on Wednesday, and for less than an hour on Thursday. To reiterate, these appearances on the witness stand represent the only time she testified in court about the murders. District Attorney Knowlton later referred to it as her "confession." Lizzie's testimony did not amount to that. Still, at times her confusion and contradictions were enough to give the judge and the handful of observers whiplash.

Dr. Bowen had prescribed a double dose of morphine at bedtime to calm Lizzie's nerves. At her trial he answered a simple "yes" to her lawyer's question about how a double dose of morphine "somewhat affect[s] memory" and also changes "the view of things and give[s] people hallucinations." But Lizzie had been unable to give police a coherent, consistent, and plausible narrative of her whereabouts and actions on August 4 before Dr. Bowen delivered a bottle of morphine the next day. Under questioning from the prosecution at Lizzie's trial, Bowen conceded that he only actually saw her take the bromo-caffeine, which would not have caused problems with memory a week later, that is, at the inquest. We simply do not know if Lizzie self-administered the morphine. She certainly did not display hallucinations at the inquest.

Knowlton eased into the interrogation by asking what Lizzie knew about Andrew's business affairs. She testified that she had learned "several years ago" that her father had made a will. She also knew of his principal real estate holdings.

Then the district attorney pivoted to the controversy over the purchase of Abby's sister's house. As Knowlton probed, Lizzie insisted that her relations with Abby remained "quite cordial," despite the uproar in the family. When Knowlton wanted to know where Abby was when Lizzie came downstairs on the morning of the murders, he asked: "Where was your mother? Do you prefer me to call her Mrs. Borden?" "I had as soon you call her mother," Lizzie replied. At this point she was very much in control and crafty in her answers.

Some early responses also indicated that she had been advised by her lawyer, offstage. Knowlton asked about Abby: "In what respects were the relations between you and her that of mother and daughter?" "That is the same question you asked me before; I can't answer you any better now than I did before." "You did not say before you could not answer, but that you declined to answer." "I decline to answer because I do not know what to say." Leaning on the shock of August 4, what we now call post-traumatic stress disorder, she could have deployed memory loss as a blunt instrument to foil the district attorney. Instead, she tried to match wits with him, sometimes leaning on the crutch of impaired memory when Knowlton cornered her.

Soon fault lines materialized and multiplied in her testimony. Lizzie denied what she had said to police and also to Bridget and Alice Russell, both of whom testified at the inquest. Then the contradictions in her testimony began to pile up like the firewood in the cellar. Lizzie started refuting her own testimony from moment to moment. The examples are too numerous to repeat. They are also too important to skip and require some lengthy quotations of testimony to demonstrate how Lizzie seemed to tie herself in a hangman's knot. For example, Lizzie squirmed answering Knowlton's question about whether she had discussed washing windows with Maggie.

Q. Did you say anything to Maggie?
A. I did not.
Q. Did you say anything about washing the windows?
A. No, sir.
Q. Did you speak to her?
A. I think I told her I did not want any breakfast.
Q. You do not remember of talking to her about washing the windows?
A. I don't remember whether I did nor not; I don't remember it. Yes, I remember; yes, I asked her to shut the parlor blinds when she was done. . . .

Knowlton let this jumbled answer pass. He had more important issues to press.

Next he wanted to know where Lizzie was when her father returned from down street and who let him in the secured front door. Lizzie first told Knowlton that she was in the kitchen reading an old copy of *Harper's Magazine* and waiting for her ironing flats to heat.

Q. Are you sure you were in the kitchen when your father returned?

A. I am not sure whether I was there or in the dining room.

Q. Did you go back to your room before your father returned?

A. I think I did carry up some clean clothes.

Q. Did you stay there?

A. No, sir.

Q. Did you spend any time up the front stairs before your father returned?

A. No, sir.

Q. Or after he returned?

A. No, sir. I did stay up in my room long enough . . . to sew a piece of tape on a garment.

Q. What was the time when your father came home?

A. He came home after I came downstairs.

Q. You were not upstairs when he came home?

A. I was not upstairs when he came home; no, sir.

Q. What was Maggie doing when your father came home?

A. I don't know whether she was there or whether she had gone upstairs; I can't remember.

Q. Who let your father in?

A. I think he came to the front door and rang the bell, and I think Maggie let him in, and he said he had forgotten his key, so I think she must have been down stairs.

Q. His key would have done him no good if the locks were left as you left them?

A. But they were always unbolted in the morning.

Q. Who unbolted them that morning?

A. I don't think they had been unbolted. Maggie can tell you.

Q. If he had not forgotten his key it would have been no good?

A. No, he had his key and could not get in. I understood Maggie to say he said he had forgotten his key.

Q. You did not hear him say anything about it?

A. I heard his voice, but I don't know what he said.

Q. I understood you to say he had forgotten his key?

A. No, it was Maggie said he had forgotten his key.

Q. Where was Maggie when the bell rang?

A. I don't know, sir.

Q. Where were you when the bell rang?

A. I think in my room upstairs.

Q. Then you were upstairs when your father came home?

A. I don't know sure, but I think I was.

After such unmoored testimony about Bridget's washing windows; whether the servant, and Lizzie herself, was upstairs or downstairs when Andrew returned; what her father said; and whether the front door was bolted, among other things, Lizzie seemed close to the breaking point. "I don't know what I have said," she told Knowlton. "I have answered so many questions and I am so confused I don't know one thing from another. I am telling you just nearly as I know."

The district attorney exposed more inconsistencies in Lizzie's testimony of her whereabouts when Andrew returned. Then he moved on to Abby. Since Lizzie was the only person in the house when her stepmother was killed, Knowlton prevailed upon her to account for her time and Abby's movements. In the process, Lizzie radically revised, even repudiated, what she had told Bridget, neighbor Mrs. Churchill, and the police.

Lizzie said Abby went upstairs to change "pillow shams." This took place shortly after Lizzie came down for breakfast. Knowlton established that the task would only take "two minutes." He wanted to know about Abby's movements from that time "until II o'clock." Lizzie claimed to be downstairs, except "for two or three minutes" when she visited the cellar water closet and a "few minutes" upstairs in her room. She suggested that Abby might have gone to her room. Knowlton pounced on this shaky response, and for good reason: Abby would have had to come down the front stairs from the guestroom, cross the first floor and climb the back stairs to her room. Then she would have had to retrace her steps to return to the guestroom, where she was found bludgeoned. Lizzie would have seen her at least once.

Then Lizzie trotted out the note that was never found, written by someone who was never identified, and carried by a messenger who was never seen.

Q. Had you any knowledge of her going out of the house?

A. No, sir.

Q. Had you any knowledge of her going out of the house?

A. She told me she had a note, somebody was sick. . . .

Q. Then why did you not suppose she had gone?

A. I supposed she had gone.

Q. Did you hear her come back?

A. I did not hear her go or come back, but I supposed she went.

Q. When you found your father dead you supposed your mother had gone?

A. I did not know. I said to the people who came in "I don't know whether Mrs. Borden is out or in; I wish you would see if she is in her room."

On the morning of the murders she had actually said to Bridget and Adelaide Churchill, according to their testimony, that she heard Abby come in.

Knowlton was almost through with Lizzie for the day after some questions about Abby's mysterious sick call. When the session ended Lizzie found herself immersed in testimony that was unpersuasive, contradictory, or inconsistent with what she told other witnesses and the police. The inquest then adjourned until the next morning. If Lizzie thought the worst was behind her, she was badly mistaken. If Knowlton believed she would easily become undone the next day, he misjudged the suspect. Yet Lizzie found herself in an unprecedented predicament for a privileged lady. Like the trespass of the police, especially its Irish contingent, on her bedroom, the district attorney exercised a free hand prying into her private life.

Ensnared

Knowlton started the next day's long interrogation with the happenings in the house after Lizzie came downstairs feeling ill and lacking an appetite for breakfast. Lizzie claimed that Abby said she was going out and would purchase food for dinner. "I told her I did not want anything"; that is, Lizzie didn't expect to eat dinner because she had no appetite.

Knowlton would return to this testimony in the inquest's most spirited exchange.

In the meantime, Knowlton established that if Lizzie was downstairs for most of the morning, not only would she have seen her stepmother cross back and forth between the guest room and her bedroom; Lizzie would have also likely encountered, or heard, anyone who entered the house and climbed the front stairs to cut down Abby. Lizzie also changed a crucial aspect of her testimony from the day before concerning what she did after her father left in the morning. "I went upstairs before he went out." . . . "Do you remember you did not say that yesterday?" "I don't think you asked me. I told you yesterday I went upstairs directly after I came up from down cellar, with the clean clothes." "You now say after your father went out, you did not go upstairs at all?" "No, sir. I did not." Why did Lizzie change her story? One answer is that much of what she had said the day before seemed to be composed as she went along. Knowlton barraged her with questions. His queries and her apparent improvisations overloaded Lizzie's cerebral circuitry. Then again, perhaps she *did* take morphine and its effects were catching up with her. Lizzie's lawyer had a ready explanation for her erratic answers: a wily, hard-charging prosecutor tripped her up because he believed the young woman was guilty.

When Knowlton turned to her actions while someone murdered Andrew, the focus of Wednesday's testimony, the tinny sound of Lizzie's testimony irritated him. On the day of the murders, to the police and others, such as Bridget and Alice Russell, she had put forth multiple versions of what occupied her as the murderer crushed the left side of Andrew's face and skull. Once again she shaved time off her visit to the barn, claiming she was there "fifteen or twenty minutes." Lizzie had intended to vacation in Marion with her friends. She also expected to fish, though, as she testified, it had been "five years" since she had done so at Swansea. That coincided with the sisters' cold war against Abby when they stopped visiting the farm in Swansea. Lizzie turned to the barn to find sinkers.

Knowlton challenged Lizzie by insisting that it would have taken no more than "three minutes" to search a box in the loft for sinkers. Lizzie responded that she ate "three pears" while standing in the loft. Knowlton seized on this admission and it led to a near-blistering exchange.

Q. You were feeling better than you did in the morning?

A. Better than I did the night before.

Q. You were feeling better than you were in the morning?

A. I felt better in the morning than I did the night before.

Q. That is not what I asked you. You were then, when you were in that hot loft, looking out the window and eating three pears feeling better, were you not, than you were in the morning when you could not eat breakfast.

A. I never eat breakfast.

Q. You did not answer my question, and you will, if I have to put it all day. Were you then when you were eating those three pears in that hot loft, looking out that closed window, feeling better than you were in the morning when you ate breakfast?

A. I was feeling well enough to eat pears.

Q. Were you feeling better than you were in the morning?

A. I don't think I felt very sick in the morning, only—yes, I don't know but I did feel better. As I say, I don't know whether I ate any breakfast or not, or whether I ate a cookie.

Q. Were you then feeling better than you did in the morning?

A. I don't know how to answer you, because I told you I felt better in the morning anyway.

Q. Do you understand my question? My question is whether, when you were in the loft of that barn, you were feeling better than you were in the morning when you got up?

A. No, sir. I felt about the same.

Q. Were you feeling better than you were when you told your mother you did not care for dinner?

A. She asked me if I wanted any meat.

To the district attorney's frustration Lizzie successfully fended off this round of dogged questioning. She was not going to wilt or to confess no matter how scorching Knowlton's interrogation. Still, the district attorney would not let go of her suspect, even bizarre, tale of eating pears in the stifling barn loft while her father perished in a house only feet away.

The front end of the barn, which faced Second Street, stood only 15 feet from the screened side door. Knowlton plunged into Lizzie's account of how she spent her time in the loft at that end. Once again she revised previous testimony.

> Q. You observe the fact, do you not? You have put yourself in the only place perhaps, where it would be impossible, for you to see a person going into the house?
>
> A. Yes sir, I should have seen them from the window.
>
> Q. From anywhere else in the yard?
>
> A. No sir, not unless from the end of the barn.
>
> Q. Ordinarily in the yard you could see them, and in the kitchen, where you had been you could have seen them?
>
> A. I don't think I understand.
>
> Q. When you were in the kitchen, you could see persons come in the front door?
>
> A. Yes, sir.
>
> Q. When you were in the yard, unless you were around the corner of the house, you could see persons who came in the back door?
>
> A. No, sir, unless I was at the corner of the barn; the minute I turned I could not.
>
> Q. What was there?
>
> A. A little jog like, the walk turns.
>
> Q. ... Going into the barn, going upstairs into the hottest place in the barn, in the rear of the barn, the hottest place, and there standing and eating those three pears in the morning?
>
> A. I beg your pardon, I was not in the rear of the barn. I was in the other end of the barn that faced the street.
>
> Q. Where you could see anybody coming into the house?
>
> A. Yes, sir.
>
> Q. Did you not tell me that you could not?
>
> A. Before I went into the barn, at the jog on the outside.
>
> Q. You now say when you were eating pears, you could see the back door?
>
> A. Yes, sir.

Knowlton's interrogation exposed several incongruous aspects of Lizzie's testimony beyond the fact that she admitted that the barn loft "was the hottest place on the property," as he put it once more. She picked up pears from the ground. Instead of eating them under the shade of the tree, she retreated to the loft. Lizzie conceded that the house's side door was within her sight while she ate the pears. Thus from the kitchen to the backyard to the barn's front loft—for nearly all of the time surrounding Andrew's murder, Lizzie would have seen anyone entering or leaving the house from the side door. Consequently, the minutes consumed in the failed search for sinkers in the box on the bench away from the window became crucial to her alibi. Lizzie insisted that it did not take Knowlton's "three minutes" to search the box containing "nails," "old locks," and a "door knob" but "ten minutes." She then spliced into her narrative that she "pulled over quite a lot of boards in the looking." Yet no one noticed any dust on her hands or face when she returned to the house and summoned help. The search for old sinkers, which could be had for pennies, sounded like a necessary fiction to fill out her time in the loft, which also struck Knowlton as an absurdity.

After relating her discovery of Andrew's body in the sitting room and sending for help, she again disavowed what she had told Bridget and Mrs. Churchill about Abby. "Did you tell Maggie you thought your mother had come in?" "No, sir." "That you thought you heard her come in?" "No, sir." "Did you say to anybody that you thought she was killed upstairs?" "No, sir." "To anybody?" "No, sir." "You made no effort to find your mother at all?" "No, sir." On the day of the murders Lizzie never visited the guestroom to see Abby's body, collapsed face down on the floor in a pool of blood. In fact, Lizzie admitted, she had only peeked in the door at Andrew's corpse rather than entering the sitting room where her father lay. The police and Knowlton drew their own conclusion: she had no need to revisit what she had done.

Lizzie jumbled her previous testimony when the district attorney returned to Abby a few minutes later. "I want you to give me all that you did, by way of word or deed to see whether your mother was dead or not, when you found your father was dead?" "I did not do anything, except what I said to Mrs. Churchill. I said to her: 'I don't know where Mrs. Borden is. I think she is out, but I wish you would look.'" "You did ask her to look?" "I said that to Mrs. Churchill." Lizzie had changed course in her testimony yet again, now admitting that she did try to find Abby but omitting that she had claimed she heard her stepmother come home.

Knowlton was almost finished with Lizzie for the day. One of his final questions dealt with the skirt that Lizzie claimed she wore on the day of the murders. At the police's request two days later, she had given them a skirt. It had a "smooch" that looked like blood; tests had not yet been completed on the garment. Lizzie did not know that. (When the tests were finished, the stain turned out not to be blood.) He asked Lizzie: "Do you know whether there was any blood on the skirt?" Knowlton worded his questions carefully; he was probing, not claiming that the skirt was soiled with blood. "Assume, that there was, can you give any explanation of how it came there on the dress skirt?" "No, sir." "Assume there was, can you suggest any reason how it came there?" "No, sir." . . . "Have you said it came from fleabites?" "On the petticoat I said there was a fleabite." . . . "You said you meant the dress skirt." Knowlton never would have asked the last delicate question about menstruation in open court.

There was one small drop of blood on the petticoat, not the skirt; its significance would be disputed at the trial. With his hypothetical questions Knowlton seemed to be trying to unsettle Lizzie, to perhaps bait her into some damning admission. His strategy failed. The outfit Lizzie handed over to police was in all likelihood not the one she wore before she changed into the pink wrapper during the midday maelstrom of August 4. Lizzie had a ready refuge from the minimal taint of any blood found outside the death settings. As she informed Knowlton: "I told those men [the police] that were at the house that I had had the fleas; that is all." The second day of the inquest soon adjourned.

Jailed

For all practical purposes the proceeding was over for Lizzie after the second day. She testified briefly the next day. She denied visiting Smith's Drug Store and trying to purchase prussic acid. Eli Bence and his two associates testified otherwise. Lizzie referred to the murders as "the affair." Given the opportunity to add anything to her testimony that might help find the murderers, she described a man in the Borden yard on two nights when she returned home. Lizzie then left the witness stand for good.

She returned to the matron's room, where Emma and a friend waited.

Witnesses testified into the afternoon. Then Knowlton, Hilliard, Detective Seaver, and Dr. Dolan huddled in the marshal's office. The meeting concluded with Knowlton telling the marshal to have an arrest warrant issued. That is when the district attorney first learned that Hilliard had been carrying a warrant since Monday. Knowlton told the marshal to return it to the court clerk and have a new one issued.

Around 5 p.m. Knowlton and Hilliard paid a call on Andrew Jennings and informed him they had a warrant for Lizzie's arrest. Jennings came to the station and broke the news to his client. Emma and Mrs. George Brigham of Central Congregational consoled Lizzie, though the older sister may have been more in need of comforting than the accused. Then Lizzie and her attorney faced Marshal Hilliard for the reading of the warrant. "I have a warrant for your arrest for the murder of Andrew J. Borden," the marshal announced. "Do you wish me to read it?" Jennings advised Lizzie to waive the reading. One week after the murders Lizzie found herself in police custody, charged with a capital crime for which there was no bail. She was held overnight in the matron's quarters.

The next morning Judge Blaisdell presided over her arraignment in district court. Overnight the news of Lizzie's arrest had shaken The Hill and trickled down to Spindle City's flatlands. The crowd swelled outside the police station, despite a drenching rain. "When the doors opened," the *Herald* reported, "only enough to fill the seating capacity of the room was allowed to enter, and officers were placed at both entrances to keep all others out."

Lizzie came into the courtroom on the arm of Rev. Buck. The clerk asked her how she pleaded to the complaint charging her with homicide. In a subdued, barely audible voice she said, "Not guilty." The clerk could not hear her. She repeated her plea forcefully, with an emphasis on "Not."

Judge Blaisdell called for a preliminary hearing as the next step. He could have skipped this legal stage and referred the case directly to the grand jury. Given the accused and the crime, he chose to proceed more deliberately. Since the inquest had been held in private, the preliminary hearing would allow Jennings to discover the evidence against Lizzie and mount a defense.

Jennings protested that the inquest had biased the judge against Lizzie. Twice he referred to his client as a "girl." "This girl," he argued, "is called to plead to a complaint issued in the progress of an inquest now in its early stages." The judge had said that the inquest remained open. Jennings repeated his dissent using the same language, including the reference to Lizzie as a "girl." "Miss Lizzie" or this "girl" were the preferred ways lawyers for the accused as well as her supporters and sympathetic papers referred to Lizzie. Knowlton used the more adult "Miss Borden." In an important sense, the thirty-two-year-old Lizzie had remained a girl, unmarried and dependent on a domineering father. In and outside of court her advocates consciously and unconsciously deployed "girl" and "Miss Lizzie" to suggest her virginal incapacity to carry out a bloodbath.

Jennings claimed that by presiding over the public hearing and thereby "acting in a double capacity," Judge Blaisdell would deprive Lizzie of "her constitutional right to be heard before a court of unprejudiced opinion." Knowlton countered by citing "statutes" and "precedent" to argue that there was nothing "extraordinary" in the court's proceedings. Judge Blaisdell overruled Jennings's plea—but not without consequences. It gave Lizzie's partisans grounds to protest that she was being railroaded. Secrecy had surrounded the inquest. The only public information dispensed each day was who testified. The inquest transcript remained in the hands of the district attorney and the court. All of this fell within the scope of the law. But The Hill now had three targets to assail who seemed to be part of a conspiracy to attribute the crime to Lizzie Borden: the judge, the district attorney, and the police.

Judge Blaisdell made two other important rulings at the arraignment. He denied Jennings's bid for an immediate hearing. Instead, the date was set for August 22, ten days from the arraignment. Second, John Morse and Bridget Sullivan were required to post $500.00 bonds to ensure their appearance in court. The *Herald* reported that the proprietors of the Republican *Evening News*, one of whom had been Andrew Borden's friend and served as one of his pallbearers, became the bondsmen for Morse and Bridget. In fact, the newspaper proprietors did nothing for Bridget, a poor Irish immigrant servant "girl" who was unable to pay. They probably hoped she would escape to Ireland, thereby undermining the case against Lizzie and confirming suspicions that the servant was the murderess. Marshal Hilliard and Detective Seaver came forward and offered surety for her. They arranged for Bridget to work as a servant for the jail keeper in New Bedford. Bridget was in a kind of protective custody, but she was allowed to stroll the streets of New Bedford. As for Lizzie, she was ordered to the county jail in Taunton, 16 miles north of Fall River, where there were facilities to accommodate women prisoners.

Late Friday afternoon Lizzie slipped into a hack at the side entrance to the police station, disappointing the crowd that had continued to brave the heavy rain for a glimpse of the prisoner. Marshal Hilliard, Detective Seaver, and the ever-present Rev. Buck accompanied Lizzie in one hack. Emma and Jennings traveled in another. Crowds lay in wait for her at the train stations in Fall River and Taunton. Whatever the consequences of the upcoming legal proceedings, Lizzie had become a curiosity, a shrouded lady who fascinated the public. She would never escape that scourge.

In Taunton she met up with an old friend. Mrs. Isabel R. Wright, jail matron and wife of the Bristol County Sheriff, had known Lizzie in childhood. When Mrs. Wright had lived in Fall River Lizzie had been a playmate of her daughter. Lizzie was extended courtesies that were not available to other prisoners. Among other things she often ordered her meals from a local hotel. Nevertheless, Lizzie found herself confined to a cheerless 9.5- by 7.5-foot cell. It would become her home for the next nine months.

"Star Chamber" and Women's Groups

The *Herald* reported that journalists from four New York dailies left Fall River on Friday afternoon. Representatives of four Boston newspapers had also begun to return home after Lizzie's arrest. The round-the-clock buzz at the Western Union and Postal Telegraph offices subsided. Between the two, it was estimated, "100,000 words a night were the average." A swollen river of ink on the case was still to come. Press commentary after her arrest offers one measure of Lizzie's early notoriety. It also suggests the so-called fourth estate's overwhelming sympathy for a virtuous Victorian woman, a "girl" scapegoated as the perpetrator of unspeakable crimes.

Three days after her arraignment, the anti-Lizzie *Fall River Globe* claimed that "three-fourths of the New England papers were sneering at the police and expressing a belief in the defendant's innocence." Even allowing for a bit of exaggeration, the regional press remained solidly in the hands of the native born and decidedly well disposed toward the accused. Smaller dailies relied on wire stories and took their cues from larger newspapers in Boston. "Of course it is possible that Lizzie Borden committed the terrible crime with which she is charged and for which she is now under arrest," the Portland, Maine, *Express* observed. "It is just possible and that is all. . . . That is what the arrest is based on. Stupidity seems to be the only attribute that Fall River police have yet displayed in this matter." A minority of New England newspapers, such as the *Providence Journal*, mostly refrained from inflammatory rhetoric and took a wait-and-see stand.

The *Fall River Herald* was among the first newspapers to represent the inquest in a disparaging way that resonated with other dailies. It described Lizzie as a "girl" and applauded her attorney's demand for an immediate hearing. "By doing this," the *Herald* claimed, "the course pursued at the star chamber examination will be exposed." The star chamber, an English court abolished in 1641, had consisted of members of the monarch's Privy Council who ruled on cases without a jury and other safeguards for the accused. The term evolved into the vernacular to signify any proceeding that acted "in an unfair or arbitrary way." Lizzie's local supporters employed "star chamber" to discredit the inquest. Pastor William W. Jubb of Central Congregational Church opined: "The star chamber proceeding by which they secured this evidence which they claim to have is a relic of barbarism."

"Star chamber" offered newspapers far and wide shorthand for outrage that elicited sympathy for Lizzie after the inquest and her arrest. They dinned the loaded term into their readers' imaginations. From the *Newport Observer* to the *New York Telegram* to the *Philadelphia Record* and beyond—"star chamber" romped through the press to mock the inquest. The *Telegram*, for instance, described "a cultivated and tenderly bred young lady," who was subjected to an inquiry with "too much in the nature of star chamber proceedings." The press pilloried the judge, the district attorney, and the police. Knowlton served as the star chamber's grand inquisitor; he possessed "a cool, metallic voice," as the *New York Herald* put it. The *San Francisco Examiner* sneered at the police investigation: "Viewed from a distance it would appear that the detectives had chosen to brand Lizzie as the murderer rather from lack of evidence against any one else than by reason of evidence against her."

On the day of Lizzie's arrest Reuters telegraphed an account of the murders to London. "Shocking Parricide in America" headlined stories the next day. The inquest and Lizzie's arrest marked a watershed in the Borden murders. The case garnered national and even transatlantic notoriety. From the far corners of New England to the four corners of the United States, "Lizzie Borden" became lodged in the public consciousness.

With the inquest, Lizzie began to build up a reservoir of sympathy in the local and national press and its readership. And women's groups spoke out in her defense. On the Sunday night after Lizzie's arrest, Central Congregational Church's Christian Endeavor Society passed a resolution of support. The next day the Women's Christian Temperance Union and the Young Women's Union followed suit. After offering sympathy for Lizzie's loss of her parents, the Women's Union resolution proclaimed: "We would also declare our unshaken faith in her as a fellow worker and sister tenderly beloved, and would assure her of our constant prayers that she may be supported under unprecedented trials and sorrows now resting upon her." The resolution was reprinted in the *Woman's Journal*, the weekly newspaper of the American Woman's Suffrage Association. The *Journal* announced on August 20: "Lizzie Borden Believed Innocent."

During the fall, more suffragists would rally to Lizzie's cause. Pro-suffrage groups such as the WCTU saw respectable native-born women like Lizzie as precisely the types who needed to be empowered with the right to vote and to serve on juries. They were essential to the future of America. Lizzie and her sisters would redeem American civic life. Armed with the right to vote, Frances Willard's morally and socially refined Protestant nuns would counteract the influence of uneducated, unwashed men like Spindle City's immigrants and their offspring, who competed with the native born for political office. Put another way, women's suffrage offered one solution to what First Congregational Church's pastor William Adams had delineated as "The Spiritual Problem of the Manufacturing Town."

CHAPTER 6

"Probably Guilty"

On the morning of August 22 Lizzie arrived by train from Taunton to considerable fanfare. With the hearing open to the public, a crowd gathered in front of the police station anxious to fill one of the district court's 300 seats on the second floor. Police cordoned off what was known as Court Square. They tightly controlled access to the courtroom. Lizzie was taken to the matron's room, where she remained for the duration of the hearing. Emma carried meals from home to ease the deprivations of Lizzie's confinement. Friends and the Reverends Jubb and Buck regularly looked in on Lizzie to brighten her spirits.

The hearing's purpose was to determine if the Commonwealth possessed sufficient evidence that indicated Lizzie's guilt. If so, then her case would be referred to the next session of the grand jury in November. After hearing evidence from the prosecution and the defense, the decision fell to the judge—the much-maligned Josiah C. Blaisdell.

The preliminary hearing has been represented as a "dress rehearsal" for Lizzie's Superior Court trial. Yet all the actors with their assigned roles had not yet been determined. The hearing, in other words, fell well short of a full dress rehearsal for the final courtroom drama. Nearly all of the more than forty witnesses who testified before Judge Blaisdell would appear at the Superior Court trial. But they composed only about half of the nearly eighty witnesses who were called to testify at that famous final legal act, which lasted thirteen days, almost twice as long as the preliminary hearing. Moreover, local lawyer Andrew J. Jennings assumed a larger role in the hearing than during the trial and delivered a powerful closing argument.

Still, Jennings believed that he needed a practiced defense lawyer for the hearing. Lizzie could afford the best counsel available. Jennings secured the assistance of Melvin O. Adams. The forty-two-year-old

Adams had graduated from Boston University Law School. He became a criminal defense lawyer in Boston and then served for more than a decade as assistant district attorney in Boston's Suffolk County before returning to private practice. Thus Adams was broadly experienced on both sides of the law. He acquired a reputation as one of the most skilled criminal lawyers in Massachusetts. He cross-examined witnesses at the hearing.

A brief look at the preliminary hearing serves as a prelude to the events that followed in the fall. The prosecution encountered one critical witness who, like Mrs. Tripp, repudiated what he had told poor Officer William Medley only two days after the murders. The hearing also produced a bombshell that seemed to shift the legal momentum in Lizzie's favor.

·

———

The Matron's Story

The preliminary hearing began shortly after 2 p.m. in the packed courtroom. Its rows of seating were filled with well-dressed women who outnumbered men throughout most of the proceeding. The women represented local partisans of Lizzie who would greet the final flourish of Jennings's closing argument with thunderous applause. A herd of reporters added to the hearing's drama and the courtroom's congestion. The *Fall River Herald* informed its readers: "There are 43 reporters and sketchers inside the rail at the district court representing all the leading dailies of the east. Among them are six or more ladies." One New York paper made light of the setting as a "dingy, stuffy little court room." It was all small-time, like the judge and the Fall River police.

To the disappointment of the assembled and those hungry for court news, the hearing ended before it began. The district attorney requested a delay. Dr. Edward Wood, the Harvard chemist, had not yet submitted a full report on the axes and one hatchet taken from the Borden cellar, nor on Lizzie's clothing that had been turned over to the police two days after the murders. Jennings agreed to a postponement until Thursday, August 25, exactly three weeks after the crime.

On the day before the delayed hearing began a revealing conversation allegedly took place between Lizzie and Emma that would not be the subject of extensive testimony until the Superior Court trial. It received wide press coverage. Hannah Reagan was "tidying up" the matron's room when Emma arrived. The matron left the sisters and turned to the task of attending to a toilet nearby. She claimed to have heard "very loud talk," which drew her to the doorway. "Emma you gave me away, haven't you?" Lizzie said angrily. "No, Lizzie, I have not," Emma responded. "You have and I will let you see I won't give in one inch," Lizzie replied as she raised a finger with her thumb pinched to the top. The matron reportedly said that the sisters did not speak for the rest of the morning.

The controversy represented another Irish-Yankee clash. Matron Hannah Reagan was an immigrant who managed to secure steady public employment in the police department like her countrymen around her dressed in blue. If the story was accurate, and the lowly immigrant matron had no apparent reason to embroil herself in the Borden controversy, what could Lizzie have been referring to that Emma divulged? Most likely it was about the dress that Lizzie destroyed in the stove on the Sunday morning after the murders. Lizzie would have known that neither Emma nor Alice Russell revealed the incident at the inquest because Knowlton never asked her about it. According to newspapers at the time, though not the Superior Court trial transcript, matron Reagan also said that Emma tried to assure Lizzie: "I only told Mr. Jennings what I thought he should know." Emma must have informed him of the dress-burning episode in case it emerged at the preliminary hearing.

Reagan provoked wrangling just as the legal proceeding started. She related the story to a reporter for the *Fall River Globe*, which immediately published it; other newspapers followed suit. Lizzie's friends mustered. A delegation led by Lizzie's lawyer descended on the jail. Jennings and banker Charles Holmes, whose wife, Marianna, was Lizzie's close friend and loyal jailhouse visitor, prevailed on the Irish matron to publicly renounce her story. Reverend Buck, a police station fixture, also tried to coax and then pressure the matron. They all undoubtedly believed that the story was part of the conspiracy against Lizzie timed to have maximum effect. Reagan would stand by her account at the Superior Court trial. At the time of the controversy, however, the newspapers had probably failed to get her words exactly right. Badgered by reporters and Lizzie's high-standing patrons, the matron tried to extricate herself from conflict with members of the Yankee establishment and said the story was not true.

Holmes, Buck, and Jennings wanted a denial in writing. Jennings drafted a statement for Reagan to sign. Reverend Buck carried it to her.

> This is to certify that my attention has been called to a report <u>said to have been made</u> by me in regard to a quarrel between Lizzie and her sister Emma, in which Lizzie said to Emma, "You have given me away, etc." and, that I expressly and positively deny that any such conversation ever took place and that I further deny that I ever heard anything that could be construed as a quarrel between the two sisters.

Later at Lizzie's trial, Jennings claimed that she was willing to sign, but Marshal Hilliard prevented her. The matron said she wanted to consult with him before she did anything. The marshal declared: "If you sign that you do it without my consent." The matron rebuffed the lawyer, the banker, and the minister. The incident ended for the moment with strong words between the marshal and both Jennings and Buck. At Lizzie's trial her friends would mount an aggressive counter-offensive against the immigrant matron's credibility, claiming that she wanted to sign the document but the marshal expressly forbade her.

The Hearing

The *Fall River Herald* distilled the essence of the gender issue that loomed over the hearing. Given Lizzie's "education and training," for her "to bring down the axe again and again . . . upon the unresisting form of a father" defied her character as a delicate, refined lady. Such heartless brutality "and the shedding of blood for blood's sake are a man's perogative [*sic*]." At the hearing, the almost complete absence of blood on the clothing Lizzie handed over to police seemed to confirm the *Herald*'s judgment.

The prosecution did not have to deploy all of its evidence against Lizzie. Knowlton had to present enough to establish probable guilt in the judge's eyes. Crucial medical witnesses at first dampened then lifted the spirits of Lizzie's supporters. From the inquest the district attorney knew what Medical Examiner William Dolan would say. But even with the week delay, Dr. Wood had yet to be heard from. His testimony would undercut the prosecution's case.

Dolan spent most of the first day and part of the second day testifying to the fatal injuries, blood splattering, and the potential weapons confiscated from the cellar. He also made a revelation that sent "a shudder through the audience," according to the *New York Herald*. The murder victims had not only been disemboweled; they were also decapitated. One Massachusetts mill city newspaper, the *Holyoke Democrat*, expressed outrage. "They have had a dozen doctors hacking away at the remains," the writer sensationalized the facts. "The bodies have been made sausage meat."

Perhaps most unsettling for Lizzie's champions, Dolan enumerated the physical evidence taken from the house and from Lizzie. He described the axes and hatchets, the hairs on one of the latter, and the apparent blood stains on two of the implements. Even though he testified that he concluded at the time "that it was not blood on the hatchets," his was not the last word. Dr. Wood of Harvard would decide. The same was true of the "smooch" on the pocket of Lizzie's dress and the spot on her petticoat. Almost a week after the murders, the police had requested the stockings and shoes Lizzie wore at the time of the murders. They should have gathered up this potential evidence as soon as Lizzie became a suspect.

Before we turn to Professor Wood's dramatic testimony near the end of the prosecution's presentation, two other witnesses are of special note: Charles C. Cook and Eli Bence. Cook managed the A. J. Borden Building. Officer Medley interviewed him two days after the murders and recorded specific details of their conversation.

Q. Mr. Cook, have you any reason to believe Mr. Borden had, or had not made a will?

A. I do not think Mr. Borden had a will, unless it was made recently. I will tell you how I know. He came into my office one day when I was writing, and waited until I finished, when I told him I was just writing a will. He said, "Charles, do you know that is something I have never done yet, but I must attend to it."

How do we reconcile Cook's answer with the inquest testimony of Emma and Lizzie that their father possessed a will and John Morse's statement that Andrew tore up his will? Andrew never filed a will in Bristol County Probate Court. This would explain Morse's claim that Borden destroyed his will. He may have had a will drawn up but then locked it in the safe that he kept at home before he tore up the document. Cook must have realized that his statement to Medley put Lizzie in jeopardy. Had she surmised that Andrew was about to create a will, or change one that she thought existed, it would bolster the alleged motive for murder.

Like Mrs. Tripp of Westport, in court Cook danced around and away from his frank statement to Medley. A major investigator of the murders, Medley was no rookie beat cop. Rather, he was a twelve-year veteran of the department who would eventually rise to city marshal. Yet neither his damning interview with Tripp nor his enlightening visit with Cook enabled Knowlton to make any headway in court.

After some prodding Cook admitted that Borden said something about a will "two or three weeks" before his death.

Q. What was it?
A. He simply told me that he had not one.
Q. Told you what?
A. That he had not any will.
Q. Did he say anything more?
A. No sir.
Q. Anything about making a will?
A. No sir.
Q. At any time?
A. No sir. . . .
Q. Do you remember of talking with Mr. Medley the next day after the murder, two days after the murder?
A. I remember he was in my office one night; I think it was Saturday night.
Q. Do you remember telling Mr. Medley about what he [Borden] said to you?
A. I do not remember exactly what I told him. I know Mr. Medley

asked me a good many questions; some I answered and some I did not.

Q. Do you remember of telling Mr. Medley Mr. Borden said to you "what are you doing?" And you said you were making a will?
(objected to)

Q. Do you remember of saying to Mr. Medley that Mr. Borden told you that that was something that he had not done, and must do?

A. I did not say anything of that kind sir.

Medley had asked another question and Cook's answer offers insight into why he had conveniently forgotten what he indiscreetly said to the officer. Medley queried Cook concerning how Lizzie and her father got along. "I do not like to answer that question," Cook responded, "on account of my position as custodian of property, as I do not know what my relations may be with the family, when this thing is settled." After his absent-minded testimony Cook survived interrogation unscathed. He would serve as the sisters' financial adviser for the rest of their lives.

When it came time for drugstore clerk Eli Bence to testify, Adams rose to object. Since the Bordens had been killed with an axe or hatchet, he argued, poison was irrelevant to the case. For the prosecution, Lizzie's alleged attempt to purchase deadly prussic acid a day before the murders demonstrated her state of mind. Bence was a witness at the inquest, but no one cross-examined him. It is revealing, then, how Lizzie's lawyers planned to counteract Bence's widely publicized eyewitness account if he were allowed to testify at the Superior Court trial.

Bence repeated for Knowlton what he had first told the police about the attempt to buy prussic acid, his discovery that the woman was Mr. Borden's daughter, and his positive identification of Lizzie at Second Street on the night of the murders. Adams then launched into his cross-examination. After some preliminary factual questions dealing with Bence's background and what happened on the morning of August 3, Adams homed in on details about the drugstore clerk's lady customer.

Q. How was she dressed?
A. She had on a dark dress; that is all I could tell you.
Q. Dark blue or brown?
A. I could not tell you the color, only it was dark.

Q. Do you know the color of the gown she has on now?

A. I should call it blue.

Q. Is that the gown she had on then?

A. I know it was not blue. I am positive of that.

Q. It was some dark color?

A. Yes sir.

Q. Was it generally of one color, like this gown she has on now?

A. I could not say.

Q. Did she wear gloves?

A. I could not say. . . .

Q. Did she have on a hat or a bonnet?

A. I do not know the distinction between a hat and a bonnet, hardly.

Q. Do you see what she has on now?

A. Yes sir.

Q. Was it anything like that?

A. I could not say. . . .

Q. Did it have any feathers or anything of that sort on its trimming?

A. I could not say. . . .

After, in re-cross-examination, Adams asked about the volume of customers in the drugstore. "You are in a place where you see a great many people everyday I suppose?" "Yes sir." "Perhaps a hundred every-day of the year?" "All of that."

Adams raised doubts about Bence's ability to recall physical details of one customer in a busy store. Lizzie's lawyers and her supporters believed that she was a victim of mistaken identity. Writers who defend her innocence have leaned on the same explanation to refute Bence's testimony and that of two other witnesses in the drugstore.

On the fifth day of the trial, Dr. Wood testified. His findings beefed up the confidence of Lizzie's advocates that she was innocent. Wood found no prussic acid in the victims' stomachs. His careful examination revealed "no blood upon the hatchet, whatever, no trace of blood. The same was true of both axes." The hair on the hatchet was not human but animal. The "smooch" on the dress pocket was not blood. One other stain lower down "had a similar appearance, but that also was not blood." Wood found no blood on the shoes or stockings. Six inches from the bottom of the petticoat, Wood did detect blood, a spot the size of a pinhead—or about "1/16 of an inch in diameter." The spot was thicker on the outside, indicating that it came from an external source. In Adams's cross-examination, Wood testified that the murderer *most likely* would have been covered with blood from the waist up as a result of Abby's slaughter and from the waist down as a consequence of Andrew's.

Following Wood's testimony, the police handed over the fourth hatchet from the cellar for examination. He also took possession of the newly broken hatchet. In the end it would be offered as the murder weapon.

The *Boston Advertiser* characterized Wood's testimony as "a song of deliverance for Lizzie." The *Fall River Herald* reported, "The close of the fifth day of the trial . . . found the prisoner's friends triumphant. All morning long they had sat in the courtroom and heard blow after blow delivered to the government's theory . . . until only a ragged framework remained."

After Wood's testimony failed to produce a bloody axe or hatchet, Knowlton grabbed his most formidable cudgel from a pile of papers: Lizzie's tortured inquest testimony. He closed the prosecution's case by reading into the hearing's record her responses to his inquest questions. Then at the end of the fifth day, the prosecution rested.

Andrew Jennings now led a brief defense that began at the end of the hearing's fifth day and consumed all of the sixth. The forty-three-year-old Jennings had graduated from Brown University and Boston University Law School. He was neither as tall nor as burly as Knowlton. Instead of Knowlton's full beard, Jennings sported a large, wavy mustache. His piercing, darting eyes betokened a quick-thinking, energetic courtroom lawyer. Though his role as Lizzie's defense counsel diminished by the time of her Superior Court trial, he served her well as a day-to-day legal adviser and forceful courtroom advocate.

During Lizzie's short defense, Jennings introduced a string of nineteen witnesses before Judge Blaisdell, including a few recalled from the prosecution's case. The headstrong Borden family friend, Dr. Benjamin Handy, still insisted that he saw a strange character near the Borden house on the morning of the murders. Police claimed the suspect was "Mike the Soldier," a habitué of the neighborhood and of the tavern, who worked as a weaver in one of the Border City mills below The Hill.

Michael Graham, his real name, was reportedly seen on Second Street around 10 a.m., his gut already at high tide with liquor. Handy held out for another suspect. He sent the police scurrying around for weeks trying to track down the phantom, whom Handy could never identify.

A hack driver, John Donnelly, claimed to have visited the barn "not much after 12." He did not see Officer Medley, who had already left. Donnelly discovered a shape in the hay as if someone had been lying there.

Phebe Bowen, the doctor's wife, offered important testimony. She visited Andrew and Abby early Wednesday evening to see how they were feeling. Abby told Bowen that "Lizzie had not been out all day," challenging the testimony of Bence and his drugstore associates. Bowen also testified that she came to the Borden house after the murders were discovered. Lizzie rested on a lounge downstairs. Bowen saw no blood on her hands or on the towel that Alice Russell was using to bathe Lizzie's face.

The case for the defense finished on the sixth day, and the hearing adjourned. Closing arguments were scheduled for the next day. With the principal exception of Charles Cook, most of the prosecution's witnesses testified credibly. Eli Bence proved to be somewhat unsteady on the stand. Dr. Wood's testimony clearly favored Lizzie. Knowlton responded with her muddled inquest declarations.

For their part, the defense may have felt confident. Adams had executed some effective cross-examinations. Jennings introduced witnesses who saw suspicious characters around the Borden house. And Dr. Wood found only one minuscule spot of blood on Lizzie's clothes.

Jennings launched into his closing on the morning of September 1. He began on a personal note, describing how this case was different from any other that engaged him. "This man was not merely my client, he was my friend. I had known him from boyhood days, and if three short weeks ago anyone had told me that I should stand here defending his youngest daughter from the charge of murdering him, I should have pronounced it beyond the realm of credibility."

Then Jennings reduced this "youngest daughter" to less than a mature thirty-two-year-old woman, as Lizzie's legal team would at her trial. And Jennings hitched his plea for this "girl" to the oppressive "star chamber" to which she had been subjected.

I have stated before that I considered the inquisition of the girl an outrage. Here was a girl they had been suspecting for days. She was virtually under arrest, and yet for the purpose of extricating a confession from her to support their theory, they brought her here and put her upon the rack, a thing they knew they would have no right to do if they placed her under arrest. As in the days of the rack and thumbscrews, so she was wracked mentally again and again. Day after day the same questions were repeated to her in the hope to elicit some information that would incriminate her. Is it a wonder there are conflicting statements?

Interpreting freely what even sympathetic witnesses said or implied, Jennings asserted, "The testimony of everybody else in this case is that this girl received a terrible shock."

He denied that the prosecution had established any other motive than a five-year-old disagreement over property. The district attorney faced another, heavier burden: "This girl has got at the most ten to fifteen minutes to commit the crime and conceal the weapon." Jennings referred to Andrew's murder because Lizzie had only been charged with that crime.

Next Jennings turned to Dr. Wood's testimony as Lizzie continued to be represented as a "girl" in need of her lawyer's and ultimately the judge's patriarchal protection. "I have no doubt," Jennings observed, "that every person with a feeling of sympathy for that girl felt their hearts leap with joy as Professor Wood gave his testimony." The prosecution was unable to find blood on her clothing, produce the murder weapon, or explain a motive. "They haven't proved that this girl had anything to do with the murder."

Given the lack of evidence, Jennings appealed to Judge Blaisdell; it would be unreasonable to jail Lizzie for three months until the grand jury met. She would not flee but simply return to her home. "Don't, Your honor, . . . put the stigma of guilt on this woman, reared as she has been and with a past character beyond reproach. God grant your Honor wisdom to decide, and, while you do your duty, do it as God tells you to do it, giving the accused the benefit of the doubt." The courtroom audience responded with thunderous applause. Lizzie bit her quivering lip and strained to hold back tears. The court then adjourned until 2 p.m.

When the hearing reconvened Attorney General Albert E. Pillsbury slipped into the courtroom to hear Knowlton's closing. Two weeks earlier the Irish *Fall River Globe* had charged that "District Attorney Knowlton was prejudiced on Miss Borden's side from the first. It did not devolve on him to support the local police in their views. . . . [Thus] he never performed a harder duty [than] when he was forced to order Miss Borden's arrest."

The *Globe* offered more than overheated class rhetoric. For Knowlton all but apologized to Lizzie and her establishment patrons at the start of his closing arguments. Within the first three short paragraphs of his summing up the evidence, he invoked the call of duty in a way that appeared to validate the *Globe*'s contention. "Does not Your Honor believe my soul is filled with anguish that I must go on and believe the prisoner guilty," he confessed, "and yet the path of duty is not always the path of pleasure." What if the defendant had been Bridget Sullivan, or Hannah Reagan, or some Irish mill girl? Would duty have been so burdensome? Knowlton would return to the painful path of duty at the end of his argument, only to have Judge Blaisdell then pick up the apologetic banner and spill a few tears on it. To be fair to the district attorney, his opening words were probably intended in part to show that he was not the burly browbeater of a defenseless female Sunday school teacher portrayed by the press.

Knowlton attempted to refute the charge that he had subjected Lizzie to a star chamber prosecution. Bridget served as his cover for she also had been grilled at the inquest. "When I came to Fall River, " Knowlton claimed, "I knew no difference between honest and reputable Lizzie Borden and honest and reputable Bridget Sullivan." Consequently, the servant "was brought here to what my learned friend calls a star-chamber inquiry, and was questioned as closely and minutely as any other member of the family."

Knowlton told a partial truth. Unlike Lizzie, Bridget was not a police suspect, though Knowlton was not as convinced that her hands were completely clean. In any case, she served more as a witness. In addition, at the inquest, preliminary hearing, and finally the trial, the prosecution subjected Bridget to the third degree to dispel lingering questions, especially on The Hill, that the "stranger," not Lizzie, had something to do with the murders. Finally, to argue that an Irish immigrant servant girl and a Borden lady stood equal before the law was defied by Knowlton's apologies and some simple facts. For one thing, as Attorney Melvin O. Adams demonstrated, Lizzie could hire the best lawyers in the state. Nevertheless, the way Knowlton invoked Bridget represented an effective retort to his critics.

He challenged the defense's claim that only a man could have delivered the blows on Abby and Andrew. Many actually believed that a strong, unladylike servant girl accustomed to handling an axe was capable of the physical brutality. The hatchet landed on the victims' skulls with uneven force. As already noted, one blow even missed Abby's head and landed on her back. "You are struck with the thought that it was an irresolute, imperfect feminine hand that could strike," Knowlton argued, "and yet not with the strength of a man. . . . " Presumably, a man would have delivered fewer blows that more consistently dashed the victims' brains.

Knowlton then turned to Lizzie's inquest testimony, denying that she was "confused or dazed." After all, she shed no tears. "I asked her where she was when her father came back, and we get this story: 'I was down in the kitchen.' That's the kind of thumbscrew I apply. . . . Almost a moment after: 'Where were you when the bell rung?' 'I think I was upstairs in my room.' 'Were you upstairs when you heard the bell?' No thinking now, no daze. 'I think I was on the steps coming down.'" As to the story of visiting the barn while her father was being slaughtered, Knowlton responded caustically: "Let me say I never saw an alibi labor as this one does."

Knowlton concluded with another reference to duty's call and to the applause that followed Jennings's argument. Of Lizzie he said, "We are constrained to find that she has been dealing in poisonous things; that her story is absurd; and that hers and hers alone has been the opportunity for the commission of the crime." Courtroom sentiment must be set aside. "Yielding to clamor is not to be compared to that only and greatest satisfaction that of a duty well done." No one applauded the district attorney.

Judge Blaisdell took hold of Knowlton's final words. He had to perform his "duty," as unpopular as it might be. Then he spoke to the defendant as if she was his daughter. He used her first name. As the magistrate, "It would be a pleasure for him, and he would doubtless receive much sympathy if he could say 'Lizzie, I judge you're probably not guilty. You may go home.'" Then he asked if a man was before the court with such circumstantial evidence linking him to the crime, "would there be any question in the minds of men what should be done with such a man?" The judge caught his breath as his eyes reportedly filled with tears. "So there is only one thing to do, painful as it may be—the judgment of the Court is that you are probably guilty, and you are ordered committed to await the action of the Superior Court."

Judge Blaisdell's decision was courageous, but also precarious and condemned on The Hill. As the evidence stood, there may have been probable cause to refer Lizzie's case for trial. Yet there were also gaps in the strong circumstantial evidence as well and perhaps legal reasonable doubt about her guilt. Knowlton knew what the government faced, as his subsequent actions indicated. Even after he presented the grand jury with a major piece of new incriminating evidence, the district attorney harbored doubts about proceeding further against the accused.

Sisterhood

The Old Colony Railroad connected Taunton and Spindle City. Devoted Emma appears to have made the trip almost daily to Lizzie's barebones jail cell. Most of Lizzie's friends reaffirmed their belief in her innocence. Mrs. Charles Holmes and Mrs. George Brigham of Central Congregational Church, her constant visitors in the Fall River jail, frequently traveled to Taunton.

Women's groups and suffragists once again leaped to Lizzie's defense after her re-arrest. They expressed their outrage that Lizzie was not afforded bail. Susan Fessenden, president of the Massachusetts WCTU, appeared at Lizzie's jail cell days after her re-incarceration. On September 5, Fessenden spoke to the group's state meeting in Boston. She lauded Lizzie's virtuous activities within the Central Congregational Church, "her helpfulness in the grand army of temperance workers and her kindness to those in need of assistance." Fessenden introduced a petition to the governor. In pleading for bail, it claimed that Lizzie's "probable innocence was at least as great as that of her guilt." The petition went on to argue that Lizzie's "30 years of virtuous living should account for much in such a doubtful case." The *Fall River Globe* reported that "all but 40 or 50 of the 2500 WCTU state members stood in support of Lizzie's innocence." On September 22, the attorney general responded to Fessenden, explaining that he couldn't comment on the case.

At the WCTU annual convention six weeks later in the shoe factory city of Brockton, Massachusetts, located halfway between Fall River and Boston, Fessenden again spoke passionately about Lizzie's legal plight. She singled out a jury system in which Lizzie "is not judged by her peers." A probably innocent woman had been subjected to the "relentless rack of the law."

Other suffragists also enlisted as advocates on Lizzie's behalf. In fact, influential women's activist Mary Livermore was the first reporter to secure a jailhouse interview with Lizzie. A writer, speaker, and promoter of women's suffrage, Livermore was married to a Universalist minister. They had spent time in Fall River, where she had become friends with Lizzie's mother, Sarah Morse Borden. Livermore's interview took place within days of Lizzie's return to Taunton and was reported in the *Fall River Globe* on September 7. During that month Livermore gave interviews to newspapers from the *New York Times* to the *New Bedford Mercury*, standing up for Lizzie's innocence and speaking out against her confinement. At the same time the *Woman's Journal* professed its "Sympathy with Lizzie."

Suffragists did have genuine compassion for Lizzie. She also represented a convenient stand-in for a larger cause—discriminatory political and legal systems. Yet Lizzie's legal circumstance represented an irony. Suffragists and the New Woman challenged the cult of Victorian womanhood. But a jury composed of traditional Yankee men, who clung to the pieties of virtuous, delicate womanhood, were not likely to convict Lizzie.

Andrew Jennings, of course, controlled journalistic access to Lizzie. In the midst of the fall pro-Lizzie clamor among women, he granted an interview to a reporter for the *New York Recorder*, identified as "Mrs. M'Guirk." She was actually Mrs. Kate Swan M'Guirk, who had lived in Fall River and had known Lizzie, as she acknowledged. M'Guirk penned a long, sympathetic, even weepy account of her interview with Lizzie. It received extensive circulation.

The September 20 interview began with a quotation from the accused. "I know I am innocent, and I have made up my mind that no matter what happens, I will try to bear it bravely and make the best of it." Lizzie's words in effect answered the question that M'Guirk had posited as the basis of the interview. She had worked with Lizzie in Fall River's Fruit and Flower Mission. M'Guirk had seen "this girl," as she put it, "load up the plates of vigorous young newsboys and poor children at the annual turkey dinner provided during the holidays for them and take delight in their healthy appetites." The journalist wanted to know if the jailed "girl" was the same person she had known in the Mission.

After three short paragraphs, the third opened with M'Guirk's answer. She found Lizzie "unchanged, except that she showed traces of the great trial she has just been through." A string of uninterrupted quotations from Lizzie followed; they cast sympathetic light on the accused. "They say, I don't show any grief . . . [and that] I don't cry," she complained. "They should see me when I am alone, or sometimes with my friends."

M'Guirk left Lizzie and then located her own voice. The second part of her account recycles her friends' familiar counter-arguments to charges against Lizzie. M'Guirk repeated the dubious claim that Andrew was looking for a home on The Hill at the time of his death. Supposedly, the sisters did not desire comfort improvements at 92 Second Street because they were going to move to The Hill.

M'Guirk's interview and apologetic follow-up undoubtedly increased the volume of sympathetic women's letters Lizzie received. In particular, members of the WCTU and the Christian Endeavor from across the country wrote to her. Even such a notable novelist of the time as Elizabeth Stuart Phelps conveyed her compassion for Lizzie. Phelps later inscribed one of her novels to the now-famous Fall Riverite. Middle-class, native-born Protestant women—from suffragists to churchwomen to writers to feminists—generated something of a groundswell of support for Lizzie in the months after the preliminary hearing. This development did not go unobserved by the district attorney and the attorney general.

Is Lizzie Insane?

Neither District Attorney Knowlton nor Attorney General Pillsbury, who usually tried capital cases, wanted to prosecute Lizzie. Though Knowlton believed she was guilty, a conviction presented chancy odds, especially if the Superior Court denied the admissibility of Lizzie's inquest testimony. Something had to be done to preempt a trial yet appease a segment of the population, such as the working-class, largely Catholic readers of the *Fall River Globe*, that the legal system was not rigged to favor one class, or one family. An insanity plea or finding offered Knowlton and Pillsbury an escape from their legal bind.

At the time of the murders newspapers commented that only a demented man could have committed the atrocities. Even before the preliminary hearing the attorney general had begun to seek professional advice on whether Lizzie was insane. He wrote to Dr. George F. Jelly, the former superintendent of the pioneering McLean Hospital for the Insane outside of Boston. On August 29, Pillsbury informed Knowlton that Dr. Jelly said he did not know enough about the case and was therefore unable to make a judgment about insanity.

The attorney general then turned to Dr. Edward Cowles, who had succeeded Jelly as superintendent of McLean. He also said that he did not have enough information. However, he offered more than Jelly. He wrote: "My inferences have been *against* a theory of insanity. . . . from anything I have so far read concerning her [Lizzie's] conduct before or after the event."

The attorney general, in particular, persisted. He prevailed on the district attorney to approach Lizzie's lawyer about a joint insanity examination. Jennings refused on the grounds that he would do nothing that indicated his client was guilty. "We can make some inquiries into the family matters without him," Knowlton suggested to the attorney general, "but it would not be so thorough as it would if we had his assistance."

In November the district attorney directed a state detective to interview people who had knowledge of Lizzie's family to find out if there was any history of insanity. On November 24, 1892, the detective forwarded his discouraging report to Knowlton. The informants ranged from prominent businessmen to neighbors and former neighbors. John

S. Brayton was one of Spindle City's mandarins. He lived on The Hill and managed the business affairs of his sister Mary, the former wife of the late Bradford Durfee and the wealthiest woman in Fall River. Brayton knew of Lizzie's mother and her father. "I never heard of any one of them being Insane or having any streak of insanity," he reported. Abby Borden's half sister offered that she "never heard that any of the Morses was Insane, but Lizzie is known to be ugly." Others said the Morses, including Lizzie's mother, were "peculiar," "odd," and "of a bad disposition." Yet no one knew of any insanity among the Morses or in Andrew's family.

Knowlton sought a legal lifeline, something that would rescue him from pursuing Lizzie into Superior Court. No significant incriminating evidence had surfaced in the weeks after the preliminary hearing. The grand jury in November represented one final legal milepost before a Superior Court trial. If the grand jury chose not to indict Lizzie, it would bring about her release while leaving the case against her open, pending new evidence. Such a temporary standoff might become permanent. In the interim, perhaps, it would appease her advocates and her accusers.

A Scandal

About a month before the grand jury convened, the major journalistic outrage of the Borden case made headlines. The episode is important to the Borden drama for several reasons. The grand jurors certainly knew the details, just as they were aware of the characterization of the inquest as a star chamber proceeding. Second, the scandal further tarnished the Fall River police. And finally, the controversy revealed the sometimes-heedless competition among newspapers for scoops and particularly sensational details about the Bordens.

Edwin McHenry was a self-styled private detective from Providence. His police specialty appeared to be trumpeting his investigative skill to small-town departments with no detectives. He came to Fall River and met with Marshal Hilliard. Why the marshal and Mayor Coughlin agreed to hire him is something of a mystery. It represented a kind of no-confidence vote in the Fall River police. McHenry's unproductive relationship with the department earned him just over $100. By the time his journalistic scandal erupted, McHenry was no longer in the Fall River department's employ. But his official association with its investigation reinforced continuing disparagement of the police's competence.

McHenry duped a twenty-four-year-old reporter for the *Boston Globe* with the improbable name of Henry G. Trickey. In return for $500 McHenry agreed to divulge all the evidence the police had against Lizzie, including new sordid details about the family and the crime. Fearful that McHenry would offer the scoop to the *Globe*'s rival, the *Boston Herald*, Trickey handed over the substantial bribe. McHenry then gave an account that trampled on the truth.

Neither Trickey nor the *Boston Globe* took the time to corroborate the welter of new facts that sprang from McHenry's bottomless imagination and enthralled the reporter's fathomless gullibility. Instead, the *Globe* splashed the story on its front page on Monday morning, October 10, under the headline: "Lizzie Had a Secret, Mr. Borden Discovered It, Then a Quarrel; Startling Testimony of 25 New Witnesses." The excruciating details of McHenry's revelations went on for pages. Among the most important "new facts": Lizzie was pregnant and Andrew had issued an ultimatum, "Name the man or leave the house by Saturday." The father had supposedly drawn up a will that disinherited her. And Lizzie was allegedly "seen in [her] Mother's room with a hood on her head" at the time of the murder. The story electrified Boston and New England. The *Fall River Globe* reported the alleged new evidence and so did the *New York Times*. The *Boston Globe* reprinted its "scoop" in its evening edition.

At the time, the term "yellow journalism" had not yet been minted to describe the unbridled competition for readers between Pulitzer and Hearst newspapers in New York City, which led to flagrant sensationalizing of the news. The McHenry-Trickey incident represented outright sensational fraud. It demonstrates how the worst practices of yellow journalism preceded the term's coinage. In Boston the rivalry between the *Globe* and the *Herald* and the widespread coverage of the Borden case in general took place in a highly competitive context in which newspapers had already brought yellow journalism to a boil. In fact, after the scandal, Attorney General Pillsbury even expressed his preference for "some sort of legislation concerning unjustifiable newspaper license in murder cases."

Scores of telegrams and telephone calls from police, case witnesses, and others swamped the *Globe* and disputed its spun-out story. The editors began to waver the next morning. The story "has proven wrong in some particulars," it announced to readers. By Tuesday evening, October 11, the *Globe*'s editors had been brought to their knees. They acknowledged they had been duped by a "remarkably ingenious and cunningly contrived story." Most importantly, they offered Lizzie an effusive apology, singling out the newspaper's assault on her virtuous womanhood. "The Globe, being thus misled, has innocently added to the terrible burdens of Miss Lizzie Borden. So far as lies in our power to repair wrong, we are anxious to do so, and hereby tender her our heart-felt apology for the inhuman reflection upon her honor as a woman and for any injustice the publication of Monday inflicted upon her."

The *Globe* had made an unpardonable transgression. It had recklessly indicted Lizzie's highest virtue—her womanly purity. From then on she could count on mostly sympathetic treatment by the *Globe*, New England's largest newspaper. Once again, as in the closed inquest and in Judge Blaisdell's presiding over that proceeding and the preliminary hearing, Lizzie became extensively viewed as another victim of the Borden tragedy.

The same grand jury that labored to indict Lizzie also indicted Henry G. Trickey. By then he had fled to Canada, where he fell to his death under a train one day after the indictment. Private detective McHenry had already left Fall River for good. Lizzie's lawyers would resurrect him at her Superior Court trial to sully the Fall River police.

The Grand Jury

Between November 15 and 21, the grand jury heard the government's evidence against Lizzie. The secret proceeding took place without a judge; an elected foreman administered the oath to witnesses. After weighing the state's evidence, the grand jury determined whether the defendant was probably guilty. If so, an indictment was handed down with the defendant referred to the Superior Court for trial. Unlike a Superior Court trial, the grand jury required a simple majority, not unanimity. The twenty-one members of the grand jury who decided Lizzie's fate were heavily Yankee Protestants from Bristol County's small towns. Two lived in Fall River and one in New Bedford. But in contrast to Lizzie's Superior Court trial, several grand jurors were Irishmen.

The session adjourned on November 21 without a decision. The next day Knowlton wrote to the attorney general. "I note your suggestions about the form of the indictment, which I will adopt if we ever get that far; of which, however, I am far from certain." Undoubtedly, all that had happened in the preceding months, from the inquest to the *Boston Globe* hoax to Lizzie's support from women's groups, weighed on the jurors.

Fairness to Lizzie also burdened Knowlton. In an unheard-of action he invited Jennings to present a case for Lizzie's defense to the grand jury! Such a proposition violated the purpose of the grand jury, which was not to try a case but to determine if it warranted referral to the Superior Court for trial. Jennings appropriately refused the district attorney's offer. Perhaps Knowlton wanted Jennings's participation in the grand jury proceeding to rid himself of Lizzie's prosecution once and for all. On the other hand, he must have expected Jennings to keep his distance from the grand jury. Most likely, Knowlton directed his invitation beyond Jennings to the public—to critics of his so-called star chamber inquest when he and Judge Blaisdell denied Lizzie's lawyer access to the court.

The grand jury reconvened on December 1, and Knowlton recalled a witness: Alice Russell, the devoted friend of Lizzie and Emma. After testifying earlier to the grand jury, it now marked the fourth time she had taken to the witness stand. Russell had told the truth—but not the whole truth. She had struggled with insomnia during the months since the August murders. Her conscience gnawed at her. She consulted with a lawyer who told her she needed to testify to what she had held back at the inquest, preliminary hearing, and first grand jury appearance. She related to Knowlton and then to the grand jury how Lizzie burned a dress on the morning after Mayor Coughlin informed her that police considered her a suspect. With Bridget gone for good, only Emma, Lizzie, and Russell were in the kitchen at the time. Russell's testimony decidedly shifted grand jury sentiment against Lizzie. The jurors began deliberations at 10:30 a.m. It still took them until 5 p.m. to reach a decision, according to Knowlton. Lizzie was indicted on December 2. For the first time, Abby was officially included in the charges against Lizzie.

The next day, the *Fall River Herald* reported, "Pastor Jubb in a State of Nervous Excitement in Taunton's Court Room / Anxious to Know Result so as to Carry Joy or Consolation to the Unfortunate Prisoner." It was the worst possible message that he had to deliver: three murder indictments, one each for Andrew and Abby and another for both of them. The Hill learned the distressing news. It leaked out from the "secret" grand jury that the highly respected Alice Russell offered damaging new testimony and that the vote was twenty to one against Lizzie. She had suffered her first setback over the fall of 1892. The actions of the grand jury gave Lizzie's legion of supporters pause, though not reason for panic.

CHAPTER 7

Lizzie's Long Wait

The holidays passed and Lizzie languished in jail, growing paler and a bit heavier. Winter gave way to spring, and still there was no prospect of a trial date. Jennings pressed District Attorney Knowlton and Attorney General Pillsbury to fix a time for the start of the Superior Court trial. They resisted.

Lizzie's "Bastille"-like confinement maddened her supporters, especially women's groups. Some believed that the government was testing Lizzie's stamina. Under the physical and emotional strain of open-ended confinement, the district attorney and the attorney general attempted to break Lizzie's resolve. Then, they hoped, she would make a clean breast of things and throw herself on the mercy of the court. In reality, another reason accounted for the delay. Knowlton and Pillsbury strung out scheduling Lizzie's trial because, with no new evidence, with potential legal roadblocks in front of them, and with the most influential press arrayed against the government, neither man wanted to litigate the case. Yet that would not satisfy those who were certain of Lizzie's guilt. Moreover, Knowlton shared their conviction.

In the months leading up to the trial, legal maneuvering took place on both sides. Jennings put together a high-powered, versatile, and costly defense team. The prosecution followed a different tack. Knowlton learned that the attorney general, who usually prosecuted capital crimes, would not take part in Lizzie's trial. A recent illness enabled Pillsbury to elude the legal controversy. Instead, a young, inexperienced district attorney would replace him. In a word, the prosecution would be legally outgunned.

The Legal Sides Take Shape

On February 1, George D. Robinson joined Jennings and Melvin O. Adams as a member of the defense team. A graduate of Harvard, Robinson had skipped law school. Instead, he studied for the bar with his lawyer brother. By the time he signed on to defend Lizzie, Robinson boasted impressive political experience in Massachusetts. He had served as a state senator and representative as well as a US Congressman. Then in 1883, Massachusetts voters elected him to the first of three one-year terms as governor. Most importantly, while governor, he had appointed one of the three Superior Court judges who would hear Lizzie's case, the justice who would deliver a pro-defense charge to the jury. That judge would serve as one of the honorary pallbearers at Robinson's funeral three years after the trial.

Robinson was also well acquainted with the presiding Superior Court Chief Justice at Lizzie's trial. They had served together in the state house of representatives, including on the judiciary committee. All of this reflected the web of cozy, political-judicial relationships in Lizzie Borden's Massachusetts, where the Republican Party dominated state government and Yankees filled the ranks of appointed positions.

At the time of the trial, Robinson was fifty-nine years old. He looked his age and then some. With a heavily receded hairline and thin top, Robinson resorted to a comb-over. Court reporters commented on his paunch. As one put it, the ex-governor's "build shows that he loves the good things of life." When he questioned a witness he seemed to lead with his mid-section, which accentuated his potbelly. Robinson served as Lizzie's lead lawyer. He did not specialize in the finer points of the law. Rather, obscuring his elite prep school and Harvard background, he knew how to address a jury of ordinary men and to question a witness with that audience in mind. Deploying a different style, he complemented Adams as an effective cross-examiner. In other words, his years as a successful politician profited him in the courtroom.

Twenty-eight-year-old Arthur S. Phillips rounded out Lizzie's defense. The junior member of Jennings's law office, Phillips was an alumnus of Williams College and a magna cum laude graduate of Boston University Law School in 1892. He worked behind the scenes, conducting research, interviewing witnesses, and performing other tasks that Jennings assigned him.

An interesting legal development took place in Fall River during April just before the prosecution team was formed. Judge Josiah C. Blaisdell was forced out of the district court. The circumstances are murky, but, in part, the ouster appears to have been a consequence of the bruising he received from Lizzie's inquest and preliminary hearing. In late March a lawyer and special justice of the district court named Arba N. Lincoln resigned and filed a complaint with the Fall River Bar Association charging that he had not received "fair play" from Judge Blaisdell. He also deplored the state of affairs at the court.

The Bar Association referred Lincoln's complaint to its executive council, which included Andrew J. Jennings. On April 13, a day after the association met to hear the council's report, Judge Blaisdell submitted a letter of resignation to the governor, citing poor health. Perhaps the Borden case's early stages and their acrimonious aftermath had taken a physical toll on the elderly judge, even affecting his management of the court. Perhaps, as well, there was some retribution from The Hill, where Lincoln lived—on the very street where Lizzie would relocate after the trial.

On April 24, three days after Judge Blaisdell's resignation took effect, a disheartened Knowlton wrote to the attorney general.

Personally I would like very much to get rid of the trial of the case. . . . I feel this all the more upon your not unexpected announcement that the burden of the trial would come upon me.

I confess, however, I cannot see my way clear to any disposition of the case other than a trial. Should it result in disagreement of the jury there would be no difficulty then in disposing of the case by admitting the defendant to bail: but a verdict either way would render such a course unnecessary.

The case has proceeded so far and an indictment has been found by the grand inquest of the county that it does not seem to me that we ought to take the responsibility of discharging her without trial, even though there is a reasonable expectation of a verdict of not guilty. . . . I think it may well be that they the jury might disagree upon the case.

But even in my most sanguine moments I have scarcely expected a verdict of guilty.

No wonder the government evaded for months setting a date for Lizzie Borden's Superior Court trial. Knowlton's aversion to prosecuting Lizzie was tangible. Quashing the grand jury indictment, which he had earlier discussed with the attorney general, remained out of the question. A hung jury represented Knowlton's best hope. Lizzie would be released from jail and not face another trial unless new evidence emerged. He told the attorney general that he recognized, even respected, how the public, "whether favorable to her or not," expected a trial. Knowlton closed his dispiriting letter to Pillsbury with the recommendation that Lizzie's trial go forward in June.

Thus, Knowlton faced the trial of his career as an acutely conflicted prosecutor. Convinced of Lizzie's guilt and of his responsibility to prosecute her, he held out little hope of a conviction. For the most part, in the courtroom Knowlton rose above his warring emotions. This persistence in energetically prosecuting the case against Lizzie constitutes Knowlton's signal civic achievement during the entire Borden controversy.

After the attorney general removed himself from the Borden case, he chose a co-prosecutor for Knowlton: William H. Moody, the district attorney of Essex County northeast of Boston. The thirty-nine-year-old Moody had graduated from Harvard near the top of his class. He bypassed law school. Instead, he studied in a private law office. Moody was not a widely experienced criminal lawyer. In fact, the Borden trial marked his first murder case. Moreover, he joined the prosecution only weeks before the trial and never quite mastered all the granular details generated by the police. All of this conspired in Moody's courtroom tentativeness from time to time.

Knowlton and Moody settled on a division of labor that made them in effect co-equal prosecutors. Moody presented the prosecution's opening statement, interrogated most of its witnesses, and argued the two major evidentiary issues that were debated in the jury's absence: the inclusion of Lizzie's inquest testimony and Eli Bence's prussic acid testimony. Knowlton interrogated the prosecution's medical and prussic acid experts, cross-examined defense witnesses, and delivered the prosecution's closing argument—a long, eloquent address.

For all his inexperience and the belated assignment to the prosecution, Moody brought energy and a keen legal mind to the case. The good-looking lawyer with an erect figure possessed more than a modicum of courtroom presence. The *Boston Globe* thought he looked much younger than his age. "He is a pure blue-eyed blond, not much above 30, dressed like a New Yorker, and with a quick intelligent face. He is bright and alert and he is handsome." In his looks and attention to dress, Moody was more than a match for the defense's dashing Adams. Moody would eventually receive an appointment to the US Supreme Court from President Theodore Roosevelt, his Harvard classmate.

Moody had once worked with ex-governor Robinson on a civil case. In another of the ironies of the Borden saga, Moody had recommended Robinson to the defense team. At the time, Moody had no way of knowing he would join the case.

Only days before the start of the trial, Knowlton received some unsettling news. Dr. Frank Draper, Professor of Medical Jurisprudence at Harvard and Medical Examiner for Suffolk County, reported on a review of autopsy photographs of the Bordens' skulls. Among other conclusions, he found "on one of the cuts in Mrs. Borden's skull, near the right ear, there is a very small but unmistakable deposit of the gilt metal with which hatchets are ornamented when they leave the factory." Draper had consulted with Dr. David W. Cheever, Professor of Surgery and Anatomy at Harvard. They both agreed. Abby Borden was killed with "a *new* hatchet, not long out of the store" [emphasis mine].

Testimony concerning the professors' discovery did not emerge at the trial. In a sensationally and inaccurately titled book, *Forty Whacks*, David Kent, who exonerates Lizzie of the crimes, claims that there was a "Harvard cover-up." It is highly unlikely, however, that two well-regarded Harvard medical professors would engage in a conspiracy or that Knowlton and Moody would be parties to one. When it came to the alleged murder weapon, the handleless hatchet, the prosecution was careful how it framed questions as to the probability of its use.

The Justices

The three Superior Court justices ranged in age from fifty-seven to sixty-one. They dressed in black suits rather than robes. Full beards enhanced their grave bearing. At the opening of the trial, the *Boston Globe* described the tribunal in overstated prose. They resembled "a stern and grim-looking bench of Judges as ever sat in Puritan New England of old." In this scenario Lizzie represented a throwback to Hester Prynne. Whether convicted or acquitted, the modern maiden would bear more than a faint imprint of a scarlet letter. As Lizzie knowingly described her fate in a letter to a friend three weeks before the trial: "You know my life can never be the same again if I ever come home."

Perhaps the least distinguished of the three justices was the oldest. A native of rural New Hampshire, Caleb Blodgett graduated from Dartmouth College. He trained for the legal profession in a Worcester, Massachusetts, law office. He went on to practice law in Boston, specializing in bankruptcy. Unlike his two colleagues, he did not serve in the state legislature. Blodgett received his lifetime gubernatorial appointment to the Superior Court in 1882.

Fifty-seven-year-old Chief Justice Albert Mason of small-town Middleboro, Massachusetts, had a weaker educational background than his colleagues. He graduated from high school and then read law in a private practice. After his admission to the bar in 1860, he served in the Civil War between 1862 and 1865 and left with the rank of Captain. Mason practiced law in Plymouth and Boston. He was also elected to the state house of representatives. Appointed to the Superior Court in 1882, Mason was elevated to Chief Justice eight years later. Mason's family included daughters approximately Lizzie's age.

Justin Dewey, the junior associate justice, owed his appointment to Governor Robinson. He emerged as perhaps the most forceful, and certainly the most controversial, member of the court at Lizzie's trial. He has been denounced and defended ever since for his detailed instructions to the jury, which no doubt pleased his political patron sitting in front of him at the defense's table.

Dewey grew up in the small western Massachusetts town of Alford. He graduated from Williams College and studied law in Great Barrington, a larger town in the western part of the state. He served in the state house of representatives and the senate. In 1886, Robinson's last year as governor, Dewey was appointed to the Superior Court.

On their legal merits, the justices represented an experienced and at least competent court. It is difficult to escape the conclusion, however, that Dewey's ties to Robinson compromised the court. The justices made two major evidentiary decisions against the prosecution that were dubious, capped by Dewey's long one-sided charge to the jury.

Another Axe Murder

On May 30, five days before the start of Lizzie's trial, an axe murder in Fall River reignited the panic that had gripped the city during the first days of the Borden slayings. On a dairy farm in the far north end of the city, a twenty-two-year-old woman named Bertha Manchester was found sprawled on her kitchen floor with her skull crushed from repeated axe blows. Blood pooled beside her body and splattered the close kitchen walls. Police discovered the bloodied murder weapon on a woodpile near the house. The murderer made off with Bertha's watch and purse.

This time police roped off the murder scene and tightly controlled who entered the house. Not even Bertha's father or brother could gain admission after the police were summoned. Stephen Manchester and his son had set off at 7:30 a.m. to deliver milk. They returned at mid-afternoon. While they made their daily rounds, Bertha typically took charge of the farm, including bossing the laborers. Her father claimed Bertha was "as strong as a man." She resisted what turned out to be a robbery, not an assassination. Bertha's brother discovered her bludgeoned to death.

The Manchester murder exposed another less-than-model Spindle City family, headed by a sometimes-overbearing patriarch. Stephen was known for having been hard on his first wife, who died, and on his second, who left him. He labored long hours to keep his farm and milk business profitable. He drove himself and demanded as much of his farmhands. Police suspicions turned toward former workers. As in the Borden case, the Portuguese headed the line of suspects.

While the police searched for the murderer, emotions in Fall River ran the gamut, from uneasiness to dread. Within ten months, three bloodthirsty daylight murders had been committed in a city where the typical violent crime was assault and battery, and drunkenness and disorderly conduct represented the most common transgression. For some the conclusion seemed obvious: the Bordens' murderer had emerged once again from the anonymous immigrant hordes who were overwhelming Spindle City.

Lizzie's friends aggressively exploited the unknown axe murderer on her behalf. They underscored the striking similarities between the butchery of Bertha Manchester and the Bordens. The brutality of Bertha's attacker, in particular, recalled the rage of Abby's slayer. Dr. Dolan's autopsy reported that there were "twenty-three distinct and separate axe wounds on the back of the skull and its base." Attorney Jennings responded quickly and tartly to the crime. "Well," he told reporters, "are they going to claim that Lizzie Borden did this too?" The same person now seemed responsible for the three brutal attacks, and it was not the jailed younger daughter of two victims.

Bertha Manchester's murder placed the police on notice. As they had in the Borden murders, the police moved swiftly. This time, however, their investigation focused on a suspect who fit the accepted profile of a potentially, even likely, violent individual. Jose Correa de Mello, a recent immigrant from the Azores, had worked for Stephen Manchester and had left the farm on bad terms with the owner. The suspect believed he was owed wages. He returned to the farm to collect them or to take money that he believed was rightly his. He didn't plan on murdering Bertha. The thinly built immigrant spoke no English. The muscular farm woman brooked no compromise. An argument ensued and perhaps the only way the immigrant could subdue Bertha was with the aid of an axe. But why the brutality? Jose later claimed that Bertha struck him first, which apparently enraged him. Then, too, de Mello had built up hostility toward Bertha, not just her father. She treated him like a despised, alien Azorean who resided at the bottom of Fall River's ethnic hierarchy.

The Fall River police traced de Mello to Taunton. They enlisted the aid of his uncle and of a leader of Fall River's Portuguese community to persuade de Mello to return with them to the police station. Police prejudice against the Portuguese complicated matters. The Portuguese were perceived as untrustworthy. The police told de Mello's compatriots that he was needed as a witness on another case, not the axe slaying. Once the duped men returned to Fall River, de Mello was arrested for Bertha Manchester's murder. The immigrant confessed to the crime after hours of police interrogation.

The itinerant farm worker's arrest took place on June 4, the day before the start of Lizzie's trial. The news broke the next morning. Most of the prospective jurors were probably unaware of this development. It took the entire day to winnow the group of potential jurors, numbering one hundred and forty-five, down to twelve men. They were immediately sequestered. Whether the jurors knew of de Mello's arrest is perhaps not the crucial point. They *were* aware that an axe murderer had struck again in Fall River, and it could not have been Lizzie. Even if they read about the arrest in the morning paper, the suspect only confirmed entrenched convictions about the immigrant identity of the real Borden murderer.

Jurors could not have known that the police were unable to attribute the Second Street slaughter to Jose Correa de Mello. To the disappointment of Lizzie's supporters, the immigrant had arrived in the country after the Borden murders. Still, other potential de Mellos haunted Fall River—hordes of rootless men, with families back in the Azores, who huddled together in tenements below The Hill. For the jury, the killing of Bertha Manchester would lend credibility to the parade of defense witnesses who claimed to have seen suspicious men hovering around 92 Second Street on the morning of the Borden murders.

The Jury

Lizzie entered the courtroom dressed in black, down to her cotton gloves. She observed jury selection. Chief Justice Mason questioned each prospective juror individually. The court and the lawyers needed to know whether jurors had formed a firm opinion on the case and if they were unable to convict Lizzie because of opposition to the death penalty, especially for a woman. Many prospective jurors had strong opinions on both issues. Given the exhaustive coverage of the case, many people throughout Bristol County had conclusively made up their minds about

Lizzie's guilt or innocence. Consider the first prospective juror called by the court. His exchange with Chief Justice Mason led to a dismissal. He was asked: "Have you any opinion which, in your judgment, would prevent you from rendering a true verdict." The man replied: "I don't think, your honor, that any evidence which can be produced would induce me to change my mind in regard to this case." "You may step aside," Mason told him.

The defense was allowed to challenge twenty-two prospective jurors without giving a cause. Beyond that, challenges had to be argued. In all, the defense challenged seventeen individuals, the government fifteen. The *Boston Globe* noted, "At first it seemed that she [Lizzie] was [going] to challenge all Irishmen and Catholics, on account of Bridget Sullivan's connection with the case." A lone Irishman managed to go unchallenged, however. The *Globe* also commented that "Only three or four foreign names were called" for interrogation from the entire group of prospective jurors. Using surnames, Lizzie's challenges, and interviewee responses, one can document from the court record at least nine Irish individuals who were interrogated. Some were challenged while others were simply dismissed for having formed settled opinions about the case. Two Frenchmen were called, one of whom claimed that he could not speak or understand English well. Both were dismissed. In other words, the pool of one hundred eleven men who were interrogated did not represent Bristol County's changing population. The twelve men left standing, moreover, even failed to represent that pool, principally because of the exclusion of all but one Irishman.

By five p.m. jury selection was completed. District Attorney Knowlton recorded detailed notes on the jurymen. Most were middle-aged, in their forties and fifties. The oldest was sixty-four; he served as jury foreman. Only two men were in their thirties. The jurors were drawn primarily from the small farming towns of Bristol County. Half were farmers. Fall Riverites were excluded from the jury pool. Only one man represented New Bedford. He was not a mill worker but the owner of an iron company. Only two jurors did not identify with a church, expressing "no interest in religion." Of the remaining ten, nine were Protestant. Two jurors were Democrats and one was Independent. Nine of the twelve jurors identified with the Republican Party. Some had daughters who were approximately Lizzie's age.

Interestingly, Knowlton marked "American" next to the names of native-born Yankee Protestants. He reacted differently when it came to native-born Catholic Irishman John C. Finn. Beside his name he recorded "Irish." Even if they were second generation and had held local political office like Finn, the Irish remained lumped with other Catholic groups that were not yet fully "American."

At thirty-five Finn was the youngest juror. Given the other elements that made up his profile, Finn may have been something of a token juror, especially since he failed to make the grade as an American. Like the several other nonfarming workingmen, he was a tradesman, a painter. With no mill hands on the jury, Finn gave the group a scrap of credibility with the ethnic Catholic working class.

In sum, the Borden trial jury did not represent the changing face of southeastern Massachusetts. Nearly all the jurors were church-going Yankee Protestants from outlying farming towns, distant from the county's population center in Fall River and New Bedford. Most had probably never seen the inside of a mill. They were men of steady habits and steady employment, family men who had, with one exception, fathered children, and who surely held traditional views of Victorian womanhood. Ex-governor Robinson would turn this sentiment to Lizzie's advantage.

The Place and the Press

Lizzie wanted to be tried in Taunton, where the sheriff and his matron wife gave her special treatment. The attorney general selected New Bedford, where Knowlton lived. The city differed from Fall River in several respects. It lacked hills and waterpower comparable to the Quequechan River. New Bedford was slower to industrialize. Plowing the seas to harvest the leviathan helped make New Bedford one of the richest cities in America. Then the discovery of oil in Pennsylvania in 1859 and the destruction of whale ships during the Civil War marked the beginning of the end for New Bedford's whaling supremacy. Increasingly, profits from whaling shifted to mills, a safer investment. Yet as late as the 1890 census, New Bedford remained much smaller than Fall River.

The former "Whaling City" had a population of approximately 41,000 to Spindle City's 74,000.

The owners of whale ships, along with their successful captains and investors, built a well-to-do residential district, New Bedford's more "ancient" version of Fall River's Hill. In *Moby Dick* (1851), Herman Melville immortalized this world: "The town itself is perhaps the dearest place to live in, in all New England," he gushed. Then he turned to specifics. He enthused that "nowhere in all America will you find more patrician-like houses; parks and gardens more opulent, than in New Bedford." The shaded streets and architectural fabric of this district remained intact in 1893. But red brick mills and immigrant-filled triple-decker neighborhoods had already significantly altered New Bedford's physical and social geography. The press took no notice of this world.

The impressive courthouse stood adjacent to the stately elms and well-tended gardens that surrounded the "great mansions of the retired whaler folk," as the *Boston Herald* informed its readers on the first Sunday of the trial. The elegant Greek revival structure bestowed its own dignity on the area. It had been built in 1831 when New Bedford was known around the world. Constructed of red brick, the courthouse had four impressive classical white columns that greeted visitors and caught the eye of passersby. An expanse of lawn was filled with flowers and dotted with trees on both sides of the walkway to the court's front entrance. Officials erected fences outside the building to control the crush of people who they rightly expected would try to gain entrance to the courtroom on the second floor. Some individuals received special access to the trial, the Reverends Jubb and Buck and prominent Bristol County lawyers.

The courtroom provided strategically placed spittoons for tobacco chewers in the audience. The courtroom also contained ten large windows. They were thrown wide open when an early summer heat wave with temperatures in the mid-90s and oppressive humidity baked New Bedford for much of the trial. As a result, the sounds of daily life in the city filtered into the courtroom—the mooing of a cow and the rattle of wagons on bustling County Street where the court was located.

Behind the court a stall for carriages had to be converted to another use. It became the press nerve center. Wires were strung that connected to newspapers in New York, Boston, and Providence and to the offices of the press associations. Typists and copyboys set up shop, carrying reporters' dispatches and stenographers' accounts of testimony to large urban dailies, many of which published morning and evening editions. Near and far the public displayed a voracious appetite for news on the progress of the trial.

At first, twenty-five seats were set aside for the press. That number had to be doubled. More than forty reporters along with sketchers and stenographers tried to satisfy the impassioned public interest in the trial. Sweaty bodies packed the courtroom.

Noted reporters, such as Julian Ralph of the *New York Sun*, covered the trial. He wrote glowingly of Lizzie for nearly two weeks. She possessed "that indefinable quality which we call ladyhood," he told his readers. Some reporters wrote for more than one major newspaper. New York's Joe Howard, the best-known journalist at the trial, wrote for papers in his home city and for dailies along the East Coast, including the *Boston Globe*. Highly partial to Lizzie, Howard's pieces attempted to inform and entertain readers. He moistened his flowery writing with cartoonish coinages: "multitudinosity," "tediosity," "conspicuosity," "bedlamistic," and "cramptitude," to name several. He signed his columns with a swagger, simply ending "Howard."

If Howard was a kind of early syndicated columnist, other journalists were "stringers," that is, part-time writers for newspapers other than their own. The reporter for the *Providence News* also served as a stringer for dailies from New Haven, Connecticut, to Portland, Maine. East Coast newspapers and the press associations produced a daily deluge of words and courtroom images that spread across the nation. The growth of newspapers in cities from Fall River to Boston to New York and beyond appealed to readerships that were segmented by class, politics, and ethnicity. Readers were especially eager for exposés of Victorian life's subterranean world.

The journalists were overwhelmingly male. A few women reporters covered the trial. They included Lizzie's friend from the Fruit and Flower Mission, Kate Swan M'Guirk, who wrote for the *New York World*.

Women spectators arrived in court equipped with opera glasses, the better to study mysterious Lizzie. But it was the male courtroom gaze that counted. From lawyers to judges, jury, and journalists, Lizzie faced a courtroom where power overwhelmingly rested in the hands of men. The jury sat to her front on the right. The reporters watched the accused woman as much as the witnesses. They wrote about her clothes, her body, her face, her demeanor, her mostly stoic reaction to prosecution testimony, the flowers she brought into the courtroom, and the way she deployed her fan—now to hide, now to reveal her face.

Here lies a gender paradox of Lizzie's trial. Men reserved all the legal power and nearly monopolized the power of the press. Yet Lizzie was not a helpless maiden. She only needed to present herself as one. After her lawyers told her to dress in black at the trial, she was in costume. Her "demeanor," one paper reported, is "quiet, modest, and well-bred—from a country rather than a city view." Far from the "brawny, big, muscular, hard-faced, coarse-looking girl" supposedly imagined by people "throughout the country," Lizzie "is a lady." In other words, she was not a Bridget Sullivan, an immigrant toughened by the drudgery of servile labor.

"Little woman?" Joe Howard asked at the start of the trial, and he told his readers, "Yes." Lizzie lacked the "amazonic proportions" that he had visualized. He was convinced of her innocence from the start of the trial. Nothing the "dumpling-body little woman" in black did in the course of the trial suggested otherwise.

In fact, as the trial progressed, Lizzie mastered the role of the demure, delicate Victorian lady who possessed neither the physical strength nor the moral degeneracy to wield a hatchet or an axe as the murderer had. She displayed dignity and fortitude to rein in her emotions in public, except when testimony turned toward the gruesome or the sentimental. It would be cynical to claim that Lizzie followed a script. Still, her rare displays of courtroom emotion proved as effective as if they were cued.

CHAPTER 8

Prosecuting Lizzie

After jury selection, Lizzie's trial lasted twelve days, between Tuesday, June 6, and Tuesday, June 20, including one Saturday morning session. The prosecution's case consumed most of the trial. Led by Moody, the district attorneys presented their detailed circumstantial evidence over more than eight days. The defense questioned witnesses for less than two days. The court swore in fifty prosecution witnesses. By aggressive cross-examination Lizzie's lawyers exploited holes in the testimony of some of these witnesses. Then, near the middle of the prosecution, police testimony suddenly veered in an unexpected direction, stunning both sides and disrupting the strong, though sharply contested, circumstantial evidence that the district attorneys had been weaving into a narrative of Lizzie's guilt.

Moody's Opening Statement

Lizzie entered the courtroom outfitted in the same rich black outfit of the previous day, wearing a stylish hat. She struck the pose of a reserved Sunday school teacher attending an obligatory funeral. The Reverends Jubb and Buck sat near her. Once the jury marched in, the courtroom was "rapped into silence by jolly-hearted, stern visaged, virile-fisted Sheriff Wright," as Joe Howard put it. The court clerk, Simeon Borden, Sr., read the indictment and Moody began laying out the prosecution's case in exacting detail.

Moody spoke for ninety minutes in what Joe Howard described as a "purely conversational tone." He started with a sketch of Andrew's admirable rise to the standing of a wealthy man. Yet he paid a price for stinting his way to riches. Through force of habit, he continued to run his household on a "narrow scale."

Moody then turned to Abby, a well-meaning, warm stepmother. He outlined the rupture in the family over Andrew's assistance to Abby's sister. Presenting some of the state's evidence that supported the view that family relationships changed irreparably five years before the murders, Moody put the issue rather lamely. An "unkindly feeling" took hold between the "prisoner and her stepmother." Throughout his opening statement Moody invoked "the prisoner" as his chosen designation for Lizzie. Twice he referred to her as "Lizzie Andrew Borden," as the indictments identified her. Moody only made a slip of the tongue once and spoke of the accused as "Lizzie." "The prisoner" and "Lizzie Andrew Borden" were calculated to underscore that the defendant was a mature woman. The opposing sides represented the age and gender of the accused in clashing ways. The defense attorneys once again alluded to their client as "Lizzie" or "Miss Lizzie" or "this girl," that is, someone respectable and incapable of raising her delicate hand to commit parricide. Interestingly, Joe Howard claimed that he and his fellow journalists all developed the "habit of calling" the defendant "Lizzie."

Moody dwelled on the multitude of locks that constricted flow through the house and profoundly affected family life. Andrew not only lived on the "narrow"; he presided over a family constrained by emotional conflict. "It will appear later on in the evidence," Moody related, "that, although they occupied the same household, there was built up between them, by locks and bolts and bars, almost an impassible wall." This statement served as powerful, concrete follow-up to the earlier bland "unkindly feeling" that he said troubled the Borden household.

Moody reviewed what occurred on the morning and evening before the murders. The prosecution would introduce three witnesses to establish that the prisoner attempted to purchase prussic acid late in the morning of August 3. Friend Alice Russell was prepared to testify about the prisoner's wild predictions of doom on that Wednesday night. These events indicated the defendant's state of mind less than twenty-four hours before the murders. Russell also witnessed the prisoner's burning of a light blue dress on Sunday morning. The paint-stained garment was, the prosecution charged, what the defendant wore on the morning of the murders.

As to that morning, Moody described how only Lizzie and Mrs. Borden occupied the house at the time of the latter's slaughter. He did concede that the unlocked north-side door was out of Bridget's sight while she chatted with the Kellys' servant and washed two sitting room windows. But Bridget saw no one on busy Second Street enter or leave the Borden house or yard. No other witnesses did either. "During all that time Bridget was washing those [seven] windows," Moody stressed, "she saw neither Mrs. Borden nor the prisoner in any part of the lower part of the house, or anywhere else."

Moody then turned to Andrew's murder. In one of the frail points in his exposition, he left vague the exact time that Lizzie had to commit the murders, hide the weapon, and clean up whatever blood splattered on her. He framed the activities that occurred between approximately 10:45 a.m., when Andrew arrived home, and 11:15 a.m., when the police were notified. Moody put off establishing the time of Andrew's murder and the prisoner's subsequent actions. He told the jury, "you can fix it better and measure it better yourselves when you come to hear the evidence." Moody had other compelling arguments to make.

As to Lizzie's claim that Abby received a note to visit a friend, Moody delivered a bare-knuckled judgment. "That, gentlemen, we put to you as a lie, intended for no purpose except to stifle inquiry as to the whereabouts of Mrs. Borden." Other lies followed when the prisoner was asked by at least half a dozen people, from Bridget to police officers, where she was at the time of her father's murder. Moody then catalogued the defendant's shifting, contradictory, and improbable responses.

In the midst of this recital, Moody took a strategic swipe at Dr. Seabury Bowen. After the murders the doctor, more than her younger lawyer, had assumed something of a fatherly figure for Lizzie. The prosecution would call Bowen as a witness. He was unapologetically sympathetic to Lizzie and grudging in his testimony when Moody later questioned him on the stand. In turn, the defense did not trust Medical Examiner Dolan. For one thing he was Irish. For another, he was convinced of Lizzie's guilt. Dolan had formed medical judgments that were potentially harmful to Lizzie, such as that the blood spilled at 92 Second Street was surprisingly not indicative of the crimes' brutality.

In any case, Moody attempted to plant mistrust of the Bordens' personal doctor. He initially thought Abby died of fright. "It is to be regretted that Dr. Bowen, a witness accustomed to observation, was the family physician and friend, and therefore affected, naturally, by this dreadful series of murders, for we might expect from him something of accurate observation." Bowen supplied the defense with an important piece of testimony on the potential side effects of the morphine that he prescribed for Lizzie—side effects that he made sound as certain as the tides in Mount Hope Bay.

Near the conclusion of his opening Moody addressed the two axes and hatchets found in the cellar. None of these turned out to be the murder weapon. The police had seen, even handled, the newly broken hatchet with ashes rather than cellar dust on it. Moody admitted that it had "attracted little attention." Then he carefully advanced the prosecution's argument: "The government does not insist that these homicides were committed by this handleless hatchet. It *may* have been the weapon" [emphasis mine]. The hatchet did not have blood or human hair on it. Nevertheless the prosecution presented strong circumstantial evidence at the trial suggesting that they had the murder weapon. In the context of trial testimony, we will return to the problem of the murder weapon to assess whether Harvard medical experts engaged in a "cover-up."

On the whole, Moody delivered a workman-like, clear, logical, and seemingly effective opening. Occasionally, he hesitated when he came to some facts of the case. Yet Moody's opening was laudable given the month or so he had been engaged in the case.

And then, just as the district attorney concluded, Lizzie fainted. As the pro-defense *New York Times* described it, with her fan concealing her face, she "had sat motionless for the last hour [then] suddenly succumbed to the strain that had been put upon her nervous system and lost consciousness." Whatever the cause of Lizzie's swoon, the timing proved exquisite. It established at the very start of the trial that the young lady dressed in mourning garb did not possess a heart carved from a block of Fall River granite. Her emotions could overtake her, even in such an exposed public forum as a packed courtroom. Lizzie's fainting, Howard reported, sent a "thrill of excitement through the awe-struck spectators." The court went into a brief recess. Jennings and

Jubb, counsel and cleric, rushed to Lizzie's aid. Smelling salts revived her and then she drank water. The trial continued.

Now began days of laborious and sometimes wearisome interrogation and cross-examination of forty-nine prosecution witnesses, not counting one who was dismissed for remote testimony. Moody called his first witness—civil engineer Thomas Kieran. He provided measurements of the interior and exterior of the Borden house, the barn, and the yard. He also calculated the distance from 92 Second Street to Spindle City's civic center as well as to the cornerstones of Andrew's commercial world. The jury then adjourned for dinner and the afternoon visit to the crime scene. Lizzie held the right to accompany the jury. Through Jennings she waived it.

———

Bridget

The third day of the trial began with Kieran back on the stand, followed by witnesses who enabled Moody to establish Andrew's movements on the tragic morning. After the autopsy photographer and John Morse testified, Moody called Bridget Sullivan to the stand. The audience shook off the effects of the heat and a morning of mostly requisite and sometimes leaden testimony. The *New York Times* described how the servant "was dressed in a maroon colored, fashionably made dress, and wore a large hat, with a large feather, and black kid gloves." The implication was clear: the lowly Irish domestic with the uncultivated demeanor and coarsened hands appeared in court in the guise of a lady.

As with all witnesses, Bridget stood behind a two-foot rail, hence the term "taking the stand." She faced the justices, the jury to her right. Bridget began her testimony at the end of the morning session. It occupied almost all of the afternoon's nearly three hours of interrogation. At the second session Lizzie for the first time sat next to her lawyers fondling a cluster of "posies" and staring at "Maggie." Such a setting worked to the defendant's advantage. She sat next to three men, one tall and the other two burly. The lawyers only served to underscore Lizzie's modest physical stature and her ladylike presence.

Bridget leaned on the rail for support as she answered a torrent of questions. She had responded to most of them in court three times, as well as to the police during their investigation. For the jury's sake, Moody had to walk Bridget through her work history, her time with the Bordens, and her household responsibilities. He established the hardware store of locks in the Borden house. When Bridget returned from visiting a friend Wednesday night, the side door was triple locked. After she entered using her key, she followed the nightly custom of latching the screen door in addition to securing the other locks. Though all the Bordens locked their doors, Bridget apparently did not secure her attic room; she had few possessions.

Moody retraced the servant's movements and activities on the morning of the murders, most of which we have already reviewed. He wanted to make clear to the jury that while she washed the exterior and interior windows, Bridget neither saw nor heard anyone until Andrew returned home. "Now during all that time [outside] did anyone come to the house that you saw?" "No, sir. I did not see anybody." "When you went to the kitchen to get your dipper, did you see anyone?" . . . "No, sir."

When Andrew arrived home, Bridget let him in the door by opening its three locks. She finished washing the inside windows and ended her chores by cleaning cloths in the kitchen.

Q. Up to that time, Miss Sullivan, had you seen or heard any other person about the premises except those whom you have named [Lizzie and Andrew]?

A. No, sir, I don't remember to hear a sound of anyone else.

Q. Are you able to hear the opening or closing of that screen door from your bedroom?

A. Yes, sir: if anybody goes in and out and is careless and slams the door, I can hear it in my room.

Moody then turned to what Lizzie wore on the day of the murders. The prosecution contended that she had turned over a dark blue "afternoon" dress to the police, but that she had worn a light blue "morning" dress. The defense challenged Moody's line of questioning, and the young district attorney seemed to falter. "What was the usual dress that Miss Lizzie Borden wore mornings? Will you describe it?" Mr. Robinson: "Wait a moment; we object to that." Mr. Moody: "Not as having any ten-

dency to show what she had on that morning." Mr. Robinson: "I object."
Mr. Moody: "I don't care to press it against objection."

The defense continued to thwart Moody, disrupting the continuity
of his interrogation.

> Q. I will call your attention, not asking you when it was worn . . . to
> a cotton or calico dress with light-blue groundwork and a little
> figure. Does that bring to your mind the dress I am referring to?
> A. No, sir; it was not a calico dress she was in the habit of wearing.
> Q. I did not ask you about the habit—
> Mr. Robinson: That should be stricken.
> Mr. Moody: Certainly.
> The Chief Justice: Let it be stricken.
> Q. Do you remember a dress of such a color with a figure in it?
> A. Yes, sir.
> Q. Will you describe that dress I have referred to as well as you can.
> A. It was a blue dress with a sprig on it.
> Q. What was the color of the blue; what was the shade of the blue?
> A. Light blue.
> Q. And what was the color of what you have called the sprig on it?
> A. It was a darker blue, I think, than the other part was.

Bridget testified that the dress had been made for Lizzie in the spring
before the murders. Instead of this light blue morning Bedford cord, an
inexpensive corduroy-like garment, on Saturday Lizzie had given the
police a more expensive dark blue "Bengaline" silk outfit. It was made
of linen and a modicum of silk and not typically worn in the morning.

A little while later, as he approached the end of his interrogation,
Moody asked Bridget if she could describe the dress Lizzie was wearing
on the morning of the murders. "No, sir. I couldn't tell what dress the
girl had on." Moody was surprised. "And you couldn't describe it?" "No,
sir, I couldn't." Needless to say, Bridget's answer diminished the results
of Moody's questioning of her about the light blue dress. At the preliminary hearing, she had responded to one of Knowlton's questions about
what Lizzie wore on the fateful morning: "You have no idea at all?" "No,
sir." Moody should have known this testimony and never pursued the
subject.

In cross-examination Bridget made ex-governor Robinson earn a portion of the $25,000 fee that he reportedly billed Lizzie at the end of the trial. He skillfully managed to elicit from her testimony about the Bordens that was favorable to Lizzie. Robinson launched his cross-examination with a focus on domestic affairs in the Borden household. Bridget acknowledged that she had no trouble in the family. She liked the Bordens and they treated her well. "It was a pleasant family to be in?" "I don't know how the family was," Bridget replied; "I got along all right." Her response suggests how Bridget sometimes qualified her answers, exercising the discretion of an experienced servant.

Robinson persisted, successfully shaping Bridget's testimony so that, on the whole, her words left a positive impression of the Bordens.

Q. You never saw anything out of the way?
A. No, sir.
Q. You never saw any conflict in the family?
A. No, sir.
Q. Never saw the least,—any quarreling or anything of that kind?
A. No, sir. I did not. . . .
Q. Now the daughters, Miss Emma and Miss Lizzie, usually came to the table, did they not, as the father and mother did?
A. No, sir, they did not.
Q. Did they eat with the family?
A. Not all the time.
Q. But they did from time to time and day to day, did they not?
A. Yes, sir.

Bridget had given him what he wanted from that leading question. But now he miscalculated and continued the same line of inquiry. To the last two-word answer he strangely asked "What?" Perhaps he did not hear Bridget's reply. She occasionally responded in a low voice and had to be told to speak louder. "Sometimes the family—most of the time they did not eat with their father and mother." Robinson tried to recover, but Bridget stuck to her position, even when he quoted her inquest testimony. Bridget said she could not remember her earlier words.

Robinson then shifted to Lizzie's relationship with her stepmother.

On the morning of the murders Bridget said that "Mrs. Borden asked some questions" and Lizzie "answered very civilly." She went on to testify that, "as far as I could see," Lizzie "always spoke to Mrs. Borden" whenever "Mrs. Borden talked with her." This typified parts of Bridget's testimony—a quietly revealing statement tacked on to her responses. The jury had to listen carefully to parse such testimony.

Robinson established three important points about what happened while Bridget washed windows. First, she admitted that when she talked to the Kellys' servant, she was not only on the opposite side of the house from the screen door; she was near Second Street, the furthest point from the door. In addition, Bridget could not look into all the rooms. On the north side of the house the windows were too high. Moreover, when Bridget came into the kitchen to retrieve the dipper, she could not see into the sitting and dining rooms.

Moody followed Robinson with a very short redirect. In response to his first question, Bridget confirmed that on Wednesday morning Lizzie wore the light blue dress with the darker sprig on it. He then inquired about a time when Mrs. Borden was sick and "neither of the girls went into her room?" Bridget recalled that the sickness lasted only a day. Robinson did not rise for a "re-cross-examination" of Bridget.

The third day of the trial and the first full day of testimony ended at 4:55 p.m. The prosecution had spent hours interrogating a key witness. Both lawyers had made mistakes. On balance, when the curtain fell on that sweltering day, the defense had perhaps gained a slight edge.

From the "Turncoat" to the "Hoodoo Hatchet"

Over the next two and a half days (Thursday, June 8, through Saturday morning, June 10), the trial gained momentum—more witnesses called, more sparring between the lawyers, and more colorful language in the competing press. The prosecution and defense arrived at pretty much of a standoff by Thursday's close. Then the next day police mangled their testimony.

Thursday began with the sometimes-sullen testimony of Dr. Seabury Bowen. He described his relationship with the Bordens as "about equal" "professional and social." The doctor embroidered the facts. He seldom visited the Borden house on a social call.

Questioned by Moody about Lizzie's dress on the morning of the murders, the good doctor performed pirouettes around questions, and then he finally threw a verbal punch at his persecutor. At the inquest, Bowen had described the dress as "drab" with "not much color in it" and "indefinite." When Moody presented the blue dress that Lizzie had turned over to police, Bowen resisted saying whether it was the dress that she wore. A frustrated Moody bored in and the doctor lashed back: "I did not pretend to describe a woman's dress and I do not intend to do now." Then pointing to what Lizzie submitted, Moody simply asked: "What color do you call that dress?" "I should call it dark blue," Bowen replied. It ought to have been obvious to all in the courtroom that his grudging testimony amounted to a limp attempt to cover for Lizzie.

In cross-examination Adams replaced Robinson and asked Dr. Bowen about the side effects of the morphine he prescribed for Lizzie on Friday, doubling the 1 gram dose the next day. If Lizzie's inquest testimony was admitted, the drug would be deployed to account for her muddled-headed responses to Knowlton. Bowen reaffirmed what he had asserted at the preliminary hearing: a double dose of morphine *caused* a loss of memory and hallucinations. Of course, morphine would not explain the slippery answers Lizzie gave police and others on the day of the murders.

Bowen's testimony yielded an interesting fact. When Abby was found the shutters were partially closed in the guestroom, the north side, which faced Mrs. Churchill's house. *Fall River Globe* reporter John Manning testified that they were completely shut. Either way, someone had shuttered the guestroom's most exposed window.

To the surprise of the prosecution, the defense recalled Bridget. In the hours of interrogation the day before Robinson forgot to ask one question. Most importantly, he quoted the servant's inquest testimony to the effect that she saw Lizzie crying and leaning against the side wooden door when she returned to report that Dr. Bowen was not home. "I swear I didn't see her crying," Bridget insisted. Robinson was unable to budge her.

Next-door neighbor Mrs. Adelaide B. Churchill followed Bridget to the stand. She testified that she never saw Lizzie shed "any tears." Churchill also described the dress Lizzie wore as light blue with a "dark navy blue-like diamond printed on it." When Moody showed her the dark blue dress, Churchill testified: "It does not look like [it]." She became more resolute: "This is not the dress I described."

In cross-examination, Robinson established that Churchill could not describe what Bridget wore that morning. Nor did the neighbor see any blood on Lizzie's dress, hands, or face as Churchill fanned her. Robinson continued his effective line of questioning by getting Churchill to admit that if Lizzie was not crying when she first saw her in the side doorway, she appeared "excited" and "frightened."

So far, through skillful cross-examination the defense had stalemated the prosecution. Then the latter called the star witness of the day: Miss Alice M. Russell, friend, confidante, and houseguest—comforter of Lizzie for four days after the murders. The courtroom stirred and Lizzie stared at her former friend. The trial represented the first time Russell testified in open court about the burning of the paint-stained dress the morning after Lizzie learned she was a suspect. It was too much for Joe Howard. To his legion of readers he branded Russell a "turn-coat friend."

She rehearsed the frantic Lizzie's outpouring of words and emotions the night before the murders. Russell's testimony turned to the skirt that she saw Lizzie getting ready to burn. As we have already discussed, Russell left the kitchen and then returned. Lizzie was pulling another small garment from halfway up the cupboard shelves. She tore the piece of clothing as she prepared to destroy it in the cast-iron stove. The trial revealed that the closet was a place where "coal, wood, irons, and kitchen utensils" were stored. In other words, the police were not likely to search such a cupboard carefully.

Russell's complete narrative, including her exchange with Pinkerton Detective Hanscom and Lizzie the next morning, riveted the courtroom. "There was deathly stillness prevailing in the chamber," the *Providence Journal* reported, "as this woman recited the story of the burning of the dress." Russell's words had been enough to sway the grand jury. Unfortunately for the prosecution, there were frail aspects to Russell's testimony, which Moody inadvertently exposed. She had tried to loosen Lizzie's dress while she lay on the lounge. Interestingly, Lizzie stopped her, asserting, "I am not faint." Still, Russell could not describe the dress that she had laid her hands on!

When Moody asked Russell whether she had testified previously about the dress-burning incident, Robinson jumped to his feet and objected, though not before the question was answered. Robinson frequently took exception to points that the prosecution raised. All too often Moody responded the way he did this time. "Well, I do not press it. If you don't want it, I don't care to put it in."

Then he forgot a crucial question and interrupted Robinson just as he started his cross-examination. He asked Russell to describe the dress that Lizzie had burned. "It was a cheap Bedford cord," she said. The dress had a "Light-blue ground with a dark figure—small figure." The description perfectly matched Mrs. Churchill's. Russell had even been present when the Bedford cord was completed in the guestroom during the May preceding the murders.

Once again Robinson mounted a robust cross-examination—well aware that the dignified church-going single woman was known for her integrity. He treated her with respect. It is a testament to Robinson's skills that highly regarded co-counsel Melvin O. Adams remained fixed in place like a potted plant for most of the defense's interrogation, with the exception of medical testimony.

Robinson's cross-examination introduced several important points. As to Lizzie's overwrought discussion with Russell the night before the murders, he presented a possible explanation: she had been sick that day, presumably from menstruation and mild food poisoning. Robinson quickly established a series of seemingly exonerating facts in his measured questioning of Russell. "Now, Miss Russell, did you see any blood upon her clothing?" "No, sir." "Or any upon her hands?" "No, sir." "A speck of it?" "No, sir." "Or face?" "No, sir." "Or was her hair disturbed?" "I don't think it was. I think I should have noticed it if it was disordered." "Saw nothing out of the way at all, did you?" "No, sir." Russell also confirmed that when police conducted a thorough search of the house on Saturday, they moved freely from cellar to attic. Neither Lizzie nor Emma denied them access to anything.

As to the burning of the dress, Russell repeated Lizzie's final words on Monday morning. "Oh, what made you let me do it? Why didn't you tell me?" Russell testified, "That is all I remember that was said." This last statement, coming from a highly credible witness, is critically important. For when Emma testified for the defense near the end of the case, as we shall see, she devised another chapter to the conversation; it absolved the sisters of any dishonesty, and Russell as well.

During redirect Moody returned to the Bedford cord that had gone up in smoke. Miss Russell acknowledged that she was unable to tell if the dress was stained beyond its edge. "Could it have been soiled with a number of things without you seeing it?" "Yes, I think so." She responded. Robinson chose not to reexamine Miss Russell.

Assistant Marshal John Fleet was the next major witness to take the stand. He testified about both of his interviews with Lizzie on the day of the murders, her pointed response when he referred to Abby as her mother, and the variations in the times she said she spent in the barn. He described the axes and hatchets that Officer Mullaly had laid out on the floor as well as the handleless hatchet with the new break that he returned to the tool box in which he had found it. He related how "the dust on the other tools was lighter and finer than the dust upon that hatchet." That is, the broken hatchet had ashes, not dust, on both sides of its head.

Moody then turned to the hours-long search of the house on Saturday. "Did you see either that in the closet [at the front of the second floor] in any other closet in the house or anywhere in the house a dress with marks of paint upon it?" "No, sir." "How critically, how carefully were you examining the dresses at that time on the Saturday?" "Very closely." "Did you find any blood upon any dress?" . . . "No, sir." At least for the moment Fleet emerged as a credible witness for the prosecution. Once Knowlton learned that Lizzie had burned a dress, he executed a risky maneuver. The *absence* of blood evidence indicated Lizzie's guilt. At least part of the light blue dress apparently had been hidden under the nose of the police in an unsuspecting utilitarian kitchen closet.

From Robinson's cross-examination it emerged that some of the dresses in the large closet at the top of the front stairs may have been turned inside out and others covered with white cloth. He suggested that Fleet might have overlooked the dress stained with dark brown paint. Since Fleet and Detective Seaver had removed dresses from the closet and examined them on Saturday, sometimes Robinson shifted back and forth between the Thursday and Saturday searches to suggest the slipshod procedures of the police. Fleet allowed that the way he and his officers searched (on Thursday), they could have missed a paint- or bloodstained dress. Fleet insisted that Thursday's search focused primarily on the presence of a man or a weapon.

Robinson attempted to make a mountain out of an ash pile. Fleet told him that there were approximately "six bushels" of coal ash in the cellar. When Robinson later learned that the police had shoveled the pile to another spot as part of their search, he thought he had a plausible explanation for the coal ash on the broken hatchet. But the police took possession of the hatchet before they moved the pile. In his closing argument, Robinson would return to the bushels of ash as a reason for the condition of the handleless hatchet.

The court adjourned with Fleet still on the stand. Under intense questioning the next day his answers became boggy. Then Officer Mullaly derailed the prosecution's narrative.

Robinson entered the court on Friday morning spoiling for a showdown with the leader of the police investigation. Fleet appeared vulnerable on at least two scores: his search of Bridget's room and his handling of the broken hatchet. Fleet had been a policeman for sixteen years, the last seven as assistant marshal. He was not about to be bullied on the stand like an unseasoned beat cop, though Robinson interrogated him almost as long as Bridget Sullivan.

Robinson and Fleet constituted two heavyweights in the trial. They clashed over how Fleet searched Bridget's room on the day of the murders. She apparently had two trunks and one was locked. Robinson labored to find out what happened. "Did she have any trunk in there?" "Yes, sir." "Did you examine that?" "No, sir." Robinson half asked and half declared that the police did not open Bridget's trunk. Then Fleet shifted: "Yes, there was a trunk that we opened, that was locked, I think. Bridget went and got a key." Fleet confused Robinson. "I want to get this right now, Mr. Fleet." "We did look in a trunk," Fleet responded.

Robinson established that the police did not look carefully. "Did you take out things that were in the trunk?" "I don't think we did." Fleet went on to say that the police "just looked in" Bridget's trunk. "Was there more than one trunk in the room?" Fleet said he thought so. Then he gave an even more evasive answer: "Well did you look into them all?" "We looked into everything that we could look into, that is, just glanced over them, that is all." Robinson concluded that the police did not look very closely. "No sir," Fleet said.

Robinson wanted to know how Fleet and his men handled Bridget's dresses. The assistant marshal was caught off guard. The cross-examination seemed to shift to Saturday, when Lizzie's dresses were examined and Bridget moved out of the house for good. Robinson was not clear about the day.

Q. Was there any blood on Bridget's dresses?
A. On Bridget's?
Q. That is what I asked you.
A. Not that I discovered. . . .
Q. You did not really look for blood, did you, on her dresses?
A. No more than I did on any others.
Q. That is not quite correct. Did you look for blood on Bridget's dresses?
A. I looked at Bridget's dresses.
Q. Just tell the jury how you looked.
A. Just looked at the dresses as they were,—some were thrown on the bed.

By all but conflating the Thursday and Saturday searches, Robinson pried several grudging admissions from Fleet. The ex-governor suggested to the jury that the police hastily focused on Lizzie as the suspect while giving Bridget a cursory treatment. He didn't have to say outright that the Irish policemen displayed their solidarity with her. He only had to imply it. Of course, Bridget possessed far fewer dresses and bedroom comforts than Lizzie.

Fleet's handling of the broken hatchet, which belatedly became the alleged murder weapon, proved more problematic for the prosecution's case.

Q. You didn't take it [the broken hatchet] along with you?
A. I did not.
Q. And you didn't take it out and lay it down with these others [the two axes and two hatchets]?
A. No, sir. . . .

Q. You went off and left this [broken hatchet] in that old ashy box just as you found it, did you?

A. Yes.

Q. And you didn't think anything to it?

A. I did not, no sir.

Q. Don't you know where it was from the fourth of August down to the time when the Grand Jury sat?

A. No, sir.

Q. Hadn't heard at all who had it?

A. I heard before the Grand Jury sat. . . .

Q. Did you in your testimony there [at Lizzie's preliminary hearing] say one word about this handleless hatchet?

A. No, sir.

Robinson held the handleless hatchet and brandished it before the jury in a bit of showmanship as he interrogated Fleet. Robinson confirmed that the assistant marshal lost control, and thought, of the hatchet for months. His forceful questioning of Fleet suggested that the prosecution trotted out the handleless hatchet in an act of desperation after tests eliminated the axes and hatchets that the police first confiscated from the cellar. Moody's redirect after Robinson had finished was very short and plowed no new ground.

One police witness who followed Fleet on Friday afternoon added a new twist to the "mystery," or press mockery, of a "hoodoo hatchet." Officer Michael Mullaly took the stand. The fifteen-year Irish veteran of the police force remained a patrolman a year after the murders. Many of his colleagues who took part in the criminal investigation had been promoted to inspector and captain. Joe Howard mordantly observed that police captains in Fall River were "as thick as flies in a cow pasture." To some, these promotions looked like rewards from the Irish mayor for Lizzie's arrest. Officer Mullaly may have nursed a grievance for being passed over. Whether it affected his testimony is another matter.

After a long week in searing heat, Mullaly roused the courtroom late Friday afternoon. He dropped a bombshell, which panicked the prosecution. His testimony to Moody focused on the axes and hatchets that he found in the cellar. He also saw the broken hatchet that Fleet pulled from the box. It looked as if ashes were "rubbed on there, wiped on, would be my way of expressing it." His appearance before the prosecution was short and his answers expected. The defense took over. The questioning turned to the broken hatchet, and Mullaly said, without Robinson's probing, that there was another piece to the handle beside what remained in the eye. "Another piece of what?" Robinson asked as if he couldn't trust his ears. "Handle." "Where is it?" "I don't know."

Mullaly's testimony became progressively damaging to the prosecution. He had not heard Fleet's testimony. Witnesses were not allowed in the court until they took the stand, but they could read detailed newspaper accounts of testimony as well as transcripts produced by stenographers who were working with journalists. The patrolman now said that Fleet knew all about the piece of the handle that fit into the break. "Well, did you take it out of the box?" "I did not." "Did you see it taken out?" "I did." "Who took it out?" "Mr. Fleet took it out." "Mr. Fleet took it out?" "Yes, sir." "You were there?" "I was there." ... "Did Mr. Fleet put that back too?" "He did."

Robinson then turned to the prosecution and asked if they had the handle. Knowlton spoke up: "Never had it." The district attorney went on to inform Robinson that "this is the first time I ever heard of it." Robinson shifted back to Mullaly: "Did you ever tell anybody about this before?" "No, sir, never did."

Fleet was recalled and Mullaly stayed in court. To both the prosecution and the defense, Fleet denied that he saw another part of the broken handle in the box or that he took the piece out and then put it back. Knowlton now stood up and asked the court to designate someone to go to the Borden house with an officer and see if the handle piece was still in the box.

The *Boston Herald*, and other papers, scoffed at what happened in court: "The handleless hatchet, now generally known as 'the hoodoo hatchet,' continued its demonish pranks in the trial of Lizzie Borden for her life today." A search of the box failed to produce the handle piece that Mullaly described. Perhaps his memory played tricks on him. It is also puzzling why, once he learned the hatchet head would be presented as the murder weapon, he said nothing to anyone about the handle piece. Whatever bestirred, or more precisely, beclouded, Mullaly's memory, his testimony flustered the prosecution. Fortunately for the district attorneys, all the police witnesses summoned after Mullaly supported Fleet's contention that the box never contained a wooden handle. But then the police fell into another clash of recall involving the alleged murder weapon.

———

The Ghost of Edwin McHenry

The court held only a morning session on Saturday. It was devoted to continuing police testimony. After corroborating Assistant Marshal Fleet's words about the handleless hatchet, two officers fell into disagreement over who wrapped it and with what kind of paper. It was only a minor detail, but Robinson exploited it as another example of police ineptness. Adding to misgivings about the police investigation, Robinson burrowed into the shadowy role of the scandalous private detective, Edwin McHenry.

Inspector Joseph Medley, Captain Dennis Desmond, and State Detective George Seaver all testified that they looked into the box and saw no hatchet handle. Medley recounted his brief discussion with Lizzie before twelve o'clock on the day of the murders, his visit to the barn loft, and his discovery of the undisturbed dust on the floor. Then his testimony turned to the hatchet.

During the search on Monday, Medley took the hatchet from the box, wrapped it in paper, and showed it to "some officers." "Did you find any handle or anything having the appearance of a handle to this hatchet except the piece that was in the eye of the hatchet," Moody asked. "No, sir." Like the other police who picked up or saw the hatchet, Medley testified that it was covered with "coarse ash dust." It was not the kind of "dirt that we found throughout the cellar," as another officer had put it.

In cross-examination Medley admitted that he "didn't look to see whether the other contents of the box were in the same condition" as the handleless hatchet. Robinson then wanted to know about the paper Medley used to wrap the hatchet before he took it to the station, especially its color. "I think it was a piece of brown paper. I wouldn't be sure as to that. It was a piece of a paper, and that is all I remember surely." Further interrogation by Robinson elicited nothing new.

When Captain Dennis Desmond took the stand, police testimony began to collide. Desmond corroborated much of what Medley said. The broken hatchet had coarse dust, and there was no handle piece in the box. Then Desmond described to Moody how he wrapped the broken axe in newspaper from the stack in the water closet. In cross-examination Robinson saw an opening. "You got a piece [of paper] out of the water closet?" "Yes, sir." "Brown paper?" "No sir, regular newspaper." . . . "You wrapped it in newspaper?" "Yes, sir." For dramatic effect Robinson handed Desmond a copy of the *Boston Globe* and asked him to demonstrate what he did before he handed the hatchet to Medley.

It is clear that Medley took the hatchet to the police station. Before that, however, he unwrapped the hatchet for others to see and then rewrapped it. Perhaps Desmond did retrieve regular newspaper to replace the brown paper. Medley had described the paper equivocally, a small, essentially insignificant detail now tentatively summoned through the scrim of hazy remembrance. Whatever happened, Robinson deployed the conflicting testimony to further chisel away at police competence generally and their mishandling of the broken axe specifically.

Robinson also successfully tied the seedy Edwin McHenry around the officers' necks. In the midst of questioning Medley, Robinson had suddenly shifted.

Q. Did you know a man by the name McHenry?
A. Yes, sir. . . .
Q. And was he ever engaged with you on the case?
A. Yes.
Q. When?
A. . . . I went with him to measure the distance from the barn to the house, or something that he wanted. . . .
Q. Under whose direction did you go at that time?
A. Under his, his suggestion, I guess. . . .
Q. You were under his control?
A. No, sir.
Q. He was an associate officer, was he?
A. Yes, sir, went with any officer whenever he chose.

Medley then denied that McHenry was actually an "associate officer" on the force, but he had already handed Robinson what he sought.

Other officers were more circumspect when it came to the notorious McHenry and his relationship with the police department. Robinson lost his patience with State Detective Seaver. "Well, that don't quite answer the question," he snapped at the witness. After verbal jousting, Seaver admitted that he saw McHenry "at the station house several times." "He was in and out of there with the officers, wasn't he?" "Yes, sir."

The first week ended with Lizzie's conviction over the horizon for Moody and Knowlton. They had made progress with some of Bridget's testimony, principally her placing Lizzie in the house at the time of the murders and her failure to see any dubious characters around the Borden house. Lizzie's destruction of the Bedford cord dress was suspicious at best and damning at worst. Furthermore, both to police and to others Lizzie gave conflicting accounts of what happened while Andrew was murdered and her barn loft alibi had a decidedly hollow sound. In turn, Robinson had recorded effective cross-examinations of prosecution witnesses, getting Bridget, for example, to concede the civility of the household and to admit she was out of sight of the screen door while she was on the south side of the house. Mullaly and McHenry had also given Robinson gift-wrapped arguments to further tarnish the police. And amidst all the lawyering, the woman in black remained in character. Lizzie assisted the defense by doing nothing to suggest that she was other than a respectable, delicate, guileless Victorian lady.

Neither side had vanquished the other at the end of the first week. If it left Lizzie's conviction for the double murder still beyond the prosecution's reach, the inquest and prussic acid testimony were yet to come. Their admission might secure Knowlton and Moody at least a hung jury and some vindication.

CHAPTER 9

The Court's Heavy Hand

Much of what remained of the prosecution's case focused on legal issues surrounding the two evidentiary rulings. But these legal debates were punctuated by the most dramatic moment in the trial—the appearance of Andrew's skull and prosecution and defense efforts to match different hatchets to his wounds. It proved too much for Lizzie's delicate constitution. She had to be excused from the courtroom, but not before nearly breaking down.

One might argue that the admission of Lizzie's inquest testimony was not as critical to the trial as it seems. After all, should the court rule in favor of the prosecution, the defense would simply fall back on Dr. Bowen's testimony about morphine's side effects. Yet the prosecution had ways of countering his testimony. Their own medical experts might attest to the *potential*, not the inevitable, side effects of the drug. Also, no one actually saw Lizzie ingest the morphine. Like the important prussic acid evidence, her inquest interrogation would enable Moody and Knowlton to recover from botched police testimony.

Monday morning, June 12, was set aside for arguments over the inquest testimony. In preparation, Knowlton, Lizzie, and her defense team signed an agreement that was filed with the court on Saturday. Both sides stipulated to nine factual statements describing Lizzie's testimony and arrest. Five points formed the crux of the agreement. First, Lizzie was not under arrest, but three days before giving testimony the mayor and marshal told her that she was a suspect. Police watched the house and its inhabitants. Second, the judge and district attorney denied her lawyer access to the inquest to counsel Lizzie. Third, she was not allowed to leave the police station after the completion of her testimony. Two hours later she was arrested. Fourth, the city marshal held a warrant for her arrest on the day before the start of the inquest. It was returned, not served. Then a new warrant was issued for her arrest. Finally, neither the judge nor the district attorney informed Lizzie that she was not required to testify to anything that might incriminate her. But the district attorney told her lawyer to advise his client, and he did.

The Inquest

The judges entered court at 9:10 a.m. on Monday, and the jurors were ushered to another room. The debate over the admissibility of Lizzie's inquest testimony lasted two hours. If Robinson had out-lawyered Moody so far, the young district attorney and future Supreme Court Justice outshined the former governor in the arguments over Lizzie's inquest testimony. He had mastered case law. He warmed to debate of legal issues on a high intellectual level. Robinson, in contrast, was no learned legal thinker. He tried to keep the debate yoked to so-called common sense, leaning lightly on legal precedent.

The case boiled down to whether Lizzie testified voluntarily at the inquest. To this issue, the court harnessed the question of whether she was under arrest when she testified. The stipulation, however, established that Knowlton told Jennings that he could inform Lizzie "before defendant testified" that she did not have to respond to anything that might incriminate her. Jennings not only advised Lizzie before she testified; he consulted with her between her appearances on the stand. Lizzie could have declined to answer questions based on the advice of her counsel. In other words, it did not matter if Lizzie was arrested, which represented an arguable point itself. Her lawyer had told Lizzie of her rights. She *chose* to testify and respond to nearly *all* of Knowlton's questions.

Moody began by upholding two important legal points. First, Massachusetts law defined an inquest as a "private" proceeding and the government had the right to exclude "any or all persons." Second, Lizzie's inquest testimony involved a series of "denials." It was "not in the nature of a confession" (though, it will be recalled, Knowlton once referred to it that way in a private letter to the attorney general).

Moody then mined case law from Massachusetts and other states, especially New York, to demonstrate recent precedent for the admission of inquest testimony under similar circumstances to Lizzie's case. The issue, Moody argued, was whether a witness testified in an inquest under "compulsion" or "voluntarily." After reviewing "all the authorities of weight," Moody drew a conclusion directly applicable to Lizzie's case: when a person "under suspicion [,] and informed that he is then under suspicion, responds to the subpoena of the State, and in the eye of the law voluntarily gives testimony at that inquiry, if he is subsequently arrested upon the accusation of being guilty of that death, what he has said at the inquiry is admissible against him."

Moody made one final argument. If the court should err against the accused, "the defendant's rights are secure." That is, Lizzie possessed the recourse of appeal to a higher court. This last argument acquires added weight in light of what Judge Dewey told Joe Howard, as reported on Saturday, June 10. "In cases of serious doubt where decisions were conflicting, it was the habit of the court to favor the commonwealth as the defense had the right of appeal, which the prosecution did not." Two days later, Dewey paid no heed to his own public pronouncement.

Robinson stood up and submitted a written brief to the court. His performance raises doubts that he had read it, at least carefully. He began by dismissing the case law of his "learned brother" that did not derive from Massachusetts. Robinson's frail grasp of case law, however, soon became obvious. He reviewed all nine of the factual statements agreed to by the defense and the prosecution, exercising some license in the process. Robinson asserted that Lizzie had been "accused of crimes by the Mayor, and City Marshal [on] August 6, 1892" when Coughlin had only said that she was a suspect, as the stipulation spelled out.

Robinson injected an emotional appeal. "Denied counsel, neglected so far as the court acted or the District Attorney, to tell her that she ought not to testify to anything that might tend to incriminate herself, she stood alone, a defenseless woman, in that attitude. If that is freedom, God save the Commonwealth of Massachusetts!"

The former governor moved uneasily through some case law, not all of it from Massachusetts. In fact, when he was responding to New York precedents that Moody had cited, Robinson switched reading from one case to another without informing the court. Moody interrupted: "That does not refer to the Mondon case, what are you reading?"

Robinson concluded by referring to Lizzie's right against self-incrimination conferred by the US Constitution. Compared to his cross-examination of witnesses, Robinson's inquest argumentation offered the court thin gruel. "It is magnificent, but it is not law," Moody replied. He was only half right.

Moody rose and said that Robinson provided him little to respond to beyond some factual errors relating to the stipulation. He described the ex-governor as deploying "vocal gymnastics and fireworks," not case law. He charged Robinson with privileging presumed common sense over the law. Moody contended that the court did not inform Lizzie about her right against self-incrimination because the judge and district attorney knew that her lawyer had done so. He then made the first of two opportunistic arguments. He maintained that an explanation of Lizzie's rights "delivered by her friend and counsel" in private "would be very much more effectual" than if it had taken place in court "in the presence of strangers." Second, to the charge that the inquest was a kind of kangaroo court out to entrap Lizzie from the start, Moody turned to the ever-helpful Bridget Sullivan, who was also subjected to intense questioning. The court recognized "no distinction between any man or woman, according to their degree. . . . " Both the servant and the lady were called because by their testimony they could "clear. . . . suspicion instead of adding to it. . . . "

Moody underscored one final issue. The marshal had indeed obtained a warrant for Lizzie's arrest the day before the inquest began. But District Attorney Knowlton, who interrogated Lizzie, had no knowledge of it.

The justices left the court at 11:16 a.m. for consultation. They returned less than an hour and a half later and offered three short paragraphs explaining their decision. They reduced the challenge to a legal straw woman: whether Lizzie was arrested at the time of the inquest. In their view, she was "practically in custody" or "effectively in custody." The chief justice offered the arguable statement that "if the accused was at the time of such testimony under arrest, charged with the crime in question, the statements so made are not voluntary and are inadmissible at the trial." The marshal's unknown, unserved warrant gave the justices thin legal cover. When one totes up the following: Moody's strong argument, Robinson's poor performance, Judge Dewey's comment to Joe Howard two days earlier, and the subsequent actions of the court—it is difficult to avoid a troubling conclusion. The judges left their thumbprints on the scale of justice.

After Chief Justice Mason read the court's decision, the *Boston Herald* reported, Lizzie "burst into tears, hiding her face in her handkerchief, while her body shook with the force of her emotion." The jury did not witness this outpouring of feeling from a woman often described as cold-hearted and then cold-blooded. The justices, however, observed the full impact of their inquest decision on the defendant.

The jury returned. The trial resumed with a burden lifted from Lizzie. That day, one newspaper reported, she "brought in a posy of bachelor buttons, as an old maid might."

The Grinning Skull

District Attorney Knowlton took over the interrogation of the next four expert medical witnesses, whose testimony occupied the rest of the trial's seventh day and all the next day. Bristol County Medical Examiner William Dolan, Harvard Professor of Chemistry Edward Wood, Harvard Medical School Professor and Medical Examiner for Suffolk County Frank Draper, and Harvard Professor of Surgery David Cheever constituted a formidable body of expertise. Knowlton, interrogating witnesses for the first time, emerges from the pages of testimony as a vigorous prosecutor.

As to Lizzie, Joe Howard claimed that she was shaken as Dr. Dolan initiated the medical testimony and moved into blood splattering, disembowelments, and beheadings. The courtroom was "distracted . . . by the evident distress of Miss Borden, who sighed heavily, lowered her head far below the hand rail. . . . And sunk back in her chair as though she could stand no more." For the afternoon session, when lawyers and witnesses passed around skulls and hatchets, Lizzie was excused from the courtroom. As the jury knew, she sat in a corridor with a sheriff and listened to the testimony. If the well-bred defendant could not stomach testimony about the murders' violence, how could she have actually committed the crimes? Her courtroom reactions that day seemed to raise such a critical question.

The four medical experts agreed on several key points. Based on blood evidence, body temperature, and digestion, Abby Borden died one to two hours before Andrew. Second, after examining the skulls, they concurred that a hatchet could have inflicted the wounds. Third, where the hatchet penetrated the brains, Andrew's skull was only one-sixteenth of an inch thick and Abby's one-eighth. Therefore, these wounds "could have been inflicted with a hatchet by a woman of ordinary strength." Depending on the way lawyers posed their questions, testimony on how much of the victims' blood spilled and how it dispersed shifted back and forth.

The third medical witness, Dr. Frank Draper, offered the most important and attention-grabbing testimony for the prosecution. Because Mrs. Borden's skull was so mercilessly crushed, Draper could not determine the size of the hatchet that inflicted the wounds. His examination of Andrew's skull suggested otherwise. But he needed the actual skull, not the plaster model that the lawyers had been using. Dr. Dolan produced the jawless, grinning skull. Leaving the witness stand, Draper used a tin plate to show that a three-and-one-half-inch hatchet like the handleless one perfectly fit some of Andrew's wounds.

Even more dramatically, Draper picked up the handleless hatchet, and with Dr. Cheever holding Andrew's skull, he demonstrated to the jury how the hatchet head slid easily into the wounds. At the end of his redirect, Knowlton asked Draper "whether in your opinion these wounds that you found could have been inflicted by that [handleless] hatchet?" "In my opinion they could." Adams protested vehemently, claiming that Knowlton had already asked the question. The district attorney replied that he had only questioned Draper about a three-and-one-half-inch hatchet and had forgotten to ask about the handleless hatchet. The latter is doubtful. Knowlton saved his question about the wounds and handleless hatchet until the end so it would stick in the minds of the jurors near the close of the day. Dr. Cheever, the final witness, agreed with Draper. "I think it could," he answered to Knowlton's question about whether the handleless hatchet might have inflicted "the wounds you found."

Did the Harvard experts participate in some kind of cover-up? What about the "very small" gilt deposit, indicating a new hatchet, that Draper had discovered and had shown Cheever? Perhaps they had changed their minds. After all, there was only one gilt speck in Abby's autopsy photograph; a new hatchet was likely to leave more. Then, too, Knowlton was careful what he asked Draper and Cheever, using the conditional "could have" when he posed the question about the handleless hatchet as the murder weapon. The defense had access to the same autopsy photographs that Draper and Cheever examined. Adams never brought up the gilt speck.

Moreover, in cross-examination, Adams unveiled a brand new hatchet like the handleless one. The new hatchet failed to fit into Andrew's wounds, as Adams found out when he asked Draper to try it. "It does not fit," the doctor showed the jury. The head of the new hatchet had not been ground down, that is, sharpened. Adams blundered. Instead of proving that anyone could have carried into the house an axe off a hardware shelf, his failed experiment reinforced the prosecution's reasoning that the handleless hatchet was the likely murder weapon. If Lizzie had purchased a new hatchet, she would have needed to have it sharpened, given the nature of Andrew's wounds. Surely she would have left a trail for the police to follow.

Despite his serious miscalculation, Adams remained a skilled interrogator who proceeded by logical steps. He showed his effectiveness when it came to how the Bordens' assailant had to be covered with blood. Consider how he approached the issue with Dr. Cheever. "It is quite a usual thing for you in operations to be spattered with blood, isn't it?" "Very." "Your hand and face get it, I suppose?" "Very often." "And your hair?" "Not so much. . . . " This line of questioning continued and led to a discussion of how arteries in the head and brain spurt blood. Then Adams arrived at the crucial point: "Would not of necessity almost the assailant have been spattered with blood?" "I think he would."

After Adams finished his cross-examination, Knowlton rose and asked three pointed questions of Dr. Cheever that ended the day on a strong note for the prosecution. "Is there any spurting of the arteries after the action of the heart has stopped from any cause?" "No, sir." "The garment that you speak of, when you put it on in your surgical operations, protects your clothing entirely?" "Yes, sir." "You don't have any trouble spattering your clothes then?" "No, sir."

The day after losing the argument over Lizzie's inquest testimony, the prosecution recovered effectively, thanks largely to Knowlton. Despite his well-founded assessment that a guilty verdict was unachievable and his handing over most of the prosecution to Moody, Knowlton possessed a strong sense of public duty. Convinced of Lizzie's guilt, he was determined to salvage something from the trial.

The Prosecution Winds Down

On the ninth day, the prosecution's last full one, twelve witnesses occupied the stand. With the exception of Marshal Rufus Hilliard and especially Hannah Reagan, most testified very briefly. A short review of the day's testimony is instructive. For one thing, it suggests how the court continued to tilt the scale of justice.

Marshal Hilliard was the first witness. One question Moody asked him had to do with the note that Abby allegedly received. "Have you been able to find any person who sent or carried a note?" "Wait a moment," Robinson protested. "I object to that. It does not appear that he has done any thing at all." The chief justice quickly ruled for the defense. "I do not see how it is competent."

Robinson then conducted a pointed cross-examination. He established that during the search of the house on Saturday afternoon, the day of the funeral, Hilliard and his officers had unfettered access and that the sisters even offered their assistance when necessary. The marshal also conceded that the handleless hatchet remained in his office (until he gave it to Dr. Wood) while the preliminary hearing took place one floor above.

Both Robinson and Moody questioned Hilliard about the Saturday night visit to Lizzie, Emma, and John Morse, when Lizzie pressed Mayor Coughlin and he let slip that she was a suspect. In redirect, Moody tried to clarify what happened Saturday night when the mayor requested that the three remain in the house for a few days and Lizzie demanded to know if any one there was under suspicion. The Mayor initially said: "Well, perhaps Mr. Morse can answer that question." Moody wanted to make sure that the jury knew how Morse had been mobbed the previous night and that was the reason the mayor urged the sisters and their uncle to stay home. Robinson protested with the rickety argument that Lizzie was unaware of what had happened. The chief justice commented that it "would be a remark [Coughlin's words about Morse], which perhaps calls for information, and would make the occurrence itself an assistance to understand the remark." Robinson demurred. The chief justice yielded. He excluded the testimony. Halfway through the 2,000-page trial transcript, one becomes increasingly convinced that the chief justice too often deferred to the forceful ex-governor.

The court disallowed as too remote the testimony of Lizzie's Grand Tour cabin mate, Anna Borden. She described Lizzie's distress over returning to "such an unhappy home." The court permitted cloak maker Hannah Gifford's testimony about the incident in March prior to the murders, when Lizzie referred to her stepmother as a "mean old thing" and said that any time they could, the sisters avoided eating with Andrew and Abby.

The prosecution then dashed through the next six witnesses—one in Miss Churchill's yard next door and five occupying various angles behind the Borden house on the morning of the murders. None saw anyone leaving the Borden yard. Robinson managed to find or create gaps in much of their testimony. For example, Lucy Collett, a French-Canadian with limited English, was sitting diagonally behind the Bordens' house on Dr. Chagnon's piazza between 10:45 and 11:45 a.m. She testified that she could see the Bordens' yard and witnessed no one. Robinson probed and found weaknesses in her testimony, including the fact that she did not see Sheriff Francis H. Wixon climb over the Borden fence after the murders searching for evidence. She had probably left the piazza by then.

Police matron Hannah Reagan occupied the witness stand longer than anyone else that day. She told Moody how she was tidying up the toilet when she heard Lizzie and Emma quarreling. She came to the doorway, as we have already recounted, in time to hear Lizzie accuse Emma of giving her away and of how she vowed not to give an inch.

Jennings took over for the cross-examination. He knew he had witnesses lined up who would refute everything Mrs. Reagan claimed. Under cross-examination, the matron enlivens the trial transcript pages as feisty, but also as evasive. She damaged her credibility. It probably did not matter. Jennings's witnesses would overpower Reagan's testimony.

A short passage from the transcript suggests what happened when she was cross-examined as a witness for the prosecution. The issue Jennings raised was the statement he drafted containing a denial of the quarrel between the sisters that Reagan had related to a reporter.

Q. Didn't I come in afterwards [to the office] and say to Marshal Hilliard, 'I understand that this woman is willing to sign this paper, unless you object?'

A. I don't remember what you said.

Q. Was it not then, Mrs. Reagan, that he said that your story, whatever story you had to tell, you would tell it in Court, —when I said that to him?

A. I don't remember seeing you. . . .

Q. Didn't you hear me tell him that if he refused to let you sign that paper, I would publish him to the world?

A. No, sir.

Once he had the matron's testimony on record he would later take a blunderbuss to it.

After Dr. Dolan and Bridget Sullivan were recalled very briefly, the most important witness of the day placed one hand on the bible, raised the other, and swore to tell the truth. Moody began asking Eli Bence questions about his background. Before he advanced very far, Robinson was on his feet: "There is a question here that we consider of vital importance," he told the court. The defense did not want the prussic acid testimony in a "piece meal" way. Moody offered to tell the court the "preliminary thing and characteristics . . . that we want to prove." Again, the court sided with the defense. The jury retired, and the witness left the courtroom, too.

Moody now made his plea for the admission of the prussic acid testimony. Once more he was in his element, arguing a legal issue in a learned way with a solid knowledge of case law in 1893. One must grasp the contour, and some of the content, of Moody's argument to evaluate what ensued.

Moody began by reminding the court that the indictments accused the defendant of murdering with "a certain intent and with premeditation." The attempt to purchase prussic acid added to the weight of evidence already introduced "tending to show that this prisoner is guilty of the two homicides charged in the two counts of the indictment." Given the late stage of the case, the evidence should be considered by the jury, rather than decided by the court.

Moody then launched into a discussion that, he apologized to the justices, was necessarily "tedious." He began by citing a legal treatise on evidence: The relevancy of evidence was "to be determined by free logic unless otherwise settled by statute or controlling precedent. All facts that go either to sustain or impeach a hypothesis logically pertinent are admissible."

No precise precedent existed for the poison evidence in the Borden case. Nevertheless, Moody stressed, he found numerous cases in which evidentiary rulings buttressed the prosecution's argument for the admission of the prussic acid testimony. He began with a Massachusetts case in which a justice made a lengthy ruling on evidence, including a statement supportive of the prosecution's position: "The conduct or declarations of a party, both before and after the principal fact in issue, are admissible, provided they are sufficiently near in point of time, and sufficiently significant of the motive or intent to be proved."

Moody then went on to identify more than a dozen cases from across the country with rulings relevant to the evidence at hand. A Kansas case, for instance, included the evidentiary question: "Could it not be shown that one charged with homicide, immediately prior there to, *was providing himself with several weapons though only one was in fact used* [Moody's emphasis]?" The court ruled that such evidence could be admitted. In another case, the court allowed testimony about a failed attempt to steal a weapon prior to another burglary because it showed intent.

In all Moody discussed and quoted from six cases. He had the files in hand and available for the justices to consult. Far from tedious, Moody's legal knowledge sparkled in the courtroom.

Moody concluded his erudite argument with prussic acid itself. Earlier testimony by Dr. Wood had established that it was one of the deadliest poisons "known to human kind." Prussic acid had no practical uses except in prescriptions. Bence had never been asked for it before. Based on logic and case law and with "proper instructions as to its weight," Lizzie's attempt to purchase prussic acid ought to be considered by the jury.

Robinson acknowledged that Lizzie's unsuccessful attempt to purchase the poison was not remote in time from the crime. Rather, he took the position that such an act hardly revealed any premeditation for her to wield an axe to murder Andrew and Abby. In other words, the defense argued, contrary to the case evidence cited by Moody, that the kind of murder weapon offered by the prosecution was critical to the issue at hand. Poison had nothing to do with an axe. Robinson labored over this legal confection.

Still, the first half of his argument displayed coherence. He preferred to focus on the "facts" of the case, not legal niceties. He claimed that the only evidence the prosecution possessed that showed any animus toward Andrew or Abby consisted of words Lizzie spoke to the cloak maker a few months before the murders. The weight of the evidence revealed no tendency to whom "she meditated the malice." It could have been Bridget Sullivan. Moody interrupted: "There is a tendency to show to whom the malice is directed." Robinson responded that people "buy prussic acid to kill animals. . . . " He offered a cat as an example.

At the end of his argument Robinson made a slapdash effort to respond to Moody's case law. As to a Pennsylvania case, "I have not examined it, only heard it read," that is, by Moody. Robinson then misidentified a case and Moody corrected him: "That is the 2nd Cushing." Robinson's response marked a legal low point in his argument. "The 2nd Cushing then, at any rate, somewhere in the books," he muttered. He admitted only partial knowledge of the important Kansas case that Moody discussed. Robinson then abruptly lurched to a conclusion. "I must say I have said all the Court desires to hear, and I have made my meaning, I trust, plain."

Why wasn't Robinson better prepared; after all, he addressed the justices, not the jury? Arthur S. Phillips, the defense team's young on-call legal assistant, could have prepared a brief for the ex-governor. Maybe he did. Perhaps Robinson felt assured about where the trial stood as the prosecution moved toward its close. Or possibly he was arrogant, an overconfidence perhaps born of his personal ties to two of the justices. In the end Robinson's bumbling performance did not matter.

The justices retired for less than an hour of deliberation. They returned at 4:33 p.m. and asked Moody to repeat the limited purpose for which the testimony was offered. Moody restated that the testimony was for the sole purpose of "bearing upon the state of mind of the defendant prior to the homicide. . . . " The chief justice declared the evidence admissible—with a worrisome condition, namely, that "the preliminary evidence must be submitted before the main question can be finally determined." Eli Bence and his co-witnesses would have to testify last (if at all), after the prussic acid experts. A brief consultation with the lawyers ensued at the bench, and then the court adjourned until the next morning.

Disarray

Thursday, June 15, day ten, the prosecution and the defense engaged in the courtroom equivalent of a brawl. It often became two against one as Chief Justice Mason repeatedly ruled for the defense. In the end, Knowlton and Moody were left reeling. The court had not yet tied a ribbon on the case for the defense. The justices saved that for last.

District Attorney Knowlton called New Bedford wholesale and retail druggist Charles Lawton. Robinson, with assistance from the chief justice, managed to handcuff Knowlton. Lizzie's fatherly lead defense lawyer challenged question after question. Far more often than not the chief justice sided with him. "Mr. Lawton," Knowlton asked, "is the drug called prussic acid sold commercially for any other purpose than upon prescription of a physician?" Robinson protested. The question was excluded. When Knowlton finished, Robinson saw no need to cross-examine the druggist. Objections and court rulings had all but nullified Lawton's testimony.

The next witness, New Bedford furrier Henry Tillson, faced the same treatment. Knowlton had to rephrase his questions or endure their exclusion as Robinson repeatedly objected. Near the end of his interrogation the district attorney persisted: "I will ask you one more question, as to whether you have any knowledge of the use of acid on furs?" Robinson took exception. The chief justice excluded the question. Once again Robinson saw no need to cross-examine the furrier. Abetted by Chief Justice Mason, Robinson had crippled another prosecution witness.

Robinson allowed analytic chemist Nathaniel Hathaway to testify, though not without some challenges to Knowlton's questions. The chemist boasted strong educational credentials. Robinson had a different plan for him. To Knowlton's question whether prussic acid had "any suitability or adaptability" for cleaning furs, Hathaway answered no. He gave the same negative response to a follow-up inquiry: "Is prussic acid in any form to your knowledge used for the purpose of cleaning fur?"

Robinson took over and asked the chemist a long series of questions. Then he arrived at a point where he wrested two concessions from Hathaway. He established that prussic acid would kill "small animal life." Then he asked, "Bugs, flies, moths and all those things would go, would they?" "Yes, sir." Secondly, as to prussic acid's deadliness, "suppose you were to dilute it still more" than the common 2 percent solution? After a volley of other questions, Hathaway finally said that prussic acid's volatility would depend on the "Strength of the solution and upon the temperature."

Robinson then asked the chemist to "leave out" the problem of prussic acid's effect on anyone handling it. Hathaway was stunned. "Leaving out the effect on the person?" "Yes." Hathaway responded with another question: "Or any other person present?" "Yes." The chemist was forced to submit to the ridiculous hypothetical: "No objection under such circumstances," he answered.

Knowlton then tried to recall Dr. Dolan. He began questioning him about his knowledge of prussic acid and its use in prescriptions. The chief justice quickly ruled that the medical examiner was not an expert.

The jury now left the courtroom. Knowlton attempted to call Eli Bence. At this point the court transcript goes silent. There are conflicting accounts of what happened next. The chief justice summoned the lawyers to the bench. Muffled words flew back and forth. What matters is that the court blocked both Bence and his co-witnesses from testifying about Lizzie's attempt to purchase prussic acid. Most important, Mason gave no official reason for the decision. The transcript only records a vague three-sentence paragraph. Mason said: "The Court is of the opinion as the evidence now stands, the preliminary questions are not included. I concluded that the testimony is over. The court did not desire to rule on it piecemeal."

From the bench Joe Howard claimed to have heard the chief justice say to the lawyers, "It is the opinion of the court that the preliminary proceedings have not been sufficient; the evidence is excluded." If Howard overheard this accurately, the court seemed to conclude that the prosecution had not stayed within the terms of the offer. Knowlton had failed to disprove that prussic acid might be used for innocent ends, for example, to kill small animals such as dogs and cats. How this applied to Lizzie made little sense. Her attempt to purchase prussic acid to get rid of moths was like trying to kill a few ants with a sledgehammer—minus the poison's toxic vapors.

The chief justice had hobbled Knowlton's interrogation of the New Bedford druggist and furrier. He then dismissed Dr. Dolan from the witness stand. Finally, he ordered the exclusion of the core prussic acid testimony with no official explanation. The timing of the court's action—at the end of the prosecution's case—was astonishingly unfair. It all represented remarkable, and, one can only conclude, prejudicial overreach. What if an Irish, French-Canadian, or Portuguese mill girl had been on trial? Can there be much doubt that the court would have proved far less predisposed to the defense in the two evidentiary rulings?

The court left the prosecution's case in tatters, with Moody and Knowlton indignant and dispirited, while Lizzie "cheerily" chatted and laughed "in conversation" with friends who formed a "semicircle about her" during recess, the press reported. Edmund Pearson, who wrote extensively and pungently about the Borden case in the 1920s and 30s, stated that he interviewed a highly regarded trial lawyer named John W. Cummings, Esq. though he does not supply the date. Cummings claimed to have been consulting with Moody and Knowlton right after the court's final ruling. The younger district attorney, who had argued so effectively in both evidentiary cases, was particularly distraught, according to Cummings. Outraged by the court's action, Moody wanted Knowlton to walk out on the trial. Then the biased court would assume responsibility for freeing Lizzie.

One has to be careful evaluating such long-after-the-fact accounts as Cummings's. Still, it is not difficult to imagine how the prosecution ended with the two district attorneys embittered. Perhaps Moody wanted to quit after shouldering the prosecution's load and Knowlton had to persuade him to soldier on. It was now Knowlton's turn to assume the prosecution's burden. He would cross-examine the defense's thirty witnesses and deliver the prosecution's closing statement.

CHAPTER 10

Defending Lizzie

Andrew Jennings began Lizzie's defense at 10:50 a.m. on June 15. He concluded the next day at 3:15 p.m. During that short span, he called thirty witnesses. Lizzie's team exuded confidence. Most of the witnesses testified only briefly, and Jennings usually skipped requestioning them after the district attorney completed his cross-examination. Still dressed in black, Lizzie helped her case by weeping during Jennings's opening argument.

Her high-priced law team did not have to present a persuasive counternarrative to the prosecution's that indicated who other than Lizzie might have committed the murders and escaped undetected, spiriting away the weapon and leaving no trail of blood. Instead, Jennings only had to cast more doubt on the Knowlton-Moody-police version of what had happened. He deployed this strategy in three ways: by raising the specter of suspicious characters around the Borden house on the morning of the murders; by marshaling testimony to suggest not only that Lizzie had visited the barn but that others had inspected its loft before Officer Medley; and by presenting a flock of witnesses who refuted police matron Hannah Reagan's account of the quarrel between the Borden sisters. And then near the very end of the trial Emma took the stand and testified longer than any other defense witness. Among other things, she tried to absolve Lizzie of any duplicity in the destruction of her dress.

Jennings Opens, Lizzie Sobs

The Borden family's lawyer spoke for just over a half hour, a third of the time Moody had consumed with his opening argument. Jennings began on an emotional note, describing both his lifelong personal and professional ties to Lizzie and her father. If he exhibited too much passion over the case, it was because a counsel "does not cease to be a man when he becomes a lawyer." He tossed around "mystery" to characterize the case, attributing the murders to some "insane person or a fiend." He informed the jury, "it is not for you to unravel the mystery of how he [Andrew] died." Rather, the jury must determine reasonable doubt. Jennings defined reasonable doubt as an alternative "hypothesis" to the prosecution's "that will exclude the guilt of this prisoner and make it possible or probable that somebody else might have done this deed...."

Circumstantial evidence, Jennings argued, was often compared to a chain. Every link in the chain of evidence had to be proved beyond a reasonable doubt. "You cannot have it tied together by weak links and strong links."

Jennings proceeded to examine the circumstantial evidence against Lizzie, which he outlined as falling under "motive, weapon, exclusive opportunity, and conduct and appearance of the defendant." Already the defense had exposed fragile links in the prosecution's chain of circumstantial evidence. As to motive, for instance, Jennings claimed that "They have not a scrap of evidence in the case but that which was given by [cloak maker] Mrs. Gifford, and you have heard also the evidence of Bridget Sullivan."

Jennings chewed over motive, focusing on Andrew's murder. The government charged that Lizzie butchered both her stepmother and "her loved and loving father." The defense would establish, "if not already shown," that Lizzie lived "quietly with her father; that the relations between them were the ordinary relations that exist between parent and daughter." Jennings promised to prove "that there was nothing whatever between this father and this daughter that should cause her to do such a wicked, wicked act as this."

By now Lizzie was weeping. "She wiped her eyes furtively a few times," the *Boston Herald* reported, "but the tears came so fast that she had to put up her handkerchief." "Miss Borden's womanhood was fully established when she burst into tears," Julian Ralph of the *New York Sun* assured his readers. Lizzie's reaction augmented Jennings's effort to humanize and feminize her as he enumerated how the prosecution had no weapon, no blood, and no exclusive opportunity for her to slaughter her beloved father.

Jennings's opening suggested how the defense planned to leave the second Mrs. Borden once again shrouded in the shadow of her husband. Lizzie's lawyers calculated that it was easier to raise doubts about Lizzie's alleged murder of Andrew, the horrific patricide. Their strategy raises an interesting question. What would have happened if the prosecution had tried the murders separately, with Abby's death first on the docket?

"Mysterious" Characters

In less than one full first day, Jennings called eighteen of his thirty witnesses. Martha and Marienne Chagnon, the daughter and wife, respectively, of Dr. Chagnon, were the first to take the stand. Both testified that on the night before the murders, they heard pounding on the "fence or a board" coming from the direction of the Bordens' yard. The Chagnons' windows were closed and in the darkness they could not see anything.

They proved to be exceptionally weak witnesses to open the defense. In cross-examination Knowlton asked the daughter: "And how could you tell the direction from which the sound came?" Martha offered no answer and the district attorney wisely did not repeat the question. Other queries Knowlton posed were greeted with silence. Martha did acknowledge that she had only an "impression" of the direction of the sound. Jennings very briefly requestioned Martha after Knowlton.

Her stepmother had a rougher go. Mrs. Chagnon could not understand or speak English very well. She did not know what "pounding" meant. "All right; I can't put the question," Knowlton stressed. Jennings did not rise to re-interrogate Mrs. Chagnon.

Lizzie's lawyer interrupted his procession of witnesses with their mysterious noises and characters to call the man who had painted the Borden house in early May prior to the murders. He offered no eyewitness account of Lizzie staining her Bedford cord. But John Grouard did make clear that there was a mixing tub in the barn and Lizzie was present when he tested a new shade that she had requested. In other words, Lizzie was around paint while he worked on the house. The point of the painter's interrogation was to establish that Lizzie could have easily smeared her dress. There was only one knot in the grain of this testimony: The prosecution never argued that Lizzie did not possess a paint-soiled dress. Rather, they were unable to find the Bedford cord before Lizzie burned it.

The carousel of witnesses who observed unknown, "suspicious" characters resumed testifying. Mark Chase ran a Boston and New York Express horse barn across the street from the Kellys. He testified that on August 4 at 10:55 a.m. he saw an unfamiliar horse and carriage in front of the Borden house with a stranger in the driver's seat.

In cross-examination Knowlton clarified the scene. The carriage was actually between the Borden and Kelly houses. Chase admitted that it might have been waiting for one of Dr. Kelly's patients. Moreover, the liveryman conceded that he only saw the side of the driver's face. He could have been someone that Chase knew. It might be recalled that Dr. Kelly was not at home on the morning of the murders. The driver and the carriage were never identified. They represent a minor mystery in the case that has fueled speculation about an accomplice in the Borden murders.

Two rear neighbors saw a stranger sleeping on the side steps of their Third Street house on the night before the murders. More relevant, a Second Street resident witnessed an unfamiliar young man leaning on the gatepost of the side entrance to the Borden yard at approximately 9:45 a.m. In cross-examination Knowlton asked: "Did you notice anything out of the way about him?" "No, sir." "About his clothes or anything of that sort?" "No, sir." "Had nothing in his hand that you noticed?" "He did not."

The unrelenting Dr. Benjamin Handy surfaced again with his story of what he observed as he passed the Borden house on the morning of August 4. "I saw a medium sized young man of very pale complexion, with eyes fixed upon the sidewalk." The man wore a suit and a tie and acted "strangely." To Knowlton, Handy acknowledged that the young man "wasn't hurrying" or "staggering" and that he had nothing in his hand. "All you can tell, so the jury could get an idea, is that his eyes were on the sidewalk, and he walked very slowly, and didn't look at anything around him." "Yes," the doctor replied. Jennings didn't rise for redirect. He had stronger witnesses on other matters queued up.

———

Jennings now shifted to who visited the barn and at what time. The testimony represents a thicket of characters and estimated times. It also encompasses the feasible and the farcical. Jennings deployed a series of witnesses of widely varying credibility to plant doubts over whether Officer Medley visited the barn loft first.

Alfred Clarkson, a "steam engineer," offered the first major direct challenge to Medley's testimony. He claimed he arrived at the Borden house at 11:30 a.m. and visited the barn seven or eight minutes later. He "looked around" the loft. He found that three people, whom he couldn't identify, were already there. Clarkson remained in the barn only a few minutes and did not see Officer Medley.

In cross-examination Knowlton was at pains to budge the engineer from his testimony. He managed to get Clarkson to allow that it may have been nine minutes before he went into the barn, but he would give no more ground. Then Knowlton quoted from the preliminary hearing. "At what time, as near as you can recollect, did you arrive at the Borden house?" he had asked. "About 11:40," Clarkson had responded. His testimony began to change. Clarkson said that he "possibly [stayed] seven or eight minutes" in the barn and that there were four, not three persons in the loft.

What can we conclude from this and subsequent important testimony that implicated Medley? First, as soon as the police learned of Lizzie's alibi, they should have cordoned off the barn. Second, testimony about time represented nothing more than witness estimates, minutes that were not fixed amidst the tumult of August 4, but that shifted over the course of ten months. As Clarkson put it to Knowlton, "I didn't look at my watch, but that is the best of my belief." Third, minutes mattered about who saw whom, as police and others passed in and out of the barn. No one remained in the suffocating loft very long.

Once again, Jennings failed to redirect questioning of his witness. Instead, he paused from testimony about who visited the barn first and called an ice cream peddler, Hyman Lubinsky. The police had interviewed the immigrant, who possessed limited facility with English. They questioned his credibility. He emerged as one of the defense's most important witnesses.

Lubinsky housed his horse team in a stable a short distance up Second Street from the livery where witness Mark Chase worked. On the morning of the murders, Lubinsky testified, he left the stable "a few minutes after eleven." The stable keeper, who followed Lubinsky to the stand, would confirm the peddler's testimony as to time. Lubinsky drove his team down Second Street on the same side as the Borden house. "Whom did you see?" Jennings asked. "I saw a lady come out the way from the barn right to the stairs back of the house. . . . She had a dark colored dress." Lubinsky said that his horse "trotted a little; not fast." He knew the lady was not Bridget because he had stopped at the house "two or three weeks" earlier to sell the servant ice cream.

Lubinsky offered specifics down to the "dark" dress, though he did not identify the color of the deep blue outfit Lizzie had submitted to the police. In cross-examination, Knowlton chipped away, with some success, at the peddler's eyewitness glance from a moving team. Lubinsky said that he was past the house a little way when he saw the lady. That means he would have had to turn his head. Under questioning Lubinsky described her as "three or four feet" from the stairs and "By the side of the house." "Then where she came from, you don't know?" "No,— away from the barn," Lubinsky responded. Knowlton challenged him: "Or away from the barn?" "I know she came from the barn," Lubinsky asserted. But Knowlton emphasized that the lady's back was to the barn and he saw her very "near the steps." Lubinsky could not be so certain that she came from the barn.

Knowlton hammered away at Lubinsky: "You go down that street every day, don't you?" "Every day." "You didn't take notice any other day?" "Something made me look at it that day. What has a person got eyes for, but to look with?" Since Lubinsky had already acknowledged that his carriage had no ice cream at the time, he couldn't have been looking for customers. Knowlton kept up the barrage. "You ask too fast," Lubinsky complained. "I can't understand what you mean."

Knowlton might have buttressed his cross-examination of Lubinsky if he had referred to the trial's first witness, Thomas Kieran. The civil engineer had testified that the sightline from the street to between the house and the barn was only a foot wide. When Lubinsky was a little past the Borden house and turned his head, he could see more of the yard, but it was impossible for him to view the barn's side door.

Jennings moved on to other witnesses, leaving Lubinsky a bit bruised by Knowlton. Among those he called were two juveniles of questionable background who came to be spoofed in the press as "Me and Brownie." With them the trial temporarily descended into farce. The first, Everett Brown, proved to be an anemic witness. He said he left his house, accompanied by Thomas Barlow, at approximately 11:00 a.m. But he had trouble pinning down the time. Jennings asked Brown: "Well, would you say it was nearer eleven or twelve that you left the house?" "I couldn't say because I didn't notice the time."

Brown and his friend walked down Second Street and learned of the crime when they got to the Bordens' house. They saw Officer Doherty, one of the earliest policemen to arrive. Brown and his confederate said that they entered the barn and went up to the loft. They remained there for five minutes, and then joined others in the backyard. After Assistant Marshal Fleet reached the Borden house at 11:45 a.m., he ordered police to clear the yard. Brown and Barlow spent the afternoon in front of the house.

Knowlton exploited Brown's inability to approximate the time he left his house. "Do you know if it was after one or not?" "I don't know the time," Brown confessed. He also could not tell whether he had seen Officer Medley.

Brown's sixteen-year-old companion, poolroom boy Thomas Barlow, was more colorful and forthcoming with respect to time. Under Jennings's questioning he testified that he went to Brown's house at 11 a.m., "stayed there about eight minutes," and then headed toward Second Street. "Me and Brownie," Barlow said, attempted to enter the house by the side door. They were prevented, so they went to the barn and climbed into the loft.

Knowlton had such a go of it with Barlow that one may wonder why the defense put such a clownish figure on the stand. He and Brownie formed a twosome. Brown laid down a marker of their arrival at the Borden house—his identification of Officer Doherty—but he was in a haze about clock time. In his own antic way, Barlow supported his friend's testimony that they had been up in the barn loft before the police.

Barlow said he ate his midday dinner at 10:30 a.m.! He had testified to Jennings that the loft was "cool." Knowlton made him choke on his words. "Now, did I understand you to say it was cooler up in the barn loft than it was anywhere else?" "Yes, sir." . . . "It really struck you as being a cool place, up in the barn?" "Yes, sir." "A nice, comfortable, cool place?" "Yes, sir." Then Knowlton zeroed in on Me and Brownie's hunt for the murderer. Barlow testified that the barn door was fastened from the outside. "What made you go into the barn?" "Why, to see if anybody was there." "You thought the man had fastened himself in on the outside, I suppose." "No." "That didn't occur to you at all?" "No, sir." (Less than four months after the trial, Barlow and a friend would be arrested on a Sunday night while burglarizing their second store on Main Street.)

Refuting the Police Matron

On Friday, June 16, the last day of testimony, Jennings closed the case for the defense early, after starting late on the previous day. In the afternoon, Lizzie entered court with four roses. Their color held significance for court watchers. The roses were "pale but fresh," according to the *Boston Herald*. The reporter claimed that they were "read by the people as a sign of her rapid progress from the deep-red flowers of earlier days toward the pure white bloom of vindicated maidenly rectitude." Such widespread newspaper rhetoric emerged from the courtroom's overwhelmingly male journalists. At a time of change for middle- and upper-class women, newspapers conveyed to the nation that in Lizzie Borden the conventions of virtuous Victorian womanhood were on trial.

After Brownie and Barlow, Jennings concluded with a strong group of witnesses. First journalists and then Lizzie's stalwarts subjected Hannah Reagan's testimony to blistering contradiction. And near the end of the day, Emma took the stand. Convinced of her younger sister's innocence, Emma made important "new" revelations that echoed with the sound of desperation.

John J. Manning had been a reporter for the *Fall River Globe*, the pro-labor Irish newspaper. He now worked for the *Fall River Herald*, the moderate Democratic newspaper. Manning had interviewed Hannah Reagan about the jailhouse quarrel between Lizzie and Emma, which made that morning's headline in the *Globe*. He told Jennings that he asked the police matron whether the story was true. She answered "that there was nothing in it."

In cross-examination Knowlton made little progress with the reporter. Manning conceded that he did not hear Reagan say "that you couldn't always believe what you saw in papers." Then he retorted, "I think it is very likely" that she said those words.

Jennings now called another Irish reporter, Thomas Hickey. He wrote for the *Fall River Globe* and the *Boston Herald*. Hickey said he interviewed Reagan the day after the publication of the account of the sisters' alleged spat. When he asked her if there had been any bickering, she said "no." She also denied repeating Lizzie's words to a reporter, "you gave me away." Then Hickey said, "Mrs. Reagan, there is absolutely no truth in the story that was printed?" She replied, "No, sir, no truth at all."

Knowlton probed a vulnerability in Hickey's testimony. The *Boston Globe* and *Boston Herald* were the principal competitors in that city's journalistic free-for-all. The *Globe* had scooped the *Herald* on the story of the sisters' wrangling. Knowlton suggested that Hickey, as the local representative of the *Herald*, had gone to see Mrs. Reagan for a specific purpose. "And, of course, your object was to show that the scoop was good for nothing, wasn't it?" Hickey equivocated through a series of questions. It only stiffened Knowlton's spine until he extracted the answers he wanted. "You went to interview Mrs. Reagan so as to show that the *Globe* scoop wasn't good for anything, I suppose, didn't you?" "Yes, sir." "[You wanted] something to offset the *Globe* scoop, wasn't it?" "Yes, sir." Knowlton's doggedness revealed the journalistic pressure on Hickey when he interviewed Reagan and this called into question the integrity of his reporting. Now the district attorney faced an onslaught of witnesses who more successfully assailed the police matron's credibility.

Mrs. Marianna Holmes took the stand. This friend of Lizzie's since childhood began as a character witness. Both belonged to the Central Congregational Church, where, she said, Lizzie and Abby went to Sunday services together and sat in the same pew. Holmes rehearsed Lizzie's church and civic activities. Jennings arrived at the story of the sisters' quarrel, and Lizzie's friend testified that Reagan denied the account on the afternoon of the morning when it made headlines. As to the affidavit drawn up by Jennings that put the denial in writing, "I heard her say that she would sign it if Marshal Hilliard was willing."

Knowlton left his bulldog demeanor at the lawyers' table. There was not much he could do with Holmes or her testimony. After his skilled interrogation of Hickey, Knowlton hardly cross-examined Lizzie's friend.

Another reporter took the stand, followed by banker Charles Holmes, Marianna's husband. Defense witnesses continued to foil Reagan's testimony. Holmes said he listened as Rev. Edwin Buck read the affidavit to the police matron. She acknowledged that its statements were true and expressed her willingness to sign, unless the marshal objected. Holmes heard "part of the altercation downstairs" when the marshal prevented her from signing.

In cross-examination, Knowlton established that Holmes and Rev. Buck were close friends of Lizzie's and convinced of her innocence. He also had Holmes admit that Reagan had not been summoned by the defense to the preliminary hearing taking place one floor below the matron's room at the time of the affidavit dispute. Moreover, Reagan was only asked to deny a reporter's story at a time when the newspapers had become purveyors of misinformation about the Borden case. Knowlton offered what were important clarifying points but not contravening ones to Holmes's testimony. Jennings did not choose to redirect.

Defense testimony continued with another lifelong woman friend of Lizzie's and fellow communicant of Central Congregational Church. Still, the leading man in the affidavit episode did not take the stage against Hannah Reagan. Rev. Buck repeatedly heard his name invoked by witnesses and lawyers, but he was not called to testify. The defense had no need to summon him. Rev. Buck's daily presence in a choice courtroom seat constituted his silent witness to the jury of Lizzie's innocence.

Blood Allegiance

Emma, the defense's most important witness, followed the testimony against Mrs. Reagan. Lizzie's guardian sister remained on the stand longer than any other defense witness. Her most damaging testimony against the prosecution focused on the highly credible Alice Russell and involved Lizzie's burning of the stained dress.

Jennings began by asking Emma to describe how much money Lizzie possessed, suggesting that she had no need to kill for riches, as the prosecution argued. Lizzie's wealth consisted of a small number of shares in a Fall River bank and in the Merchant's Manufacturing Company and more than $2,800 in savings at the time of the murders, a comfortable sum for 1892. Nearly all that money came from Andrew's inflated purchase of his father's house from the sisters in mid-July before his murder. Of course, Jennings did not want the jury informed of this fact.

From money he switched to sentiment and Andrew's cheap gold ring, a gift, as we have already seen, from Lizzie. "Did he constantly wear it after it was given to him?" "Always," Emma answered. "Do you know whether it was upon his finger at the time he was buried?" "It was."

Jennings then turned to police searches of the house. Emma testified that she and Lizzie didn't show "the slightest objection" to any of their searches. The sisters provided assistance to the police when they asked for it.

Jennings shifted to Lizzie's light blue Bedford cord dress. Emma testified that the dress was made in the guestroom with Abby present. Mrs. Raymond was also the stepmother's dressmaker. Jennings and Emma created a scene of domestic bliss —the four participants in the circle enjoying their company and happily engaged in womanly things. Regarding Saturday's thorough search, when the police said they didn't discover the paint-soiled Bedford cord, Jennings asked Emma if she knew where the dress might have been found. "I saw it hanging in the clothes press over the front entry."

Then Emma said much more. Because she could not find a vacant nail on which to hang her own dress, Emma told Lizzie: "You have not destroyed that old dress yet; why don't you?" Emma increasingly took responsibility from Lizzie for the destruction of the dress. Jennings asked Emma to tell the court what happened the next morning, Sunday, when the sisters were unable to attend church because of the throng on Second Street. "I was washing dishes, and I heard my sister's voice and I turned round and saw she was standing at the foot of the stove. . . . This dress was hanging on her arm and she says, 'I think I shall burn this old dress up.' I said, 'why don't you' or 'you had better' or 'I would if I were you,' or something like that. . . . but it meant, Do it. . . . " Emma rounded out the setting by testifying that the kitchen windows and door were open, and the police were about the yard. Alice Russell also witnessed Lizzie preparing to burn the dress. Now Emma had to refute Russell's testimony but not the kind friend's integrity. Emma accepted moral limits to her apparently laundered testimony of the paint-stained dress story. Everyone emerged vindicated.

On Monday morning Miss Russell described for Emma and Lizzie the "falsehood" she had told Pinkerton Detective Hanscom, namely, that all the dresses from August 4 remained in the house. The falsehood "frightened" Emma. She and Lizzie "decided to have her [Russell] go and tell Mr. Hanscom that she had told a falsehood, and to tell him that we told her to do so. She went into the parlor and told him, and in a few minutes returned from the parlor and said she told."

Emma's story is riddled with inconsistencies. Without belaboring her own seeming "falsehoods," three are worth commentary. First, in her testimony Miss Russell said nothing about a second visit to Hanscom. She certainly would have remembered it. The second conversation would have partially redeemed her integrity after she failed to testify about the dress burning until her guilt-spurred return to the grand jury. Second, even Emma testified that Lizzie said to Alice Russell, *not* to her, "Why did you let me do it?" But according to Emma, *she* instigated the dress burning. And finally, Russell saw Lizzie take what looked like a skirt from the kitchen cupboard, not the upstairs closet, as she prepared to burn the garment.

Jennings concluded his interrogation of Emma with the widely re-ported story of the sisters' jailhouse squabble. She denied each of the alleged details of the dispute as they had appeared in the press. "Was there ever any trouble in the matron's room between you and your sister while she was there?" "There was not."

Knowlton's cross-examination of Emma represented the prosecu-tion's major confrontation with a defense witness. He had to question her aggressively but not with an exhibition of muscular masculinity. He needed to treat Emma like a lady. The *Boston Herald* described the con-testants in a story distinguished by its overblown prose. To start, the account reminded readers of New England's most notorious historical blemish. The district attorney possessed the "firm and unyielding" way of a colonial "witch burner." "He is a very large and powerful man, with a head as hard as iron set on a neck that is a tower for strength. His shoulders are a yard apart. His legs are like the foundations of a bridge. He is by nature combative, and he snorts like a warhorse." Discount-ing for the extravagant figurative flights, we can still discern Knowlton's manly presence and manner in the courtroom.

The *Herald* also penned a contrasting sketch of Emma. She looked like "the aged double of her sister," but with conspicuous differences. "Emma is weak and retreating." She lacked Lizzie's "strong and firm" chin. Yet the physically smaller older sister, who also dressed in black, shared a familiar courtroom persona with Lizzie. Both sisters fit the profile of the "typical old maid schoolmarm." The *Herald* staged the courtroom drama for its readers in a way that Knowlton couldn't win. The husky district attorney had to be careful not to overwhelm Emma physically and rhetorically. If he appeared to manhandle her, it would only earn Emma the jurors' sympathy.

Cross-examination began and Emma rewrote an important chapter in family history and in the case against Lizzie. Knowlton wound his opening questions down to the family trouble over Andrew's purchase of the house of Abby's half-sister, with the deed handed over to his wife.

Q. Were the relations between you and Lizzie and your stepmother as cordial after that . . . as they were before?

A. Between my sister and Mrs. Borden they were.

Q. They were entirely the same?

A. I think so.

Q. Were they so on your part?

A. I think not.

Q. And do you say that relations were entirely cordial between Lizzie and your stepmother after that?

A. Yes, I do. . . .

Q. Did your sister change the form of address to her mother at that time?

A. I can't tell you whether it was at that time or not.

Knowlton kept pressing the suddenly self-assertive spinster while Emma recast herself as the principal agent safeguarding the sisters' interests against the stepmother's scheming.

He began quoting Emma's inquest testimony, which was often equivocal, but not as dodgy as her current responses. Her answers irked him. "Do you mean they [relations] were entirely cordial between your stepmother and your sister?" Knowlton read what he had asked at the inquest. Emma had answered "no." She now responded, "Well, I shall have to recall it, for I think they were." Knowlton accused Emma of remembering inquest answers when she had said relations were cordial and forgetting them when she had testified they were not. Hannah Reagan had frittered away her credibility with her evasiveness. Emma was not so agile as to potentially avoid a similar end. Tractable in everyday life, she tried to establish that she, not Lizzie, fomented trouble with Andrew over the house purchase and harbored the hard feelings toward Abby at home in its aftermath.

Knowlton struggled to restrain his prosecutorial combativeness. He kept quoting Emma's earlier testimony. He had asked Emma about Andrew's gift of his father's house—the attempted appeasement of the sisters. "The giving of the property to you did not entirely heal the feeling?" Emma had answered, "No, sir." Now she said: "It didn't, not with me, but it did with my sister after." He wanted to know if she remembered making "such [a] distinction" at the inquest. "I don't remember the question nor the answer," Emma replied.

Recess for dinner interrupted Knowlton's interrogation. When the court resumed at 2:15 p.m., the case for the defense had only an hour remaining. Knowlton grilled Emma for about half that time. He wanted to know if Alice Russell was an "Intimate friend." Emma characterized her as a "calling friend," an interesting distinction that offers insight into the social mores of women who composed the Borden sisters' circle. They called on Russell and she on them.

However, through a series of questions Knowlton established facts that stood at odds with Emma's representation of Russell's relationship. As we have already noted, she stayed with the sisters for four nights after the murders. On two of those nights she moved into Emma's room. And, of course, Lizzie confided in the so-called calling friend for nearly three hours on the night before the murders. Then on the day of the bloodshed, when Dr. Bowen was not at home, Lizzie sent Maggie to summon Miss Russell. Such uncontested facts impugned Emma's depiction of the sisters' relationship with their "calling" friend.

Knowlton's questioning of the sisters' friendship with Russell served as a prologue to his focus on the dress-burning episode. In the verbal to-and-fro over what happened, Emma had trouble keeping pace with Knowlton when he asked her about Alice Russell's testimony.

Q. Wasn't the first thing said by anybody, "Lizzie, what are you going to do with that dress?"

A. No, sir. I don't remember it so. . . .

Q. Do you remember Miss Russell to so testify?

A. I think she did.

Q. Do you remember whether that was so or not?

A. It doesn't seem so to me. I don't remember it. . . .

Q. Do you remember that you did not say it?

A. I am sure I did not. . . .

Q. You swear you didn't say so?

A. I swear I didn't say it.

Q. Did you just tell me that you didn't remember of saying it?

A. I did.

Q. Do you mean to put it any stronger than that?

A. I think I may truthfully.

Q. What has refreshed your recollection since?

A. Nothing; only thinking, I am sure, I didn't.

Perhaps that last answer persuaded the jury. Still, it came in the context of Emma's often less-than-nimble responses to Knowlton's interrogation as well as her new and suspect testimony that conveniently converged to exonerate her sister.

Jennings, for one, remained confident in his case—and in Emma. He only asked her a few questions as follow-up. Then he turned to his last two major witnesses —one more credible than the other.

Mrs. Mary Raymond spent three weeks during the May preceding the murders at 92 Second Street making dresses, including the Bedford cord. It consisted of a "blouse waist and full skirt." Lizzie intended to replace an old wrapper with the Bedford cord, which soon became stained with new paint. Even after it was smudged, Mrs. Raymond testified, Lizzie wore the dress "all the time" during those three weeks in May and it faded.

As to the old wrapper, Raymond delivered some important testimony. Lizzie cut pieces from the wrapper "and said she would burn the rest." She then went downstairs and "came back without it." Thus, Mrs. Raymond's testimony indicated that the Borden sisters did burn old dresses. They also salvaged a few pieces for rags. Mrs. Raymond made one final important point. Asked by Jennings whether Lizzie could fit one dress under another, she responded: "Her dresses were always too snug for that."

Raymond's testimony stymied Knowlton. He very briefly cross-examined her and made no headway, never even pointing out that Lizzie saved no rags from the Bedford cord as she had from the wrapper. In redirect, Jennings asked a few questions, and then called his last witness.

Phebe Bowen, the doctor's wife, was among the first people to arrive on the murder scene. After her husband reached the house and saw the carnage, he told her to go home. Bowen said that Lizzie looked "white, [with] lip or chin quivering." She wore a dark blue morning dress. Her hands appeared particularly white against the dark blue. Bowen saw no blood on Lizzie.

In cross-examination Knowlton raised two questions about Lizzie's clean hands and the color of her dress. Bowen repeated the description of the white hands and the district attorney rapidly fired back. "Did they present to you the appearance of having been out in a dusty barn?" "I did not notice anything upon them." "Noticed nothing of that whatever?" "No, sir, I was not thinking of it."

Bowen had told the police and Knowlton at the preliminary hearing that she had been back and forth peering out her window until 10:55 a.m. as she waited for her daughter to arrive by train. She did not see anyone entering or leaving the Borden house or yard. The district attorney did not raise this important testimony at the trial. Rather Knowlton focused on Lizzie's dress and had Bowen describe it again. He countered by invoking her preliminary hearing testimony. "What dress did she have on?" Bowen had been asked. "A white dress with a waist with blue material, a white spray running right through." Knowlton actually misquoted part of Bowen's answer, but the defense oddly failed to protest. She had not said "A white dress" but "a dark blue" with a white spray. Nevertheless her description of a blue "ordinary morning dress" with a white spray failed to match the dark blue Bengaline silk outfit given to police. It was neither ordinary nor a morning dress, and it didn't have a white spray. Like her husband, Mrs. Bowen was an unwavering partisan of Lizzie. They both tried to be cagey about previous testimony when it came to the dress Lizzie had worn on the morning of the murders.

Wrapping Up

A few final maneuvers closed the case for the defense. Most significantly, co-counsel Robinson rose and asked the stenographer to read passages of Bridget Sullivan's inquest testimony and the assistant marshal's preliminary hearing testimony. In the servant's case, the stenographer repeated the testimony, which Bridget had contradicted earlier in the trial, that Lizzie was crying after the discovery of her father's body. As to the assistant marshal, Robinson made a less important point: until the trial Fleet had not testified that Lizzie told him how she helped her "feeble" father onto the couch.

The defense rested its case and the prosecution spent the remaining hour in rebuttal. Moody replaced Knowlton and called two witnesses. Marshal Hilliard revisited the Hannah Reagan controversy and repeated what he told the matron about the affidavit Rev. Buck wanted her to sign.

More importantly, Officer Michael Mullaly then took the stand and testified that he had interviewed Hyman Lubinsky as part of the police investigation. The ice cream peddler had insisted that he passed the house at 10:30 a.m., not shortly after 11 a.m., as he now testified. Mullaly had recorded the interview in a report book that he presented in court.

The prosecution completed its rebuttal with the preliminary hearing transcript. Moody asked the stenographer to read engineer Alfred Clarkson's testimony about what time he arrived at the Borden house on the day of the murders, Emma's testimony concerning Lizzie's relationship with her stepmother, and Mrs. Bowen's (correct) testimony about Lizzie's dress. The court adjourned at 4:15 p.m. Closing arguments would begin on Monday.

How do we evaluate the condensed case for the defense? It did not represent a compelling argument for Lizzie's innocence. But then her lawyers did not have to assemble such an array of witnesses and evidence. They only needed to scatter new seeds of doubt. After all, the court's evidentiary rulings had already created significant breaches in the narrative of Lizzie's guilt that Moody had advanced in his ninety-minute opening statement. Defense witnesses raised new, though often far from fatal, questions about the prosecution's case: the witnesses who heard sounds at night or who saw vaguely questionable figures on Third or busy Second Street; those, including the laughable Brownie and Me, who claimed, at various times, not to have seen Officer Medley on the grounds or in the barn; Lizzie's intimates who pummeled Mrs. Reagan; the dressmaker; and Emma, whose testimony conflicted with Alice Russell's and often with her own previous statements made under oath.

Knowlton knew before the defense began that the prospect of conviction had vanished. Nonetheless, he cross-examined nearly all defense witnesses vigorously and skillfully. He pursued vindication for prosecuting Lizzie. If victory had evaporated, perhaps a hung jury still remained in his grasp.

CHAPTER 11

Verdict

The trial lasted two more days. Closing arguments filled most of those hours. Ex-governor Robinson delivered a solid four-hour performance. He reviewed the prosecution's evidence in a systematic, lawyerly, and measured way. Robinson changed his persona when he made sport of the police and when he directed folksy appeals to the jury of men mostly from Bristol County's outlying towns. At some moments Robinson carried on as if he was still running for office.

In the course of his deliberate presentation, Robinson made only two significant missteps. He tried to attribute the origin of the story about Abby visiting a sick friend to Bridget, not just Lizzie. Then he told the jury that it was not the defense's responsibility to offer a theory of the murders but only to show reasonable doubt about the prosecution's theory. Nevertheless, he over-invested in a sketchy alternative hypothesis of how an assassin committed the crimes.

Knowlton responded with a five-hour closing that overshadowed Robinson's in eloquence. He displayed energy, forcefulness, even brilliance as he laid out the circumstantial evidence against Lizzie and challenged the veracity of defense witnesses, especially Emma. He even won plaudits from the leading pro-Lizzie press. Yet his closing argument was not flawless. He stumbled at two points. First, he reiterated too many times what he had declared at the preliminary hearing, to the derision of the working-class *Fall River Globe*. It was painful for him to prosecute a lady of Lizzie's background, but his public duty demanded that he do so. More seriously, he garbled his words when he discussed the absence of premeditation in Lizzie's slaughter of her father. Even the careful reader of the trial transcript, let alone the word-weary jury, might misunderstand Knowlton to say that he "hoped" Lizzie was innocent.

After the closing arguments concluded, Judge Justin Dewey, Robinson's appointee to the court, took an hour and a half to deliver instructions to the jury. It represented yet another intervention of the court on the side of the defense. Furnished with more than forty exhibits, the jury went off to deliberate.

Robinson's Close

Robinson began by portraying the Borden murders as a male crime, and the action of a "maniac or a fiend" at that. The slaughter represented the work of someone "whose heart is blackened with depravity, whose whole life is a tissue of crimes, whose past was a prophecy of that present." Robinson was preparing the jury for a shift to Lizzie's life of Christian charity. But first he had to say more about the masculine makeup of the crime. He claimed, contrary to medical testimony, that the assassin "aimed" his blows "steadily and constantly," with "none going amiss." The bloodletting was the work of a man who "knew how to handle the instrument, was experienced in its control."

Robinson turned to "Miss Lizzie" or "Lizzie" or "this girl" or "this young woman." In his telling, the crimes were "morally and physically impossible for this young woman defendant." Later he rounded out his argument by sketching Lizzie's thirty-two unblemished years as a prologue to her innocence. How could she "suddenly" become the "rankest and baldest murderess. . . ." He urged the jury to use its common sense. To believe that without warning upright Lizzie became a monster represented "a condition of things so contrary to all that our human life has taught us that our hearts and feelings revolt at the conception." He asked the jury to look at Lizzie, as they had day after day: "have you seen anything that shows the lack of humanly feeling and womanly bearing?"

Robinson effectively deployed gender throughout his closing. When he needed to, as in Lizzie's suspicious and fearless visits to the cellar on the night of the murders, he reminded the jury of her "monthly illness." The prosecution made much of the fact that Lizzie was home when Abby was murdered. Robinson scanned the jury of family men. "I don't know where I would want my daughter to be, than to say that she was at home, attending to the ordinary vocations of life as a dutiful member of the household."

Later in his closing Robinson invoked domesticity to explain how the murderer could have slipped into the house through the unlocked screen door and evaded Lizzie. She was preoccupied,

> Doing just the same as any decent woman does, attending to her work, ironing handkerchiefs, going up and down the stairs, going to the cellar, to the [water] closet. You say these things are not proved. No; but I am taking you into the house just as I would go into your house, for instance, and say, What are your wives doing now? . . . Undoubtedly they are going down cellar for potatoes, going out into the kitchen, to the sink room, here and there.

Of course, Lizzie was no wife and Bridget assumed the burden of kitchen duties in the Borden household.

Robinson seized on other opportunities to exploit gender in ways that were probably effective with the jury. Consider, Robinson asked the jury, Assistant Marshal John Fleet's two visits to Lizzie's bedroom when a scrum of police, neighbors, friends, and doctors took over the house. You saw the "distinction that he wrought in the courtroom . . . , the set of that mustache the firmness of those lips." The manly, handsome Fleet "was up in this young woman's room in the afternoon, attended with some officers, plying her with all sorts of questions in a pretty direct and peremptory way. . . ." Then Robinson appealed to the jurymen: "Is that any way for an officer of the law to deal with a woman in her own house? What would you do with a man—I don't care if he has blue on him—that got into your house and was talking to your wife or your daughter in that way?"

Robinson reproached the Fall River police in general, not just Fleet. They were simply ordinary men attired in blue. "And you do not get the greatest ability in the world inside a policeman's coat." He chided the 125-man force to find the mysterious handle to the alleged murder weapon and "carry it to the British Museum."

If Robinson dressed down the police, he also dressed up other witnesses and suspects. Ice cream peddler Hyman Lubinsky was "an enterprising young man" with an eye out for business as he rode down Second

Street. The stranger seen at the Borden gate around the time of the murders, apparently simply seeking shade from a tree on the sidewalk, became a potential co-conspirator in the crime.

Robinson was not above manipulating evidence and testimony. He claimed the screen door was open for an "hour and a half," not the hour that the trial indicated. More seriously, he misled the jury about the note that Abby allegedly received. Lizzie told Bridget, who told Mrs. Churchill. Robinson claimed that the latter's testimony proved that Abby informed Bridget as well as Lizzie. He quoted Mrs. Churchill out of context. "What did Bridget tell you about Mrs. Borden having a note? She said Mrs. Borden had a note to go and see someone that was sick, and she was dusting the sitting room, and she hurried off and she didn't tell me where she was going, she generally does." Robinson turned to the jury: "You get the idea. Both Bridget and Lizzie had learned from Mrs. Borden that she had a note." Robinson pointed out how Mrs. Churchill's testimony revealed that Bridget related more details than Lizzie about what Mrs. Borden said. Yet no one questioned whether the servant was telling the truth. This misrepresentation of trial testimony marked a low point in Robinson's closing remarks.

Still, he posed many plausible answers to questions raised by the prosecution. Lizzie visited the barn looking for "sinkers and tin or iron to fix a screen." She spent time in the yard *and* the barn. The "groan" and the "scraping" she heard came from the street. Only if someone mounted the stairs looking for Abby would her body be visible at eye level with the floor. The house and rooms were kept under lock and key because of the burglary two years earlier. On the witness stand Martha Chagnon also referred to her stepmother as "Mrs. Chagnon." Robinson poured scorn on the police: "Well, I advised the City Marshall to put a cordon around that [Chagnon] house, so that there will not be another murder there."

Robinson wove folksiness into his arguments as a counterpoise to his sarcasm. The shutters were closed in the guestroom because Abby wanted to shield the carpets from the fading effects of the sun. "I remember with some reflections," Robinson turned wistful, "about my old mother how she looked after the carpets and the boys, that they didn't get the light in." At one point, the Harvard-educated lawyer gave a short history of rag-use in New England households to explain Lizzie's burning of the Bedford cord dress. "In the olden days" the rags were saved because they were used in papermaking. Ragmen went from house to house and purchased the content of bags that families kept. Now, he claimed, papermakers no longer needed rags, and "a common way of getting rid of old things is to put them into the fire and burn them up to save being annoyed and pestered by tramps." Why would tramps "pester" families, however, if there no longer was a market for rags?

Robinson stood on much firmer ground when he reminded the jurymen that the prosecution had not proven major claims presented by District Attorney Moody in his opening statement. The court excluded both Lizzie's inquest testimony and the alleged purchase of prussic acid with evil intent. The jury was not to consider either of these opening claims during its deliberation, Robinson informed them. Nor, under the law, were they to draw any inference from the fact that Lizzie did not testify.

The prosecution had no direct evidence of Lizzie's involvement in the murders. There was no blood except one pinhead-sized spot; its source was obvious, he suggested. There was no weapon, except a "last resort" to the handleless hatchet, which the prosecution presented "timidly and haltingly": It *could* have been the instrument of death. Lizzie did not have exclusive opportunity because the screen door was unhooked. As to motive, all the prosecution presented were the words of cloak maker Hannah Gifford that Lizzie expressed animosity toward her stepmother. Motive in the double murder trapped the prosecution in a bit of a contradiction, Robinson insisted. For they asserted that Lizzie decided "to kill Mrs. Borden because she did not like her, and to kill her father because she liked him but she wanted his money."

The ring that Andrew took to his grave was summoned one last time. Though Emma said that Lizzie gave it to her father ten or fifteen years earlier, Robinson put it in the hands of a "little girl." What the ring meant to Andrew—and to Lizzie—was clear. "He loved her as his child, and the ring stands as the pledge of plighted faith and love, that typifies and symbolizes the dearest relations between father and daughter."

Robinson turned to Emma at one point. He shrewdly tried to preempt the prosecution's argument that the blood bond with Lizzie compromised Emma's testimony. "They will say her sisterly affection carries her along to swing her from the truth." Instead, Robinson offered up

Emma's loyalty to her sister as what should be the natural path of relations. "It is creditable that she does stand by her [Lizzie] and it will take a long time for a man to say in his heart she is untruthful for telling what she does here."

Over the course of his closing Robinson actually presented a defense theory of the crime. The assassin entered the house through the open screen door to kill Andrew. Abby surprised him. Apparently she did not have enough time to leave in response to the note. She had to be sacrificed. Then the fiend hid in the house until Andrew returned, dispatched him and slipped away unseen, carrying away the note and bloody weapon.

Robinson advanced this narrative too aggressively. Then, as if catching himself, just before the noon break he repeated to the jury that their duty was not to judge his theory but the government's. At the beginning of the afternoon session he made the point more forcefully. "We are not bound to furnish you with any theory of it [the crime]. I said at the outset, that is not our duty...." Robinson claimed that his theory was merely to show that someone other than Lizzie had "reasonable opportunity."

Earlier Robinson led the jurymen to believe that Lizzie would hang if found guilty of the crimes. Like the press he interjected an old chestnut: that ineradicable dark chapter in Massachusetts history. "We do not even burn witches now...." (In fact, they were hanged.) He assigned the jury the burden of redeeming Massachusetts' past. Robinson concluded with an appeal to the jurymen's paternal side. "Take it; take care of her as you have and give us promptly your verdict 'not guilty' that she may go home...."

Robinson had earned the praise of the press and surely the respect of the jury for his cross-examination of prosecution witnesses. The *New York Times* claimed, however, that his closing disappointed many in the audience. "They had expected an eloquent address; what they heard was a calm analysis of the evidence." Yet his competent closing, punctuated by humor and ridicule at the expense of the police, suggested the defense's confidence in its case. Moreover, Robinson's performance probably had his desired effect on the jury.

Knowlton's Close

Knowlton confronted his last opportunity to secure the only vindication at hand—a hung jury. After the prosecution's setbacks, he still pursued cross-examination vigorously. Now he wrapped up the case with a well-crafted set of arguments that he delivered with conviction and passion. After two hours even Joe Howard reluctantly acknowledged that "Knowlton's plea is not only ingenious and forcible, but in a certain degree effective."

The district attorney began with the recognition that the defendant held the "rank of a lady." He "hoped" that in presenting his arguments he would never "lose sight of the terrible significance of that fact." He struck an apologetic pose three times at the beginning of his address. Knowlton indulged in a bit of pandering to the jury. Perhaps he overdid it. He described his "painful duty," "this terrible duty," and "the saddest day of my life." Apparently, Knowlton calculated that he needed to acknowledge the reality of what the jury observed in court day after day: from dress to demeanor, Lizzie cultivated the art of Victorian ladyhood. Then he could show that women, even ladies and particularly this lady, were capable of committing grisly crimes.

He launched into a discussion of women's dark side, cobbling together a theory of female criminality from familiar literary sources— even to late nineteenth-century common folk like the jurymen. Though ladies may "lack in strength and coarseness and vigor," he argued, "they make up for it in cunning, in dispatch, in celerity, in ferocity. If their loves are stronger and more enduring than those of men, . . . their hates are more undying, more unyielding, more persistent." He appealed to the "great poet" of the English language, without naming Shakespeare. Knowlton must have had in mind Lady Macbeth, who prodded her husband and king into committing regicide. Knowlton also referred to the widely read Charles Dickens. He did not identify the author or the novel, but simply mentioned a major character who was slain by a woman in *Bleak House*.

The district attorney brought sensational women murder cases very close to home by reminding the jurors of Massachusetts' own Sarah Robinson. She had poisoned "a whole cart load of relatives for the sake of obtaining a miserable pittance of a fortune." Knowlton's opening strategy amounted to trying to wean the jury away from allowing the defendant special standing because of her gender. "You have been educated to believe, you are proud to recognize your loyalty, your fealty to the [female] sex. Gentlemen, that consideration has no place under the oath you have taken." As a hypothetical proposition Knowlton's argument conceivably registered with the jury. But how could they screen out gender when they had seen a prim Christian lady before them for nearly two weeks?

Preparatory to tackling the substance of the case, Knowlton raised another important preliminary issue—circumstantial evidence and the chain that supposedly represented its compulsory form. "Direct evidence is the evidence of a man who sees and hears; circumstantial evidence is all other kinds of evidence." He claimed that "chain" was a "misnomer" for circumstantial evidence. What mattered was a "sufficiency of circumstantial evidence," not an unbroken chain or one whose links were all strong. Knowlton turned to a simple literary reference to make his point. When shipwrecked Robinson Crusoe discovered a footprint, he had sufficient circumstantial evidence that someone else was on his "Island of Despair."

Knowlton now turned to the crime's circumstantial evidence. Typically, he referred to Lizzie as "this woman," "the defendant," and "Lizzie Andrew Borden." In the prosecution's narrative Abby Borden, who "had not an enemy in all the world," was the assassin's target, not Andrew. Knowlton cited the testimony of Assistant Marshal Fleet and cloak maker Hannah Gifford, who described Lizzie's pointed or disparaging statements about Abby. He reminded the jury of the five-year-old corrosive discontent between the sisters and Abby.

Then Knowlton shifted to Emma, professing his sympathy for her plight. In effect, he accused Emma of perjury. He handled her genteelly, however, treating her as a lady who was overcome by loyalty to Lizzie and fear of losing her only sister. Knowlton professed to "admire" the "fidelity of that unfortunate girl to her still more unfortunate sister." Knowlton claimed that he "could not find it in my heart to ask her many questions." Poor Emma was "in the most desperate strait," consumed with fright because "her only sister stood in peril and she must come to the rescue." Knowlton almost forgave Emma for not telling the truth, especially about relations within the family, which were far from "peaceful."

He then returned to Abby's murder; it was not the deed of a thief. "No, Mr. Foreman, there was nothing in those blows but hatred, but hatred and a desire to kill." Something else distinguished the brutality: "The hand that held that weapon was not the hand of masculine strength." Rather the blows came from "the hand of a person strong only in hate and desire to kill." Moreover, sounds carried throughout the narrow house. Was Abby's murder not accompanied with "groaning and screaming?" Did she fall "without a jar?"

Knowlton scoffed at the idea that a phantom murderer entered the house and avoided the "cordon of Lizzie and Bridget." How could such an invader hide in the most "zealously guarded house I ever heard of?" Even the large clothes closet at the top of the stairs, the most likely place for a murderer to conceal himself, was locked.

Similarly, the note represented another fiction. On a busy street no witnesses saw it delivered. Knowlton insisted that "no note came; no note was written; nobody brought a note; nobody was sick." The district attorney seized the opportunity to correct Robinson's misrepresentation of Bridget's testimony about the note, which she only learned of from Lizzie, not directly from Abby, as Robinson asserted.

Knowlton had now addressed the jury for two hours. The court adjourned at 5:05 p.m. until 9 a.m. the next morning, the last day of the trial. "So far as he has gone," the *New York Times* commented on Knowlton, "he has spoken with great force and eloquence." Joe Howard maintained, "Down to the opening of Governor Robinson the bets were 2 to 1 in favor of an acquittal; now they are 2 to 1 in favor of a disagreement." And Knowlton still had three hours of closing arguments to present.

The next morning, Tuesday, June 20, marked the trial's thirteenth and final day. Knowlton offered the prosecution's explanation of Lizzie's need to slay her father. In the process he lapsed into his closing's most serious slip of the tongue. "There may be that in this case which saves us from the idea that Lizzie Andrew Borden planned to kill her father. I hope she did not. I should be slow to believe she did. I should be slow to ask you to believe she did." It was a cumbersome argument about premeditation that the jury may have reduced to Knowlton's "hope" that Lizzie was innocent of killing her father.

Though the district attorney did not stop to disentangle his awkwardly presented point, he did quickly recover the clarity that characterized his closing. Lizzie failed to think through the double murder. "There is cunning in crime, but there is blindness in crime too." Lizzie had not planned to kill Andrew. She saw "no escape" after she dispatched Abby. Given the ill will in the family, Lizzie's father would immediately grasp the murderer's identity. Andrew had to be sacrificed. It was an act of "wicked and dreadful necessity."

He now confronted Lizzie's alleged behavior while Andrew was being butchered. She abandoned ironing a small number of handkerchiefs when she was almost finished. "And you are asked to believe, and it is addressed to your credible understandings as men ... that [she] went out of the house and up in the barn, to the hottest place in Fall River, and there remained during the entire time that was covered by the absent Bridget upstairs." Why was the defense unable to produce a piece of iron that she needed to fix a screen? Knowlton pressed the point; Lizzie could not even identify the screen that required repair. "In all your observation and experience," Knowlton appealed to the twelve men, "have you heard an attempt to create an alibi which was more unreasonable and less within the credence of jurors?"

Yes, but Hyman Lubinsky saw Lizzie coming from the barn, the jurors must have told themselves. Within days of the murders, the police had interviewed Lubinsky twice and did not find him credible. Then Arthur Phillips, Jennings's assistant, questioned Lubinsky on August 22, three days prior to the beginning of the preliminary hearing. Yet the defense did not introduce him as a witness. Furthermore, Knowlton reminded the jury that Lubinsky could not have been scouring the neighborhood for customers. "His cart was empty then [of ice cream] and he was going to have it filled. . . ."

Before he moved on to other defense witnesses, Knowlton paused to stand by Officer William Medley, the defense's punching bag. Did the "gentlemen" of the jury really believe that Medley did not tell the truth? Was it believable that he "can take the oath of God upon his lips and stand upon that stand and face that unfortunate woman and deliberately commit perjury to send her to an ignominious doom [?]" Knowlton insisted defense witnesses were either muddled or simply mistaken about the times when they visited the barn. He brought up "Brownie and Me" only to dismiss them as empty sacks.

Knowlton returned to Lizzie and when she "discovered" her father's body. She sent Bridget for Dr. Bowen and then for Miss Russell and remained in the house unafraid. "A single cry would have alarmed the street and brought crowds to her assistance." Knowlton asked the jury to recall "strong man, Charles Sawyer." He was stationed inside the screen door with "qualms of fear that agitated him." The sign painter locked the cellar door, fearful that the murderer might be skulking there. Lizzie stood alone in the same place.

Knowlton then moved on to what Lizzie wore at the time of the murders, certainly not the dark blue afternoon dress, made of both silk and linen. He fastened on the testimony of Dr. and Mrs. Bowen, questioning their trustworthiness. Knowlton portrayed Dr. Bowen as a witness who "would cut his heart strings before he would say a word against that woman if he could help." Mrs. Bowen contradicted her preliminary hearing testimony about Lizzie's dress. Knowlton feigned sorrow for her. "It may be that you observed that when Mrs. Bowen raised her hand to take her oath it shook like an aspen leaf."

The district attorney next juxtaposed Emma's questionable testimony against Alice Russell's rectitude as to what happened with the Bedford cord on Sunday morning, "while the church bells were ringing people to come to divine worship." First he argued for Miss Russell's integrity. She possessed a "Puritan conscience." A "confidante" of the family, "all the wealth of the Indies could not persuade that woman to twist the inflexion of a voice against" the defendant. Russell testified that Emma was surprised when she saw Lizzie in front of the stove getting ready to burn the Bedford cord. Who was believable—a woman who bore witness "from her conscience" or "from her interest?" He urged the jurors to search their own "consciences and tell me which of these two women you think is entitled to credence." One wonders why Knowlton did not recall Miss Russell at the end of the trial to refute Emma's testimony about the entire Bedford cord incident. Perhaps he didn't want to subject the shaken woman to the distress of further cross-examination. The defense would only claim that Russell didn't remember what Emma said.

Knowlton discussed two more women witnesses near the end of his presentation: Bridget Sullivan and Hannah Reagan. He made a powerful point about class, and by implication about ethnicity, that recalled Andrew Jennings's argument at the preliminary hearing. Lizzie's lawyer had asked, in the "natural course of things," who was more likely to be suspected, the "stranger" or the Christian lady who had led an unblemished life? The way Knowlton turned this argument on its head is worth quoting.

> Now, if you please, supposing those things that have been suggested against Lizzie Borden had been found against Bridget Sullivan, poor, friendless girl? Supposing she had told the wrong stories; supposing she had put up an impossible alibi; supposing she had put up a dress that never was worn that morning, at all, and when the coils were tightening around her had burned a dress up that should not be seen, what would you think of Bridget? Is there one law for Bridget and another for Lizzie? God forbid.

Of course, if the evidence had incriminated Bridget rather than Lizzie, Knowlton would not have been so apologetic about prosecuting her. Nevertheless, Knowlton might have concluded his closing on this high-minded invocation of class to a jury of mostly common men. But, among other things, he needed to defend Hannah Reagan's ravaged integrity.

Knowlton claimed that she would not have told the story of the Borden sisters' quarrel to the *Fall River Globe* if she had known the reporter intended to publish it. The uproar it provoked unnerved her, especially after Lizzie's friends "came around in troops to harass Mrs. Reagan into taking it back." She stood by the "extremely significant" story on the stand in the face of a "slur such as my distinguished friend in courteous words imposed upon her." To be sure, Knowlton was also skilled at clothing sharp points in a gentleman's language, particularly when referring to a lady such as Emma.

As the clock drew toward the noon hour, Knowlton summarized the prosecution's case and assured the jurors that the "wells of mercy" had not gone dry in Massachusetts. Lizzie did not face the death penalty. Now was not the time for mercy. Knowlton finished his closing at 12:05 p.m.

Of the two opening and two closing arguments, Knowlton's was by far the most stirring. Once he had moved beyond his apologies, Knowlton argued compellingly and coherently for Lizzie's guilt. He only misstepped temporarily on the absence of premeditation in Lizzie's murder of Andrew. The *Boston Advertiser* singled out his final "eloquent appeal to the jury." Joe Howard told his legion of readers that Knowlton's performance "entitles him to rank with the ablest advocates of the day." The two district attorneys' hopes must have brightened that Lizzie would not be acquitted. They could not have anticipated what Justin Dewey, the junior justice, had prepared for the jury—and for the prosecution.

Charge and Decision

The court recessed after Knowlton finished and reconvened at 1:45 p.m. Chief Justice Mason informed Lizzie, "It is your privilege to add any word you may desire to say in person to this jury." Lizzie stood and looked directly at the now familiar twelve faces in the jury box: "I am innocent. I leave it to my own counsel to speak for me." Now Justice Dewey unveiled the text of his ninety-minute charge to the jury. In the process, he took his own hatchet to the prosecution's case. One wonders why the justice with the closest ties to the lead defense attorney was assigned to charge the jury. Perhaps Dewey lobbied for the role. Either way, the justice did not disappoint the man responsible for where he sat.

Dewey began by describing his duty, which was defined by Massachusetts statute. It required the court "not to charge juries with respect to matters of fact" but to explain "testimony and the law." The statute prevented judges "from expressing any opinion as to the credibility of witnesses or the strength of evidence." Then came some legal sleight of hand. Dewey issued a torrent of words—an outpouring of law, opinion, and especially highly prejudicial questions. Dewey seemed to forget that he was a judge, not an advocate for the defense. Even the pro-defense *New York Times* acknowledged, "Clearly he departed from his role and went beyond the limits of judicial action. Dewey's expressions of opinion were sometimes subtle, sometimes direct."

He did clarify legal issues: what constituted first-degree murder and premeditation; the distinction between essential and helpful facts; and the legal definition of reasonable doubt, for example. At the same time

Dewey did not shrink from interjecting his opinions. He accomplished this, while trying to cover his tracks, by proposing leading questions and comments that poisoned the jury's charge and foiled Knowlton's closing. Three examples among many should suffice to suggest Dewey's judicial overreaching: cloak maker Hannah Gifford's testimony, the note that Lizzie claimed Abby received, and Lizzie's unburdening of herself to Alice Russell on the night before the murders.

According to Dewey, the prosecution relied on Gifford's testimony about Lizzie's harsh words for Abby "largely as the basis" for its claim of bad blood in the family. Dewey's position diminished or rendered completely irrelevant testimony of Bridget Sullivan, Assistant Marshal Fleet, and Emma herself from the inquest, which Knowlton quoted at the trial. Dewey questioned the "significance attached" to Mrs. Gifford's testimony. Lizzie's words represented the "language of a young woman and not a philosopher or jurist." And young women were in the "habit" of using "intense expression" that could easily be misinterpreted. In the next breath, Dewey summoned dressmaker Mary Raymond and reminded the jurors of how she described the three Borden women sewing together with her in the guestroom.

Dewey was still in his opening act. He plunged headlong into one of the knottiest problems the defense faced—the note allegedly sent to lure Abby from the house. The prosecution claimed Lizzie lied. Dewey outlined their argument. Then he posed a series of questions to the jury, seeming to advocate reasonable doubt as he proceeded. What motive did Lizzie have to "invent" such a note? "Would it not have answered every purpose to have her say, and would it not have been more natural for her to say simply, that her stepmother had gone out on an errand or to make a call?" She would then have no note to explain. Dewey suggested that the jury seriously weigh the defense's theory that a hidden assassin carried it away with him against the prosecution's claim that Lizzie was a lying murderess.

Dewey sketched the prosecution's argument about the note in two sentences—one short, the other long. They totaled less than 90 words. He devoted 500 words to laying out the case for the defense and concluding with the "chain" of essential evidence, which was actually metaphor, not law. Dewey shackled the jury to his compulsory chain, requiring each essential fact to be unbroken by reasonable doubt. As to the note, "if one essential fact fails to be proved, the connection is broken, a gap arises in the process of proof and it cannot be legally affirmed that the conclusion aimed at [Lizzie's guilt] is established beyond a reasonable doubt."

The argumentative justice questioned Lizzie's "presentiments" to Miss Russell. He set aside the defense's explanation of Lizzie's "monthly illness" as the cause of her agitated state. He wanted to know if the jury considered it "reasonable and probable that a person meditating the perpetration of a great crime, would, the day before, predict to a friend, either in form or in substance, the happening of that disaster." That, to be sure, was not quite the point that the prosecution made. Lizzie's "foreboding," in the context of her father's supposed problems and the strange characters lurking about the backyard, was calculated to divert suspicion away from her.

Near the end of Dewey's charge, Knowlton challenged the justice when he took issue with Mrs. Reagan's testimony. The district attorney knew that his powerful closing argument had been thwarted. Dewey grasped the consequences of his charge. Never one to shy away from the press, he was interviewed the day after the verdict. "I was satisfied when I made my charge to the jury that the verdict would be not guilty," he informed the *Boston Globe*, "although one cannot always tell what a jury will do."

Joe Howard saw the significance of Dewey's handiwork. "The judge's charge was remarkable," he wrote; "it was a plea for the innocent." Not surprisingly, the jury acted swiftly. They reached a unanimous decision in ten minutes. Then they sat for an hour to make a show that they had actually discussed the evidence and arguments that had occupied them for almost two weeks. The jury's action suggests how, from Lizzie's inquest testimony to the prussic acid evidence to Dewey's charge, the court grounded the prosecution's case whenever it threatened to take flight. The jurymen did not even trouble themselves with the more than forty exhibits in the deliberation room. Dewey had all but excused them from handling crucial exhibits. He called into question the prosecution's medical witnesses, even though the defense hadn't produced its own experts to challenge their testimony. And when it came to exhibits such as the broken hatchet and Andrew's dented skull, he seemed to discourage the jury from attempting to match up blade and blow: "You may think you can apply them to each other and judge as well as an expert."

The jury returned to the courtroom shortly after 4:30 p.m. Before the clerk could ask, "What say you, Mr. Foreman?" he was interrupted. An eager Charles I. Richards blurted out, "Not guilty." The courtroom erupted in applause with Lizzie's partisans waving their handkerchiefs. She dropped to the chair, her head and arm stretched forward to the railing as she cried. According to the *Boston Advertiser*, "The stately judges looked straight ahead at the bare walls." Julian Ralph claimed in the *New York Sun*, "Judge Blodgett's face contorted with violence of his effort to repress his strong emotion." Sheriff Wright did nothing but shed tears.

The jurors surely congratulated themselves. After the trial they met at a studio in their best three-piece suits. They sat and stood for a group photograph, a memento of a moment when they stepped out of obscurity, into the early summer sunlight, and through a publically charged experience they would remember for the rest of their lives. Less than three weeks after the trial, one prominent juror, accompanied by another man, presented the group photograph to Lizzie. Surviving evidence indicates that she wrote letters of gratitude to each member of the jury.

Reaction

Since the major newspapers believed in Lizzie's innocence from the start, they welcomed the trial's outcome and praised the justices. "The acquittal of the most unfortunate and cruelly persecuted woman," the *New York Times* huffed, despite its criticism of Justice Dewey, "was by its promptness, in effect, a condemnation of police authorities of Fall River and of the legal officers who secured the indictment." Julian Ralph summoned a now hackneyed journalistic historical reference. Lizzie's acquittal demonstrated that "witches are out of fashion in Massachusetts and that no one is to be executed there on suspicion and on parrot-like police testimony." Persecuted Lizzie "was no longer friendless," Howard enthused. The *Boston Globe* showered praise on everyone. "The Borden Jury was as prompt in action as the court itself," it applauded. "Massachusetts lawyers and Massachusetts judges gained a reputation throughout the country that will not soon be lost."

Closer to Fall River the *Providence Journal*, Andrew Borden's favorite newspaper and the most widely read daily in Bristol County, adopted a more skeptical position. Its reporters expected a hung jury. As one put it, "The verdict of the jury was not in accordance with my opinion, not in accordance with my expectations, not in accordance with my views." Another reporter expressed his surprise at the verdict. "I did not expect conviction but an acquittal was farthest from my thoughts."

In Fall River, one reporter claimed, people were "surprised and indignant." The Irish-controlled *Globe* never reconciled itself to the verdict. "The 'THING' That Butchered the Bordens Still at Large," a *Globe* headline ridiculed the jury's decision three days after Lizzie's acquittal. On the opposite side of the political spectrum, the *Evening News* embraced Lizzie's innocence and her return home.

Lizzie's acquittal elated the women's rights leaders who had protested her arrest. Susan B. Fessenden, president of the Massachusetts Chapter of the WCTU, told the press that the trial was "one of the most surprising revelations of the possibilities of gross injustice. . . . Is she guilty? No, a thousand times no. There has not been a shred of evidence of guilt." Lucy Stone, former president of the Massachusetts Woman Suffrage Association, said that "every testimony brought against her by the government has been refuted. . . ." She urged Lizzie to "stay in Fall River." Mary Livermore, the new president of the Suffrage Association, sent Lizzie a telegram the day after the trial: "Thank God, dear Lizzie, that you are acquitted. Everybody is rejoicing and the wires are freighted with the good news." In the days after the trial, supporters from around the country inundated Lizzie with letters of support. Cranks added to the volume of correspondence.

Hosea Knowlton also received his share of letters from across the country, many from lawyers offering accolades for his closing argument. He and Marshal Hilliard were also the targets of letters from indignant correspondents, some of whom threatened violence. In the fall of 1893, the Massachusetts voters elected Knowlton attorney general. They reelected him five times, significant acknowledgment of his dutiful performance at the trial and some consolation for the judicial intervention that secured Lizzie's acquittal.

The court's actions did not escape criticism. In his *Collection of Articles Concerning the Borden Case* (1894), based on letters to the *Boston Advertiser*, retired Massachusetts District Court Judge Charles G. Davis spared no words in criticizing Justice Dewey's charge to the jury. He accused the judge of "arguing the case upon the evidence to the jury," precisely what Dewey said he could not do. "It was not the prisoner but the Commonwealth which did not have a fair trial." Dewey encouraged "the jury to distrust every important item of evidence offered by the prosecution in the case." Davis also claimed that the two evidentiary rulings confounded nearly all the members of the Massachusetts Bar.

Professor John Wigmore, of the Northwestern University Law School and a renowned scholar on evidentiary law, also examined the trial. In an essay, "The Borden Case," that appeared in the *American Law Review* in 1893, Wigmore gave no quarter to the court. He agreed, for example, with Judge Davis: The court's decisions on Lizzie's inquest testimony and the prussic acid evidence were simply wrong. "Is there any lawyer in these United States," Wigmore asked, "who has a scintilla of a doubt, not merely that her counsel fully informed the accused of her rights, but that they talked over the expediencies, and that he allowed her to go on the stand because he deliberately concluded that it was the best policy for her, by so doing, to avoid all appearances of concealment or guilt?"

The Fall River police closed their investigation after the trial. They had no credible suspects in hand and no belief they would find one. Andrew Jennings claimed in 1894 that he had "found a clue that promised to reveal all" about the case. Jennings said he worked "diligently on it for two months" only to arrive at a dead end. The crime remained "a puzzling mystery" to him. Judge Dewey had used the words "mystery" and "mysterious" in his charge to the jury. For many on The Hill "mystery" served as code for "I don't want to talk about the crime," at least in public. Yet Fall River had to deal with the return of its now most famous, or infamous, native bloom.

Epilogue

When the jury acquitted Lizzie, she was one month shy of turning thirty-three years of age. She had lived half of her allotted days. She died in 1927, before she reached her sixty-seventh birthday. A detailed examination of those decades falls beyond the scope of this study. Yet some salient facts about her life after the trial help round out the preceding account. Lizzie returned to Fall River yearning for acceptance, respect, privacy—and a home on The Hill. She fulfilled only the last long-standing desire.

Lizzie became a stranger in her native country. Her acquittal constituted a kind of public vindication of the Bordens, of The Hill, of Spindle City. Still, in so many ways Lizzie had provoked unwanted scrutiny on the world the Borden clan and their associates had created. Then, too, reasonable doubt had secured Lizzie's acquittal but it had not erased suspicion that she was in some way implicated in the crime if not the actual axe murderess. Many former friends and acquaintances shunned Lizzie rather than go on with life on The Hill and in the Central Congregational Church under the pretense that the earth had not shifted. Moreover, off The Hill Lizzie became Fall River's sideshow, its curio, a spectacle wherever she went. The Borden vein of obstinacy ran deep. Lizzie refused to leave Fall River, which would have been received with relief and also as tacit admission of guilt.

The sisters could not return to Second Street. The house had become a macabre magnet for visitors to Fall River. Hacks greeted trains from Boston, offering travelers a close-up view of the house. A week after the acquittal, Lizzie and Emma purchased a large Victorian in the bosom of the coveted Hill. They moved during the first week of September. Lizzie called their new house "Maplecroft." She eventually had the name engraved on the face of the top step to their new abode, an ornate gesture at odds with the sensibility cultivated by Hilltoppers. After all, the roomy Victorian house fell well short of a mansion, even after substantial additions were made to the back of the dwelling. The sisters found no respite from the plague of hackers who added a stop at Maplecroft to Second Street for their out-of-town customers.

Before Lizzie moved to The Hill members of the Central Congregational Church signaled that she was no longer welcome. After the trial Sunday crowds gathered outside the church hoping to catch sight of her. She did not appear until the end of July, chaperoned by Dr. Seabury Bowen and Charles Holmes. Worshippers had vacated the pews in front of hers. That evening she showed up for services escorted by Mrs. Charles Holmes. Then she stopped attending Central Congregational or, it appears, any house of worship at all.

Following her acquittal, members of the Christian Endeavor and the WCTU from across the country inundated Lizzie with letters of support. Members of her local sorority reacted differently. Many distanced themselves from Lizzie. She also perceived slights where none existed. In June 1894, a revealing controversy erupted concerning what happened to Fall River's WCTU.

The local president of the organization told the *Boston Advertiser* that Andrew Borden had permitted the members to sublet their rooms, which helped reduce the monthly rent. Now the society would no longer have that privilege. The president paid a call on Lizzie, who refused to see her. The *Fall River Globe* played up the incident. "Lizzie Borden Turns a Cold Shoulder on Former Associates," one headline proclaimed. Another stirred the pot: "That Bounce Given by Lizzie Borden to Her Tenants Has Set the Whole Town to Talk Again."

The Republican *Evening News* disputed the reports of Lizzie's mean-spirited retaliation against her former Christian sisters. The *Globe*, it claimed, misstated the facts: "That Miss Borden never ordered the society out, as alleged; that had the Union had a lease, as stated, it could not have been forced to vacate; and third, that, indirectly, the Borden sisters were practically contributing $120.00 a year to the work of the association." Of course, it was Charles Cook, who continued as manager of the Borden building, and not Lizzie who directly told the WCTU that they would no longer be permitted to sublet their rooms. The president claimed Cook repudiated a recent promise of a seven-year lease. They now had use of the rooms for only three years at a rent they could not afford. The women were obliged to find cheaper quarters.

Lizzie and Emma could not stroll downtown without exciting Fall Riverites as if the circus had come to town. Two weeks after the acquittal, the sisters visited Charles Cook, who served as their financial adviser. The *Fall River Herald* described what happened. "It did not take long to pass the word that Lizzie Borden was on the street. Out of offices and stores rushed the clerks, and people appeared in upper windows, all curiously watching the movements of the celebrated people." The sisters braced for more hostile than curious scrutiny when they left. "The street hoodlums fell into their wake and when the party returned up Main Street, there was a small crowd of urchins following them." The sisters found refuge in Dr. Bowen's house.

On The Hill, neighborhood kids sometimes pestered the sisters. They rang the doorbell at night and ran away. Or they tied the door and threw sand or gravel at the windows. At other times the house became the target of rotten eggs and Lizzie the object of "vile names." She complained to police, who were unable to make arrests.

The *Fall River Globe* added accelerant to anti-Lizzie emotions in Fall River. Within two months of Lizzie's acquittal, reporter Edwin Porter published the first book on the case based on the articles he had written while covering the trial for the *Globe*. Despite its substantial flaws, *Fall River Tragedy: A History of the Borden Murders* stood for decades as the major account of the crime and the trial. Like Porter, the *Globe* was convinced of Lizzie's guilt. It commemorated the anniversary of the murders with carefully crafted headlines that fostered this conviction throughout Spindle City. On August 4, 1893, the *Globe* announced: "One Year Ago Today the Borden Murders Startled and Astounded the Civilized World and Yet the Murderer Is Free to Walk the Street, or Visit the Scene of the Carnage." In 1900 the *Globe* produced a more biting headline: "Eight Long Years, Since Justice Was Foiled in Borden Butchery, Lizzie Sees That Her Father's Grave Is Kept Green, but She Hasn't Paid That $5,000 Reward Yet."

The *Globe*'s anniversary onslaught continued until 1914, when an influential Irish priest prevailed on the paper's directors to abandon their more than two-decade-old tradition. Yet for Lizzie, the *Globe*'s yearly account and Porter's book confirmed old and kindled new sentiment in Fall River that she had given justice the slip. The newspaper and the book shaped local opinion. Beyond Fall River, however, Lizzie retained support among thousands of women who had rallied to her side.

After many people on The Hill withdrew from Lizzie, she retreated from public life in Spindle City to the private world of Maplecroft, where she enjoyed her Boston terriers, watched birds in her yard, fed squirrels, and read in her library. Lizzie's coachman drove her around Fall River and the countryside with curtains frequently drawn. Shortly after the turn of the century Lizzie purchased a car and her coachman became her chauffeur. Lizzie came to cherish her single life and, like a New Woman, her autonomy. But she had not earned her independence. And unlike New Women she boasted no educational or professional accomplishments.

Often Lizzie escaped Fall River on visits to Providence, Boston, New York, and Washington, D.C. She stayed at the best hotels and ate at premier restaurants. Above all, she indulged in her love of theater. Had she been more attractive and not burdened with her background's moral reservations about a life in the theater, Lizzie, the woman of many faces, might have been an actress. The trial offered a taste of the theatrical.

Lizzie was clearly taken with stage performers, especially women. Her relationship with a well-known actress contributed to Lizzie's permanent estrangement from Emma. Nance O'Neil (born Gertrude Lamson) was single and fourteen years younger than Lizzie. By the fall of 1904, Lizzie had come to know the thirty-year-old actress very well. Their association appears to have been nothing more than a friendship; some have speculated otherwise. O'Neil performed in two plays in Fall River between October 15 and November 1, 1904. Lizzie entertained the cast at Maplecroft, and the celebration stretched deep into the night, scandalizing some on The Hill. It was too much for Emma. She resolved to leave Maplecroft for good, though she did not actually move out until the following June.

As Emma indicated to a *Boston Post* reporter in 1913, she had been considering leaving Lizzie for several years and had sought the counsel of Reverend Buck. "I did not go until conditions became unbearable." Emma failed to specify the nature of those conditions. They certainly involved conflicting personalities and Lizzie's over-attachment to theater people. Of Maplecroft, Emma vowed never "to set foot in that place again." She kept her word. To the *Boston Post* reporter's question about

Lizzie, Emma responded: "Queer? Yes, Lizzie was queer, but guilty on that terrible charge made against her—no—emphatically, No."

Surprisingly, the sisters held on to their Second Street horror house for twenty-five years. They rented it to tenants who put up with endless prying visitors. The sisters finally sold the house in 1918. In such financial matters, Charles Cook served as the sisters' go-between.

Emma moved between Fall River and Providence, finally settling in Newmarket, New Hampshire, by the early 1920s. In the meantime, Lizzie went on with life at Maplecroft, where two maids served her, and her chauffeur stood on call. She also continued the purchase of property on the sides of and across the street from Maplecroft. These acquisitions of land and houses had actually begun before Emma moved from Maplecroft and lasted until 1926, a year before Lizzie died. Suffering from a self-described "nervous condition," Lizzie's purchases strike one as an attempt to control her surroundings.

After her death, Lizzie's maids and chauffeur expressed their fondness for her. She was not above kindness to them and some of the neighborhood children whose families remained friendly toward her. Those who knew Lizzie claimed she quietly helped students pay for college. Lizzie's life after her acquittal perhaps represents an argument against the strong circumstantial evidence that she was a vicious axe murderess. Over the course of her life after the trial, she offered no hints of guilt, expressed no twinges of remorse, committed no acts of violence. She lived a mostly quiet life as a well-to-do spinster, albeit a nerve-racked one. Could her secret guilt have been the source of that condition? We will never know.

What we do know is that one-time murderesses who achieve a specific objective with calculated actions fill the annals of crime literature. Moreover, Lizzie displayed aspects of a dissociative personality, a capacity to detach herself from reality, which she demonstrated to police immediately after the murders. She seems not to have allowed the permanent rupture with Emma—her lifelong confidante, her protector, her deliverer at the trial—to interfere with the enjoyment of wealth. There is nothing in criminology that suggests the moral necessity of a tortured conscience in a murderess of Lizzie's profile. In other words, on her psychic terrain Lizzie could have avoided the kind of tormenting guilt of Raskolnikov, the axe murderer in Dostoevsky's *Crime and Punishment.*

Lizzie died on June 1, 1927, less than two months short of her sixty-seventh birthday. There was no funeral. An Episcopal minister from the Church of the Ascension on Rock Street read biblical passages that had been preselected by Lizzie. Verses were sung from her favorite hymn, "My Ain Countrie," that had also been chosen by Lizzie. A hearse transported the body to Oak Grove Cemetery. Lizzie was interred next to her father, with a simple stone engraved "Lizbeth." Emma was too ill to travel from New Hampshire. She had become so disaffected from Lizzie that she may not have returned to Fall River anyway. Emma died nine days after Lizzie and was buried in the Borden plot.

At the time of the sisters' deaths, the industrial order that the Bordens, Durfees, and others had built from the labor and lives of immigrants had begun its own spiral toward demise. Lizzie and Emma were spared the worst. The Great Depression arrived ahead of schedule in Spindle City. The closure of mills gathered force in the four years after the sisters' deaths. Scores of smokestacks no longer blackened the sky with their constant plumes of soot. A death rattle echoed through mills that hung on. As early as 1931 the city raised the white flag of insolvency. The State Finance Board ran Fall River for a decade. Few people referred to the place as Spindle City anymore.

Rather, Fall River endured in American cultural memory as Lizzie Borden's hometown. The famous rhyme "Forty Whacks" secured that legacy. Fall River schoolchildren had recited the ditty long before 1924, when Edmund L. Pearson first published it. A Harvard-educated New York City librarian turned true crime writer, Pearson helped revive interest in the Borden case and tilt public opinion against Lizzie. Absorbed by and angered about the case, Pearson included important Borden chapters in his crime books between 1924 and 1937. He wrote with flair and assailed Lizzie and her defenders the way Joe Howard had championed her innocence, though in better if biting and biased prose. Still, Pearson only initiated a new national awareness of the Borden case. How "Forty Whacks" infiltrated American popular culture and how Lizzie persisted as one of the country's most notorious alleged murderers are subjects worthy of another book.

CHRONOLOGY

1822	Andrew Jackson Borden born in Fall River, Massachusetts
1823	Sarah Anthony Morse born in Somerset, Massachusetts
1845	Andrew Borden and Sarah Morse marry at Central Congregational Church
1851	Emma Lenora Borden born in Fall River
1860	Lizzie Andrew Borden born in Fall River
1863	Sarah Morse Borden dies
1865	Andrew Borden marries Abby Durfee Gray (b. 1828) at the Central Congregational Church
1872	Family moves to 92 Second Street
1875–1877	Lizzie attends Fall River High School, completing only two years
1878	Andrew retires from Borden, Almy & Co (furniture and funeral business) to manage his investments
1887	Lizzie is confirmed in the Central Congregational Church and begins her society work
1887	Andrew buys Abby's mother's share of house
1887	Andrew gives Lizzie and Emma Ferry Street house
1890	Andrew pays for Lizzie's Grand Tour and Emma exchanges bedrooms upon her sister's return
1891	Day robbery of Borden house
July 15, 1892	Andrew repurchases Ferry Street house for $5,000
August 4, 1892	Murders of Andrew and Abby Borden
August 9–11, 1892	Inquest; Lizzie arrested
August 12, 1892	Lizzie arraigned and jailed in Taunton
August 25–September 1, 1892	Preliminary Hearing: Lizzie judged "probably guilty" and returned to Taunton jail
September 1892	Women's religious groups and reformers rally to Lizzie's support
October 10, 1892	*Boston Globe* Henry Trickey scandal
November 15, 1892	Grand jury in Taunton begins murder investigation and on the 21st adjourns with no indictment

December 1, 1892	Grand jury reconvenes and Alice Russell testifies about Lizzie's burning of a dress
December 2, 1892	Grand jury indicts Lizzie
May 8, 1893	Lizzie arraigned in New Bedford
June 5–20, 1893	Superior Court Trial and acquittal
August 1893	Edwin Porter publishes *Fall River Tragedy: A History of the Borden Murders*
September 1893	Lizzie and Emma move to The Hill
February 1897	Reports of alleged shoplifting in Providence
June 1905	Emma Borden moves from Maplecroft
June 1918	Second Street home sold
June 1, 1927	Lizzie dies at age of sixty-six and leaves an estate of $347,930.76
June 10, 1927	Emma dies at age of seventy-six and leaves an estate worth $447,009.35
1931	Fall River declares bankruptcy

BIBLIOGRAPHICAL ESSAY

Note from the Series Editors: The following bibliographic essay contains the major primary and secondary sources the author consulted for this volume. We have asked all authors in the series to omit formal citations in order to make our volumes more readable, inexpensive, and appealing for students and general readers. In adopting this format, Landmark Law Cases and American Society follows the precedent of a number of highly regarded and widely consulted series.

The basic primary sources for this study are the inquest, preliminary hearing, and Superior Court trial transcripts, which comprise 3,000 pages of testimony. Writers on the case have not always used all of the sources, often skipping over the preliminary hearing, for example. For a time it was not readily available. The published version of the trial is so flawed as to render it virtually useless. Edmund Pearson, *The Trial of Lizzie Borden* (Garden City, NY: Doubleday, Doran, 1937) was the most accessible source for the trial. It was reprinted in 1987, with a brief introduction by Alan M. Dershowitz in *The Notable Trials Library*. For publication, Pearson had to reduce the 2,000-page transcript. He strongly believed in Lizzie's guilt. He left out crucial material, sometimes to the detriment of Lizzie's defense.

Very reliable transcripts of the inquest and trial are available at Lizzie AndrewBorden.com. This site is maintained by Stefani Koorey, Ph.D., in Fall River. I have checked her transcripts against other sources to confirm their reliability. The first volume of the inquest, which contains the testimony of Bridget Sullivan and Lizzie, has been lost. But Lizzie's testimony was published by the *New Bedford Evening Standard* on June 12, 1893, while the trial was underway. It has been widely reprinted. In addition to the judicial proceedings, LizzieAndrewBorden.com also has a transcript of police witness statements as well as the wills of Lizzie, Emma, and John Morse. A transcript of the preliminary hearing is available from Koorey's Pear Tree Press, a reference to the tree that grew in the Bordens' backyard.

Joyce Williams et al., *Lizzie Borden: A Case Book of Family and Crime* (Bloomington, IN: T.I.S. Publications Division, 1980) contains important primary sources. These include police arrest records for the week in August 1892 when Lizzie was charged with the crime; Assistant Marshal Fleet's notes of interviews with Lizzie, Bridget, and John Morse; the *Fall River Daily Herald*'s early reports on the crime; and the *New York Times* coverage of the trial. There are three bulky collections of newspaper articles. For the local dailies see Philip T. Silvia, Jr., ed., *Victorian Vistas: Fall River, 1886–1900* (Fall River, MA: R. E.

Smith, 1988). In the *Lizzie Borden Sourcebook* (Boston: Branden Publishing, 1992; rpt. 2010) David Kent in collaboration with Robert A. Flynn produced a large volume of wide-ranging newspaper articles covering all the events down to Lizzie's acquittal and its aftermath. The collection is especially strong on Boston dailies. Like Joyce Williams, Kent failed to include the *Fall River Globe*. Other writers have over-relied on the *Globe* for its biting comments. One needs to read all three of the local dailies as well as also consult the *Providence Journal* and the Boston and New York newspapers. In *Chronicling America*, the Library of Congress has made available for the researcher hundreds of newspapers from across the country. As of this writing New England newspapers are almost totally absent from the project. See http.www.chroniclingAmerica .loc.gov.

A very valuable source of information on the Borden case is a collection of District Attorney Hosea Knowlton's papers. See Michael Martins and Dennis A. Binette, eds., *The Commonwealth of Massachusetts vs. Lizzie A. Borden: The Knowlton Papers, 1892–1893* (Fall River, MA: Fall River Historical Society, 1994). The Fall River Historical Society possesses other important primary sources, principally Marshal Rufus Hilliard's "Journal" and the papers of Andrew J. Jennings, known as the "Hip-bath Collection," a reference to how Lizzie's lawyer stored the papers. The society has a "proprietary claim" on these collections and restricts access. The curators intend to publish volumes based on the papers of Hilliard and Jennings. We do have a description and some transcriptions of Jennings's material from someone who was offered access more than twenty years ago. See Barbara M. Ashton, "The Hip-Bath Collection: How It Influenced the Legend of Lizzie Borden," in Jules R. Ryckebusch, ed., *Proceedings: Lizzie Borden Conference* (Fall River MA: Bristol Community College, 1993), 211–221.

Finally Leonard Rebello, *Lizzie Borden Past and Present* (Fall River, MA: Al-Zach Press, 1999) is a bulky essential "handbook" about the Bordens, the case, and Lizzie's life after the trial. Rebello does not offer a narrative. Rather he compiles information from primary sources such as numerous newspaper and journal articles; he also maps both the Bordens' Second Street neighborhood and Lizzie's street on The Hill, and offers the researcher countless other pieces of information.

There are scores of secondary works on the Borden case, many of them fictional and others self-published or originating with obscure presses. Only a handful of Borden books warrant commentary; they range widely in quality. The curators of the Fall River Historical Society authored the most recent volume; it is 1,000 pages long. Michael Martins and Dennis A. Binette, *Parallel Lives: A Social History of Lizzie A. Borden and Her Fall River* (Fall River, MA: Fall River Historical Society, 2010) does not deal with the trial or directly with Lizzie's guilt or innocence. Rather the mammoth, well-documented, and lavishly illustrated book focuses on Lizzie's life and offers elaborate, sometimes excruciating, detail about legions of people and social activities on The Hill, where the historical society is located. Among the work's signal achievements, it offers the best biographical information on Lizzie that we are likely to achieve, especially on her life after acquittal. I found the work especially helpful in writing chapter 2. The book is assertively and sweepingly revisionist, challenging every major point that has been made about Lizzie and Andrew. Long before the authors claim on page 993 that "no evidence of her guilt has ever surfaced," we know that they are convinced of Lizzie's innocence.

David Kent in the sensationally titled *Forty Whacks: New Evidence in the Life and Legend of Lizzie Borden* (Emmaus, PA: Yankee Press, 1992), agreed with the curators. Kent felt betrayed by Edmund Pearson's edited *Trial of Lizzie Borden*. Kent's reading of the record (excluding the preliminary hearing, which he skipped) led him to believe Lizzie was innocent. Like most writers, he had to come up with a new angle. Thus, he argued for the alleged "Harvard cover-up" of the single piece of gilt in Abby Borden's autopsy photograph.

A year earlier Arnold Brown proposed a much more provocative theory. In *Lizzie Borden: The Legend, the Truth, the Final Chapter* (Nashville: Rutledge Hill Press, 1991), Brown argued for a more expansive conspiracy. Lizzie, the prosecution, and the defense all knew that Andrew's alleged illegitimate son, a William Borden, committed the murders. Lizzie wanted to protect her father's reputation. She agreed to go through the inquest and preliminary hearing to protect her father's name. The secret grand jury would then fail to indict her. Brown did a lot of research with his conclusion already in hand. He read the court transcripts, often selectively, sometimes perceptively, and frequently perversely. For example, he suggested that Lizzie, not Knowlton, was in control at the inquest. Brown's book was published as a Dell paperback with blood splattered over the cover. The sensational book mixes fact and fiction.

In 1992 Bristol Community College in Fall River organized a conference to commemorate the centennial of the crimes. The papers were published in Ryckebusch, ed., *Proceedings, Lizzie Borden Conference*. On the whole the essays are disappointing but some raise important questions and the description of the "Hip-bath Collection" is valuable. The book also has an excellent annotated bibliography.

A helpful portrait of Borden family life, first published in 1984, has been widely read by students. See Stephen Nissenbaum, "The Lizzie Borden Murders," in R. Jackson Wilson, et al., *The Pursuit of Liberty*, 3rd edition, 2 vols. (New York: Harper Row, 1996), 2: 164–182. It contains some glaring factual errors such as two different, incorrect ages for Andrew. Frank Spiering, *Lizzie* (New York: Dorsett Books, 1984) found another sensational hook. He claimed that Emma, not Lizzie, committed the murders. Emma slipped back into Fall River from vacationing in Fairhaven, fifteen miles away, and killed Abby and Andrew. Then she managed to return to Fairhaven without leaving a trail. In Spiering's telling, Lizzie endured accusation and trial to protect Emma. The book shades over into fiction.

Massachusetts Superior Court Judge Robert Sullivan wrote a solid book on the Borden case that focused on legal issues. In *Goodbye Lizzie Borden* (Brattleboro, VT: Stephen Green Press, 1974), Sullivan concentrated on the trial and was sharply critical of the court, especially the two evidentiary rulings. Sullivan even argued that Lizzie's inquest testimony would be admitted in 1974, that is, even after the evidence rulings of the Warren Supreme Court (1953–1969) such as Miranda (1966). The major flaw of Sullivan's valuable book is that it is top-heavy with extensive quotations from the trial and short on context.

Perhaps the book on the case most read and referred to by casual readers and academic nonspecialists is Victoria Lincoln, *A Private Disgrace: Lizzie Borden by Daylight* (New York: G. P. Putnam's Sons, 1967). The book was a selection of the Book of the Month Club and it won the Edgar Allan Poe Best Fact Crime Book Award in 1967. Lincoln was a Fall River native and a novelist. *A Private Disgrace* is very well written. Unfortunately, her novelistic skills were not always put to good use. Her book is filled with imaginative leaps and abundant speculation. Her novelty was the claim that Lizzie committed the crimes while suffering from the effects of temporal lobe epilepsy. Lincoln grew up on The Hill and drew on her "insider" knowledge—stories that she had heard about Lizzie growing up and that she uncritically accepted as true. I have found serious factual errors in *A Private Disgrace* that raise questions about how carefully she read key sources. For example, she claims that drugstore clerk Eli Bence stood outside the house and below a window to identify Lizzie's voice when police took him to Second Street. She apparently did not read the entire inquest testimony, which establishes clearly that he was brought into the doorway of the kitchen and made a visual and voice identification of Lizzie. Among other things, Lincoln asserts that the jury was all Yankee when, as we have seen, there was one Irishman among the twelve men.

Edward Radin was a true crime writer of note. He conducted a great deal of research in Fall River, and published a well-written, informative book: *Lizzie Borden: The Untold Story* (New York: Simon & Schuster, 1961). Radin attacked Edmund Pearson, who had replaced the *Fall River Globe*'s Edwin Porter as the leading authority on the Borden case. Radin's good work was marred by his conclusion that Bridget Sullivan had committed the murders and Lizzie was innocent. Bridget had no motive and no opportunity to kill Abby, though Radin devised timelines that suggested the servant did.

An interesting defense of Lizzie appeared with the publication of Arthur S. Phillips, *The Phillips History of Fall River*, 3 volumes (Fall River, MA: Dover Press, 1944–1946). In volume three (97–109) Phillips, the junior lawyer on Andrew Jennings's legal team, described himself as the only remaining survivor of all the "professionals" who participated in the trial. Yet more than fifty years after the crime, he surprisingly added only a bit of detail to the theory that Robinson laid out at the trial: a boy came to the side door with a note for Abby; the killer entered the house by the same unlocked door; Abby hadn't left the house yet; he killed her and hid in the very small closet at the bottom of the stairs, butchered Andrew, and escaped undetected. The killer was most likely someone the prickly businessman had angered.

Phillps's defense of the deceased Lizzie was in part a response to how public opinion, both within and beyond Fall River, had swelled against her over the decades. His argument for her innocence may also be considered as a reply to the work of Edmund L. Pearson. Pearson wrote extensively on the case, and he did so with verve and wit. He wrote a long introduction to his edited transcript of *The Trial of Lizzie Borden* in 1937. This was preceded by chapters of up to 119 pages in his works: *Five Murders* (Garden City, NY: Doubleday, Doran, 1928); *Murder at Smutty Nose and Other Murders* (New York: Page, 1926); and *Studies in Murder* (Garden City, NY: McMillan, 1924). The last volume published the rhyme "Forty Whacks." Though Pearson did his own research, in many respects his work represented a more graceful, wry retelling and filling-out of what Edwin H. Porter had said in *The Fall River Tragedy: A History of the Borden Murders* (Fall River, MA: Press of J. D. Monroe, 1893). Pearson made some claims that I have been unable to substantiate. For instance, he said that a group of ministers met with the justices and called for a fair trial for Lizzie.

A handful of writers have focused on gender in the trial with varied results. The first to raise gender issues was Kathryn Allamong Jacob, "Why She Couldn't Have Done It, Even If She Did," *American Heritage* (February 1978): 42–53. Jacob's sketchy essay briefly discusses popular perceptions of gender, which worked on Lizzie's behalf to give shape to belief in her innocence. The essay is marred with factual inaccuracies, such as that Lizzie purchased most of the copies of Edwin Porter's *Fall River Tragedy*. Ann Jones discusses the Borden case in *Women Who Kill* (1980; new edition, New York: The Feminist Press, 2007), 241–269. Jones is a good writer and a perceptive student of the case. She weaves gender into a broader analysis of how a guilty Lizzie escaped justice. Janice Schuetz devotes a chapter to Lizzie Borden in *The Logic of Women on Trial: Case Studies of Popular American Trials* (Carbondale and Edwardsville: Southern Illinois Press, 1994), 61–85. Schuetz raises some helpful points about gender in the case, but her discussion is far less incisive and helpful than Jones's analysis. Walter L. Hixson, in *Murder, Culture, and Injustice: Four*

Sensational Cases in American History (Akron, OH: University of Akron Press, 2001), 5–66, begins with the Lizzie Borden case. He offers an examination that discusses gender as one contextual issue in the trial. He gets some major facts wrong, even describing patrolman and later captain Philip Harrington as city marshal. Far less informed is the chapter on Lizzie in the thin book of communications specialist A. Cheree Carlson, *The Crimes of Womanhood: Defining Femininity in a Court of Law* (Urbana: University of Illinois Press, 2007), 85–110.

The longest, most informative, and most complex work on gender and the Lizzie Borden case has been produced by Cara W. Robertson, "Representing 'Miss Lizzie': Cultural Convictions in the Trial of Lizzie Borden," *Yale Journal of Law and Humanities* (Summer 1996): 351–416. Robertson analyzes a range of gender issues, from Lizzie versus Bridget, to theories of female criminality, to Lizzie's behavior in court. Robertson pushes too hard her view that the opposing lawyers consistently advanced different, coherent narratives of gender. But her rich essay, written from the perspective of cultural studies and based on her Harvard undergraduate honors thesis, represents the most detailed work completed to date on the Lizzie Borden case and gender.

A number of works were helpful in understanding the changing lives of native-born women in late Victorian America. I found the following the most informative. For an important and detailed discussion of nineteenth-century representations of the physical bodies of native-born and immigrant New England women, see Bluford Adams, *Old and New New Englanders: Immigration and Regional Identity in the Gilded Age* (Ann Arbor: University of Michigan Press, 2014), ch. 3. Other important works help put gender aspects of the case in context. On the spinster, Zsuza Berend offers some important revisionist arguments in "'The Best or None': Spinsterhood in Nineteenth-Century New England," *Journal of Social History* 2, no 4. (Summer 2000): 935–957. She stresses the continuing influence of Protestant religion and culture, even on New Women who sought self-service as much as self-achievement and fulfillment. Berend responded primarily to Lee Virginia Chambers-Schiller's important book: *Liberty, a Better Husband: Single Women in America: The Generations of 1780–1840* (New Haven, CT: Yale University Press, 1984). She stressed how women in the Northeast adopted the individualism of the revolution and the Enlightenment, though not to the exclusion of religion. Interpretations of the origins and definition of the New Woman vary. A good starting point is Jean V. Matthews, *The Rise of the New Woman: The Women's Movement in America, 1875–1930* (Chicago: Ivan Dee, 2003). I found especially helpful Carroll Smith-Rosenberg, "The New Woman as Androgyne: Social Disorder and Gender Crisis, 1870–1936," in her important collection of essays, titled *Disorderly Women: Visions of Gender in Victorian America* (New York: Alfred A. Knopf, 1985), 245–296.

Other important works include: Elaine Abelson, *When Ladies Go A-Thieving:*

Middle Class Shop Lifters in the Victorian Department Store (New York: Oxford University Press, 1989). See also Cynthia Eagle Russett, *Sexual Social Science: The Victorian Construction of Womanhood* (Cambridge, MA: Harvard University Press, 1989), and Carroll Smith-Rosenberg and Charles Rosenberg, "The Female Animal: Medical and Biological Views of Woman and Her Role in Nineteenth-Century America," in *Women and Health in America: Historical Readings,* ed. Judith Walzer Leavitt, 2nd ed. (Madison: University of Wisconsin Press, 1999).

On Frances Willard and the WCTU, see *Let Something Good Be Said: Speeches and Writings of Frances Willard,* edited by Carolyn De Swarte Gifford and Amy R. Slagell (Champaign-Urbana: University of Illinois Press, 2007); and Ruth Bordin, *Frances Willard: A Biography* (Chapel Hill: University of North Carolina Press, 1985). On Lucy Larcom see Shirley Marchalonis, *The Worlds of Lucy Larcom, 1824–1893* (Athens: University of Georgia Press, 1989).

Books that I found helpful in thinking about ethnicity in late nineteenth-century New England include Adams, *Old and New New Englanders,* cited above, and Barbara Miller Solomon's classic *Ancestors and Immigrants: A Changing New England Tradition* (Cambridge, MA: Harvard University Press, 1956). On race and American immigrants, see Matthew Frye Jacobson, *Whiteness of a Different Color: European Immigrants and the Alchemy of Race* (Cambridge, MA: Harvard University Press, 1999). Mary Blewett touches on ethnicity in her detailed account of politics, labor, gender, and the industrial system in late nineteenth-century Fall River. See *Constant Turmoil: The Politics of Industrial Life in Nineteenth-Century New England* (Amherst: University of Massachusetts Press, 2000). Finally, for a comparative work on Fall River and Lynn, Massachusetts, see John T. Cumbler, *Working-Class Community in Industrial America: Work, Leisure, and Struggle in Two Industrial Cities* (Westport, CT: Greenwood Press, 1979).

INDEX

Adams, Melvin O.
  background, 104–105
  as defense attorney, 127
  at preliminary hearing, 104, 105,
    110–111, 112, 113
  at trial, 149, 151, 165, 166
Adams, William W., 14–15, 103
Allen, George, 66–67
American Printing Company, 13
American Woman's Suffrage
    Association, 103
Andover Review, 5, 14
arrest warrants, 82, 99, 160–161, 163
attorney general, Massachusetts,
    Knowlton as, 209
  See also Pillsbury, Albert E.
Auriel, Antonio, 20
axe murder, Manchester, 132–134
axes
  blood stains, 68, 78, 108
  found in cellar, 68, 72, 78, 108, 143,
    152
  scientific analysis, 105, 111

Barlow, Thomas, 181–182
barn. *See* Second Street house, barn
Beattie, John, 42–43
Bence, Eli, 73–74, 98, 110–111, 113, 169–171,
    173
Benson, Horace, 30, 35
Blaisdell, Josiah C.
  at arraignment, 99
  background, 85
  inquest, 82, 83, 84, 99–100
  preliminary hearing, 99, 104, 116–117
  resignation from district court, 128
Blewett, Mary, 11

Blodgett, Caleb, 131, 208
Borden, Abby Durfee Gray
  allowance, 23, 31, 42
  autopsy, 18, 57–58, 72, 76, 108, 130, 133
  on day of murders, 55–56
  death, 57–58
  domestic life, 30, 31
  estate, 87
  family, 29, 30, 31
  fear of poisoning, 52
  food poisoning, 51–52, 55–56
  funeral, 75–76
  jewelry, 38–39
  marriage, 29–30
  note allegedly received, 59–60, 61,
    75, 92–93, 142, 167, 196, 198, 201,
    206–207
  personality, 30, 42
  physical appearance, 30
  skull, 18, 130, 164–165
  See also Borden murders
Borden, Abby Durfee Gray, relations
    with stepdaughters
  Andrew's attempts to improve,
    23–24, 31
  Emma's testimony, 187–188
  increasing tensions, 21–22, 31–32, 41,
    49–50
  jewelry theft and, 38–39
  Lizzie's comments to others on, 32,
    38, 81, 168, 197, 206
  Lizzie's testimony on, 89–90
  Moody's description, 141
  observers on, 30, 147–148
  Whitehead on, 86–87
Borden, Abraham, 25
Borden, Alice Esther, 28

Borden, Andrew
  autopsy, 18, 60, 72, 76, 108, 130
  business activities, 11, 24–26, 49–50,
    53
  on day of murders, 55–56, 58–59,
    60
  death, 60, 63
  dominant role in family, 23–24, 39,
    41
  Emma's education and, 33
  estate, 62, 81, 87
  farm laborers and, 19, 20, 24
  farms, 24, 30, 52, 88
  father, 25, 27
  food poisoning, 51–52, 55–56, 58
  funeral, 75–76
  gifts to daughters, 23, 24, 31, 38, 40,
    41, 188
  household, 23–24, 30–32
  lack of will, 62, 88, 108–110
  marriages, 28, 29–30
  Morse and, 43–44, 52, 88
  obituary, 13, 30
  personality, 23, 26–27
  physical appearance, 26
  real estate, 11, 24–25, 26, 27–28, 31, 58
  reputation, 11
  skull, 18, 130, 164–165
  wealth, 2, 11, 21, 23, 24, 25, 48
  See also Borden, Lizzie, relationship
    with father; Borden murders;
    Second Street house
Borden, Anna, 38, 168
Borden, Charles F., 13
Borden, Emma
  allowance, 23, 31, 33
  bedroom, 45
  birth, 28
  confined to house, 78–79, 167
  death, 216
  education, 32–33, 41

  gifts from father, 23, 24, 40
  house on The Hill, 211–212
  inquest testimony, 187–188
  murder investigation and, 3, 18, 72
  in New Bedford, 52
  physical appearance, 33, 187
  preliminary hearing testimony, 191
  relationship with uncle, 88
  as single woman, 4, 33, 34
  stepmother and, 21–22, 23–24, 30,
    31–32, 187–188
  trial testimony, 32, 151–152, 182,
    184–189, 197–198, 200–201
Borden, Emma, relationship with
    Lizzie
  bedrooms exchanged, 45
  estrangement, 32, 214–215, 216
  protectiveness, 32, 33, 34, 197–198
  quarrel in matron's room, 105–107,
    168, 182–184, 186, 204
  support during legal proceedings,
    98, 101, 104, 117
Borden, Lizzie
  alibi, 68, 69, 71–72, 76–77, 94–97, 159
  allowance, 23, 31, 33, 39
  arraignment, 99, 100
  arrest, 2, 82, 99
  bedroom, 44–45, 47, 68–69, 70–71,
    195
  birth, 28
  in cellar on night of murders, 73
  church and civic activities, 15, 21,
    35–37, 50, 119
  confined to house, 78–79, 167
  on day of murders, 56, 57, 59–61
  death, 211, 215, 216
  demeanor at funeral, 76
  demeanor after murders, 53, 61, 62,
    64, 66, 67–68, 69–72, 74
  education, 35, 38
  European trip, 38

friends, 24, 27, 35, 37–38, 81, 87–88, 117, 183–184, 212
as "girl," 99–100, 102, 113–114, 119, 141
help offered to police, 77
imprisonment, 2, 101, 105–106, 117, 126
inconsistent stories, 68, 71–72, 76–77, 94–97, 159, 196, 202
indictment, 124–125, 177
insanity plea possibility, 120–121
interest in theater, 214
as kleptomaniac, 39–41
as lady, 3, 4, 139, 199
life following trial, 13, 211–215
newspaper interviews, 118–119
notoriety, 101, 103, 213
personality, 24, 35, 45, 215
physical appearance, 34–35
physical strength, 16, 21
poison sought by, 52, 54, 55, 73–75, 98, 110–111, 169–171, 173
police interviews, 18, 67–72, 152, 159, 195
reaction to verdict, 208
relationship with uncle, 44, 88–89
Russell and, 52–54, 61, 188
sedative and morphine, 71, 76, 89, 143, 149, 160
self-presentation, 3, 4, 62–63, 139
as single woman, 4, 37, 100, 214
social identity, 3, 5, 62–63
statement to jury, 205
state of mind before murders, 53–54
suspect theories, 53, 70, 71, 98, 207
suspicion of, 64, 65, 74–75, 78–79, 85, 162
wealth, 5, 39–40, 184–185
See also Borden, Abby Durfee Gray, relations with stepdaughters; Borden, Emma, relationship with Lizzie; clothing; trial

Borden, Lizzie, relationship with father
Andrew's gifts, 23, 31, 38, 40, 41
Andrew's suspicion of Lizzie's theft, 39
discussion of moving to The Hill, 49
Jennings on, 176
names, 28
possibility of incest, 41
ring given by Lizzie, 28, 29, 41, 67, 185, 197
Borden, Matthew Chaloner Durfee (MCDB), 12–13, 25
Borden, Philip H., 18
Borden, Richard (17th century), 6
Borden, Richard B., 7–8, 12, 25
Borden, Sarah Morse, 28, 32, 35, 43–44, 118
Borden, Simeon, Sr., 140
Borden (Andrew J.) Building, 24–25, 58, 59, 212–213
Borden family
background, 6–7
in Fall River, 7–9, 10, 12–13, 21
reputation, 6
rumors about financial support of Lizzie's defense, 82
wealth, 7–8
Borden murders
anniversaries, 213–214
books on, 213–214
brutality, 1–2, 41, 62–64, 66, 107, 116, 133, 201
charges, 124–125, 177
controversies, 3, 63–64
crime scene, 64, 65, 67, 73, 144
description, 57–58, 60
discovery of bodies, 61–62
documentary sources, 51
events preceding, 51–54, 55–57, 58–60

Borden murders (*continued*)
  intruder theory, 20–21, 57, 198, 206
  legend, 1
  Lizzie's alibi, 68, 69, 71–72, 76–77,
    94–97, 159
  masculinity, 16, 20–21, 107, 194
  motives, 41, 55–56, 63, 81, 176, 197,
    201–202
  as mystery, 1–2, 3, 176
  newspaper stories, 8, 18, 23, 73, 82,
    101–103
  number of blows, 1, 58, 60
  suspects, 3, 20, 112–113, 134, 178, 196
  timing, 51, 57–58, 62, 63
  See also evidence; investigation; trial
Boston Advertiser, 112, 205, 208, 209, 212
Boston Globe, 74, 122–123, 130, 131, 135, 138,
    158, 183, 207, 208
Boston Herald, 122, 137, 156, 164, 176, 182,
    183, 186–187
Boston Post, 32, 43–44, 214–215
Bowen, Phebe, 113, 190, 191, 203
Bowen, Seabury
  Abby's food poisoning and, 52
  at Borden house after murders, 67,
    68, 69
  description of Andrew's body, 60
  on furnishings of Bordens' house,
    46
  house, 48
  inquest testimony, 149
  morphine prescribed for Lizzie, 76,
    89, 143, 149, 160
  prosecutors on, 142, 143
  relationship with Borden sisters,
    142, 143, 212
  sedative administered to Lizzie, 71,
    76, 89
  sent for after discovery of
    Andrew's body, 16, 60–61
  on sequence of murders, 62

  trial testimony, 89, 142, 143, 148–149,
    160, 203
Brayton, John S., 120–121
bribery scandal, 122–123
Brigham, Mrs. George, 49, 99, 117
Bristol County Medical Examiner, 18
Brown, Everett (Brownie), 181, 203
Bryant, Charles A., 46, 80–81
Buck, Edwin A.
  at Borden house after murders, 67,
    68, 69
  police matron and, 106–107, 184, 191
  relationship with Lizzie, 36, 80, 99,
    101, 104
  at trial, 137, 140, 184

Catholic schools, 14–15
Central Congregational Church
  Andrew Borden's marriages, 28, 29
  Andrew Borden's membership,
    26–27
  Borden family donations, 13
  building, 10
  Christian Endeavor Society, 36, 103
  City Missionary, 36, 67, 80
  female members, 38
  Lizzie Borden's activities, 21, 35–36,
    50
  pastors, 80, 102, 104
  supporters of Lizzie Borden, 2, 18,
    36, 37, 80, 103
  treatment of Lizzie Borden after
    trial, 212
  See also Buck, Edwin A.; Jubb,
    William W.
Chagnon, J. B., 16, 168
Chagnon, Marienne, 177
Chagnon, Martha, 177, 196
Chase, Mark, 178, 179
Cheever, David W., 130, 164, 165, 166
child labor, 12, 14

Chinese immigrants, 15
Christian Endeavor Society, 36, 103,
   119, 212
Churchill, Adelaide, 48, 61–62, 66, 77,
   97, 149–150, 196
City Marshal. *See* Hilliard, Rufus
Clarkson, Alfred, 179, 191
class
   divisions in Fall River, 36, 82–83, 86
   elites, 6, 8, 10–11, 14, 17
   legal system and, 115–116, 204
   of Lizzie Borden, 3, 86
   of women, 4–5, 204
clothing
   blood stains, 98, 108, 111–112
   dress changed after murders, 67, 98
   dresses owned by Lizzie, 38
   dress given to police, 78, 98, 106, 107,
      108, 145, 146, 149, 190, 203
   dressmaker, 151, 185, 189–190, 206
   light blue Bedford cord dress, 77,
      141–142, 146, 151, 152, 185, 189
   Lizzie's inquest testimony on,
      97–98
   Lizzie's lies about, 80
   police searches, 77–78, 152–153
   rags made from, 196–197
   stockings and shoes, 108, 111
   Victorian, 34–35
   witness descriptions of Lizzie's
      dress on day of murders, 77,
      145–146, 148, 149–150, 190, 203
   worn by Lizzie at trial, 139, 140
clothing burned by Lizzie Borden
   Emma's account, 106, 185–186
   light blue Bedford cord dress, 151,
      152
   in past, 189–190
   Russell's testimony on, 79–80, 124,
      141–142, 150–151, 152, 188–189, 203
Collett, Lucy, 168

Cook, Charles C., 108–110, 113, 212–213,
   215
cotton industry. *See* textile mills
Coughlin, John, 16, 17–18, 78–79, 85,
   121–122, 162, 167
Cowles, Edward, 120
Cummings, John W., 174
Cunningham, John, 66

Davis, Charles G., 209–210
defense attorneys. *See* Adams, Melvin
   O.; Jennings, Andrew J.; Phillips,
   Arthur S.; Robinson, George
   D.; trial
de Mello, Jose Correa, 133–134
Desmond, Dennis, Jr., 77, 157–158
Dewey, Justin, 131–132, 162, 205–207,
   209–210
Dickens, Charles, 199
district attorney. *See* Knowlton, Hosea
   M.
doctors, 16
   See also Bowen, Seabury; Chagnon,
      J. B.; Kelly, Michael
Doherty, Patrick, 42, 67, 68, 69, 74, 86,
   87, 181
Dolan, William
   autopsies, 18, 72, 133
   on crime scene, 64
   at inquest, 85, 99
   murder investigation, 67, 77, 78
   preliminary hearing testimony,
      107–108
   on sequence of murders, 62
   trial testimony, 164, 169, 173–174
   view of Lizzie's guilt, 142
Donnelly, John, 113
Draper, Frank, 130, 164, 165
dresses. *See* clothing
Durfee, Bradford, 8
Durfee family, 8–9, 10, 12

education
  of Emma Borden, 32–33
  of Lizzie Borden, 35, 38
  of women, 15, 32–33, 34
  See also schools
Episcopalian Church of the
    Ascension, 10
ethnicity
  of grand jurors, 123–124
  hierarchy, 18–20
  of jurors, 135–136
  tensions in Fall River, 1, 4, 20
  See also immigrants; native born
    Americans
evidence
  autopsy photographs, 130, 166
  bloody cloths, 45–46, 68–69
  "chain" of, 176, 200, 206–207
  circumstantial, 21, 77, 84, 140, 176,
    200
  excluded from trial, 160–164,
    169–174, 210
  grand jury deliberations, 123–124
  made up by McHenry, 122
  medical, 72, 164–166
  mishandled, 65, 72, 158
  at preliminary hearing, 107–108
  skulls, 18, 130, 164–165
  See also axes; clothing; hatchets
Express (Portland, Maine), 102

Fall River, Mass.
  Borden family history in, 7–9, 10,
    12–13, 21
  churches, 10
  class divisions, 36, 82–83, 86
  crime, 66
  elites, 6, 8, 10–11, 14, 17
  ethnic tensions, 1, 4, 20
  image, 6
  incorporation, 8

industries, 7–10, 11–14, 21
location, 7, 9
Manchester axe murder, 132–134
mayors, 13, 16, 17–18
native born residents, 3–4, 6, 10, 11,
  14–16, 17
newspapers, 17–19, 23, 82
Oak Grove Cemetery, 18, 76
philanthropy, 13, 36
population growth, 19
river and falls, 7–9
sentiment against Lizzie after trial,
  212–214
social change, 21
supporters of Lizzie Borden, 2, 15,
  18–19, 37, 48–49, 100, 106
textile mills, 9–10, 11–14, 48, 216
See also The Hill; immigrants
Fall River Bar Association, 128
Fall River Evening News, 18, 66, 75, 82,
  100, 209, 212
Fall River Globe, 17–18, 42–43, 60, 65, 66,
  67, 74, 82, 86, 101–102, 106, 115, 118,
  122, 149, 182–183, 209, 212, 213–214
Fall River Herald, 17, 20, 27, 31, 36, 46, 47,
  49, 58, 64, 69–70, 75, 76–77, 81, 86,
  99, 100, 101, 102, 105, 107, 112, 213
Fall River High School, 35
Fall River Hospital, Women's Board, 36
Fall River Industrial System, 11–13, 21
Fall River Police
  annual picnic, 60
  burglary investigation, 39
  criticism of, 65, 102–103
  Irish immigrants, 4, 18, 42, 65, 68, 83
  Manchester axe murder
    investigation, 132–134
  McHenry hired by, 121–122
  mistakes, 65, 72, 77–78, 108
  promotions, 155
  See also investigation

farm workers, 19, 20, 132, 133–134
Fessenden, Susan B., 117–118, 209
Finn, John C., 136
First Congregational Church
    Andrew Borden's membership, 27
    Borden family donations, 13
    building, 10
    pastors, 5, 14, 103
    supporters of Lizzie Borden, 18, 37
Fleet, John
    interviews of Lizzie Borden, 69, 70,
      71–72
    mishandled evidence, 72
    murder investigation, 67, 68, 70, 72,
      73, 77, 181
    preliminary hearing testimony, 191
    trial testimony, 152–155, 156
"Forty Whacks" rhyme, 1, 2, 216
French Canadians, 14, 16, 19, 20
French immigrants, 74–75, 135
Fruit and Flower Mission, 36, 119, 138

gender issues
    legal power, 139
    murders as male crime, 16, 20–21,
      107, 194
    patriarchy, 40
    at trial, 69, 139, 186–187, 194–195,
      199–200
    See also Victorian womanhood;
      women
Gifford, Hannah, 32, 168, 197, 206
Graham, Michael (Mike the Soldier),
    112–113
grand jury, 104, 121, 123–125, 186
Grouard, John, 177

Handy, Benjamin, 24, 67, 112–113, 178
Hanscom, O. M., 78, 80, 150, 186
Harrington, Hiram, 27, 31, 76–77
Harrington, Lurana Borden, 27, 28

Harrington, Philip, 70–71, 74, 87
Harvard Medical School scientists, 130,
    143, 164–166
    See also Wood, Edward S.
hatchets
    blood and hair on, 68, 78, 108
    found in cellar, 68, 72, 78, 108, 143,
      152
    gilt metal on new, 130, 165–166
    handleless, 72, 81, 112, 143, 152, 153,
      154–158, 165–166, 167
    probable murder weapon, 72, 112,
      143, 164–166, 197
    scientific analysis, 105, 111, 143
Hathaway, Nathaniel, 172–173
hearings. See preliminary hearing
Hickey, Thomas, 183
The Hill, Fall River
    churches, 10
    Lizzie's house, 13, 211–212, 213,
      214–215
    police force and, 83
    political power, 17
    residents, 10–11, 21, 48, 82–83
Hilliard, Rufus
    arrest warrant for Lizzie Borden,
      82, 99, 160–161, 163
    bond posted for Sullivan, 100–101
    at inquest, 85, 99
    McHenry hired by, 121–122
    murder investigation, 66–67, 75, 77,
      78–79
    police matron and, 107
    trial testimony, 167, 191
History of Fall River, 10
Holmes, Charles, 27, 106–107, 184, 212
Holmes, Marianna, 106, 117, 183, 212
Holyoke Democrat, 108
Howard, Joe, 138, 139, 140, 141, 143, 150,
    155, 162, 164, 173, 199, 201, 205,
    207, 208

Hutchinson, Anne, 6
Hyde, John, 73

immigrants
    arrests, 20, 66
    in Bordens' neighborhood, 48
    children, 14–15
    ethnic hierarchy, 18–20
    in Fall River, 1, 3, 4, 14–15, 17, 18–20
    farm workers, 19, 20, 132, 133–134
    French, 74–75, 135
    French Canadian, 14, 16, 19, 20
    Portuguese, 14, 19–20, 21, 132, 133–134
    prejudice against, 14–15, 133–134
    servants, 5
    Swedish, 19
    women, 5, 15
    workers, 14
    See also Irish immigrants
incest, 41
inquest
    circumstantial evidence produced,
        84
    criticism of, 102
    judge, 82, 83, 85, 99–100
    observers, 85–86
    results, 84
    secrecy, 100, 102
    witnesses, 81
inquest testimony
    of Augusta Tripp, 87–88
    of Bridget Sullivan, 86, 115, 149, 163,
        191
    of Dr. Bowen, 149
    of Emma Borden, 187–188
    of John Morse, 88, 109
    of Sarah Whitehead, 86–87
inquest testimony, of Lizzie Borden
    agreement to testify, 85
    alibi for Andrew's death, 94–97, 116
    as basis for arrest, 84

on clothing, 97–98
contradictions, 84, 90–97, 116
exclusion from trial, 79, 160–164, 210
on parents' marriage, 29–30
on possible suspect, 98
read at preliminary hearing, 112, 116
on relations with stepmother, 89–90
rights not read, 79, 82, 161–163
investigation
    arrest of Lizzie Borden, 2, 82, 99
    arrest warrants, 82, 99, 160–161, 163
    autopsies, 18, 57–58, 60, 76, 108, 130,
        133
    beginning, 66–67
    closure, 210
    initial, 64
    interviews of Lizzie Borden, 18,
        67–72, 152, 159, 195
    McHenry and, 121–123
    mistakes, 65, 67, 72, 77–78, 152–153,
        179
    newspaper stories, 74
    police visits to Lizzie's bedroom,
        68–69, 70–71, 195
    rewards offered, 75
    scope, 65
    searches of house, barn, and yard,
        67, 68–69, 75, 77–78, 80–81,
        152–158, 167, 179
    suspicion of Lizzie Borden, 64, 65,
        74–75, 78–79, 85, 162
    witnesses, 65, 67, 73–75
    See also evidence; inquest;
        preliminary hearing
Irish American jurors, 136
Irish immigrants
    arrests, 66
    Catholic schools, 14–15
    doctors, 16, 18, 48, 57, 178
    in ethnic hierarchy, 19
    mayors, 16, 17–18

newspapers, 17–18
police, 4, 18, 42, 65, 68, 83
prejudice against, 4, 14–15
prospective jurors, 135
servants, 5, 16–17, 42
stereotypes, 16–17
workers, 14
See also immigrants; Reagan,
Hannah; Sullivan, Bridget

Jelly, George F., 120
Jennings, Andrew J.
at arraignment, 99–100
background, 112
defense team, 126–128
grand jury and, 124
inquest and, 85, 90, 99–100, 161
insanity examination refused,
120
on Manchester axe murder, 133
murder investigation and, 77, 78,
106, 210
opening statement, 175–177
police matron and, 106–107
at preliminary hearing, 43, 104,
112–114
relationship with Borden family,
175–176
reporters and, 118
at trial, 143–144, 168–169, 175–190
trial preparations, 126
Johnson, Lizzie, 81
Jubb, William W.
on Andrew Borden, 27
sermons, 80
support of Lizzie, 80, 102, 104, 125
at trial, 137, 140, 143–144
juries
Borden trial, 134–136, 144, 207–208
grand, 104, 121, 123–125, 186
women excluded from, 103, 118

Kelly, Michael, 16, 48, 57, 178
Kent, David, 130
Kieran, Thomas, 144, 180
kleptomania, 39–41
Knowlton, Hosea M.
aversion to prosecuting Lizzie,
128–129
background, 85
challenges in prosecution, 84, 174
closing argument, 130, 193, 199–205
criticism of, 102
election as attorney general, 209
grand jury and, 124
hung jury as goal, 128, 129, 159, 192,
199
inquest, 29–30, 81, 82, 83, 86–88,
89–98, 106, 161
jury instructions and, 207
jury selection and, 135–136
at preliminary hearing, 100, 107–108,
109–110, 112, 113, 115–116
summer home, 78
trial delay, 2, 126
trial preparations, 117, 120–121,
128–130
witness cross-examinations, 177, 178,
179, 180, 181–183, 184, 186–189, 190,
192
witness questioning, 69, 164–166,
172, 173

Larcom, Lucy, 34
Lawton, Charles, 172
Lincoln, Arba N., 128
Livermore, Mary, 118, 209
Lubinsky, Hyman, 179–180, 191, 195–196,
202

Manchester, Bertha, 132–133
Manchester, Stephen, 132, 133
Manchester axe murder, 132–134

Manning, John, 149, 182–183
Martel's Drug Store, 74–75
Mason, Albert
  background, 131
  jury selection and, 134–135
  relationship with Robinson, 127, 167
  during trial, 163, 164, 172, 173–174, 205
Massachusetts Woman Suffrage
    Association, 209
MCDB. *See* Borden, Matthew
    Chaloner Durfee
McHenry, Edwin H., 66, 121–123,
    158–159
McLean Hospital for the Insane, 120
medical examiner. *See* Dolan, William
Medley, William
  interviews of Lizzie Borden, 68–69
  murder investigation, 81, 87, 108–109
  searches of house, barn, and yard,
    45–46, 158, 179
  testimony, 157, 158, 202
Melville, Herman, *Moby Dick*, 137
men. *See* gender issues
menstruation, 40, 45–46, 53–54, 69,
    98, 207
M'Guirk, Kate Swan, 118–119, 138
Moody, William H.
  arguments on inquest testimony,
    161–163
  arguments on prussic acid
    testimony, 169–171, 174
  opening statement, 140–143
  physical appearance, 130
  as prosecutor, 129–130
  rebuttal witnesses, 191
  on US Supreme Court, 130
  witness questioning, 144–146,
    148–151, 152, 155–156, 157–158, 167
Morse, John V.
  alibi, 43, 56, 67
  bond, 100

  in Borden house after murders, 43,
    67, 78–79, 167
  on day of murders, 55, 56
  as horse trader, 43
  inquest testimony, 88, 109
  on Lizzie's personality, 35
  relationship with Andrew Borden,
    43–44, 52, 88
  seen as suspect, 75
  trial testimony, 144
  visit to Bordens, 43, 44, 52, 88
Mullaly, Michael
  murder investigation, 46, 67, 68, 72,
    152
  trial testimony, 153, 155–156, 191
murders
  Manchester axe murder, 132–134
  poisonings, 54
  See also Borden murders

native born Americans
  Fall River residents, 3–4, 6, 10, 11,
    14–16, 17
  industrialists, 11, 14
  jurors, 135–136
  newspaper editors and reporters,
    102
  support of Lizzie Borden, 2, 119
  See also ethnicity; The Hill;
    Victorian womanhood
New Bedford, Mass., 10, 52, 101, 136–138
newspapers
  competition for scoops, 23, 121, 122,
    183
  in Fall River, 17–19, 23, 82
  investigation coverage, 74
  sensationalism, 5, 23, 108, 122
  supporters of Lizzie Borden, 2,
    101–103, 112, 118–119, 123, 138, 208
  See also specific papers
New Woman, 4, 15, 34, 36

Women's Journal, 103, 118
Wood, Edward S., 72, 78, 105, 111–112,
        113, 164
Woonsocket Call, 30, 35
workers
    in Fall River, 12
    farm, 19, 20, 132, 133–134
    immigrants, 14
    in textile mills, 5, 11, 14, 15

wages, 12, 19, 31
women, 5, 15
    See also class; servants
Wright, Isabel R., 101

Yankees. *See* native born Americans
yellow journalism, 122
Young Women's Christian
        Temperance Union, 36, 103